A History of the Metropolitan Railway and Metro-land

A History of the Metropolitan Railway and Metro-land

Irene Hawkes

© Irene Hawkes 2018

ISBN 978 0 86093 674 9

First published in 2018 Oxford Publishing Co
an imprint of Crécy Publishing Ltd

All rights reserved. No part of this book may be reproduced or transmitted in any form or by any means, electronic or mechanical, including photocopying, recording or by any information storage without permission from the Publisher in writing. All enquiries should be directed to the Publisher.

A CIP record for this book is available from the British Library

Publisher's note: Every effort has been made to identify and correctly attribute photographic credits. Any error that may have occurred is entirely unintentional.
Printed in Poland by Opolgraf.

Crécy Publishing Limited
1a Ringway Trading Estate
Shadowmoss Road
Manchester M22 5LH

www.crecy.co.uk

Front cover: Met Vickers No 16 at Neasden 6 May 1933 AW Croughton, SLS Collection

Back cover: Back cover bottom right:
The City Line and the Widened Lines (right) north of Farringdon Street Station. *Crecy Heritage Library*

Back cover bottom left:
Front cover of Metro-land, 1921, with an idealised suburban squire's half-timbered residence.

Back cover main:
'F' class locomotive No 92. *Crecy Heritage Library*

Contents

Introduction 6

Part One: The History of the Metropolitan Railway, 1863-1948 10

1 The Underground Project 12

2 The construction of the first underground railway 16

3 The first extensions 28
   Extension to Moorgate
   The Hammersmith & City line
   The Widened Lines
   The Metropolitan & St John's Wood Railway

4 The Inner Circle 33

5 The East London Railway 39

6 The Metropolitan tries to become a main-line railway 42
   Sir Edward Watkin
   Extension to Harrow
   Extension to Aylesbury
   Extensions to Verney Junction and Brill
   The Metropolitan Railway's attempts to advance northwards
   Rolling stock

7 The Metropolitan Railway's last extensions 57
   Uxbridge branch
   Watford branch
   Great Northern & City Railway
   Improvements to the Finchley Road-Wembley Park section
   Relief line project
   Stanmore branch

8 Electrification 65
   The last of the steam rolling stock
   New electric stock

9 Amalgamation and nationalisation 75

Part Two: The Development of 'Metro-land' 78

10 The Metropolitan Railway Surplus Lands Committee 80

11 The Metropolitan Railway Country Estates Limited Company and Metro-land 84

12 The suburban development – Why? How? Who? 107

13 Wembley: an example of suburban development 122

Conclusion 144

Appendix
   The locomotives of the Metropolitan Railway 146

Bibliography 151
Further reading 156
Notes 157

Index 158

Introduction

The dominance of London is nothing new. From the time when the Romans established a base on the Thames, at a spot as near to the sea as possible, where it could be forded and where the banks were firm enough to unload ships and build roads, London has been the largest city in Britain. It became, and still is, the meeting point of all main roads and railway lines, a commercial, financial, industrial, political and educational centre – in other words, the heart of England. The Roman historian Tacitus, in the first century AD, described London as 'a busy emporium for trade and traders', but of course the London of Tacitus was not as big as the London we know today; as centuries went by, more people came to the capital, causing it to expand and, as H. P. White points out:

London Bridge photographed in the second half of the 19th century. The severe overcrowding on the bridge, the main thoroughfare across the River Thames, is clearly evident. *Andrew Dickson Wright Architectural Photograph Collection, Cornell University Library*

'In the early seventeenth century, it was considered to be such a phenomenal size as to be socially and economically undesirable. James the First, himself an immigrant, attempted Canute-like to stem the flood-tide of growth by decree. But a century later Defoe was asking "wither will this monstrous city then extend?" In the 1820s, when the city numbered over 1.25 million, William Cobbett was castigating its growth as draining provincial England of wealth, culture and talent: "the increase of London, the swellings of the immortal Wen". Yet his Great Wen was on the threshold of unparalleled expansion.'[1]

Indeed, towards the end of the 18th century London's population started to grow rapidly, and increased sixfold, from 1,110,000 to 6,580,000 during the 19th century. As more people were coming to the capital, more accommodation was required, and it was provided by building outwards rather than upwards, like nowadays. Thus, bricks and mortar soon started to invade green fields and market gardens, and London ceased to be confined within its city walls.

The causes of this explosive expansion were numerous, but one of the most important was the transport revolution brought about by the steam railway. The railways brought more goods and more passenger traffic but, as the railway termini were on the outskirts of the capital, all the merchandise and people had to be carried to their destination, in the centre of the town by other means of transport, thus causing a lot of traffic on the roads, which soon became congested.

By bringing more trade and industry, the railways created more opportunities for employment. Improved educational facilities also gave more children the opportunity to reach standards that opened the way to white collar employment. This economic growth brought higher income to quite a number of people and, with the help of the railways, which had made possible the separation of home and work, it encouraged all those with a good job and good wages to move out of the crowded districts, in order to live in the lovely green suburbia outside London since the capital was no longer a pleasant place to live in.

Indeed, from the 1850s onwards, London was getting overcrowded and circulation in the metropolis was becoming more and more difficult, as the highways were clogged up with traffic.

We can thus see that road congestion was not the result of the motor car age, since London already suffered from it in the 19th century; but in those days the roads were fewer and narrower, and the vehicles more ponderous and slower. Though most Londoners travelled by foot, all sorts of vehicles were crowding the streets: sedan chairs, coster's barrows, gigs, buggies, phaetons, wagonettes, hackney coaches, various private carriages, horse-drawn omnibuses and big vans purposely obstructing the traffic so passers-by could read their slogans. Most of these vehicles were iron-tyred, and as the streets were paved with cobblestones the resulting noise was deafening. In those days a horse-drawn vehicle took more time to cross London than a train going from London to Brighton or Oxford; and, according to W. J. Passingham:

'The man living in Hackney and about to make a journey to Hammersmith took affectionate farewell of his family, and his wife was regarded by the neighbours as a widow until they saw him again with their own eyes. London jogged along at the average speed of about six miles per hour, and if people reached their destination – well there was something to write home about.'[2]

Crossing the Thames was the worst part of the journey, since most of the bridges charged tolls. As to the streets, they were very bumpy, and on rainy days they were transformed into little lakes, causing the vehicles to plunge into them, to splash causing the vehicles to plunge into them and splash in all directions. Walkers were not happy as they would arrive at work covered in mud and muck.
With the increasing number of traffic jams, many

'The Crystal Way', a suggestion of 1855 to ease traffic congestion around London, from a contemporary architect's drawing.

Cross-section of 'The Crystal Way.

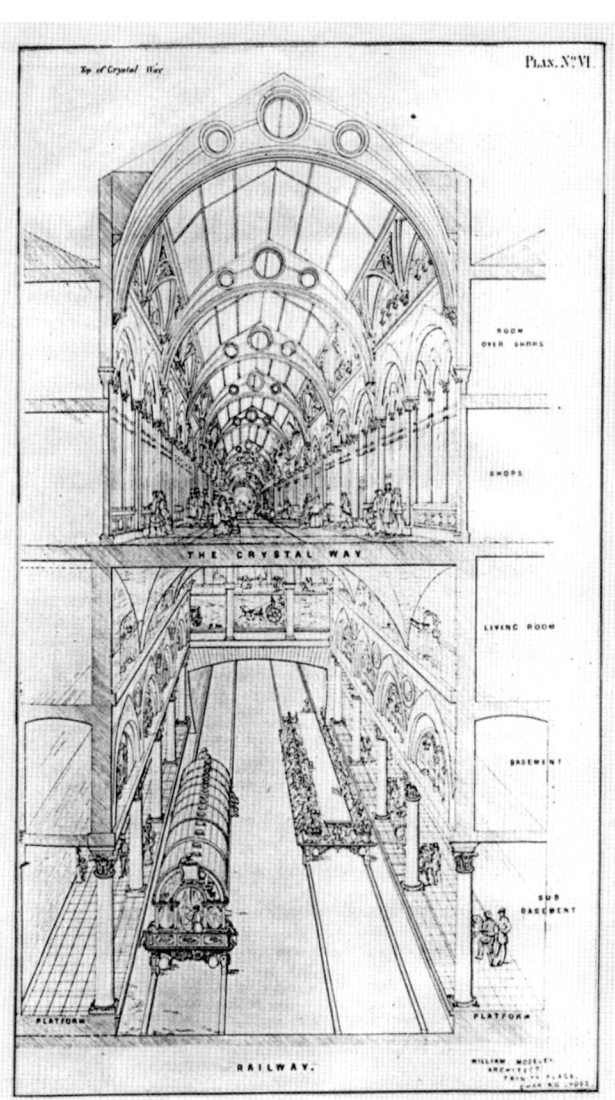

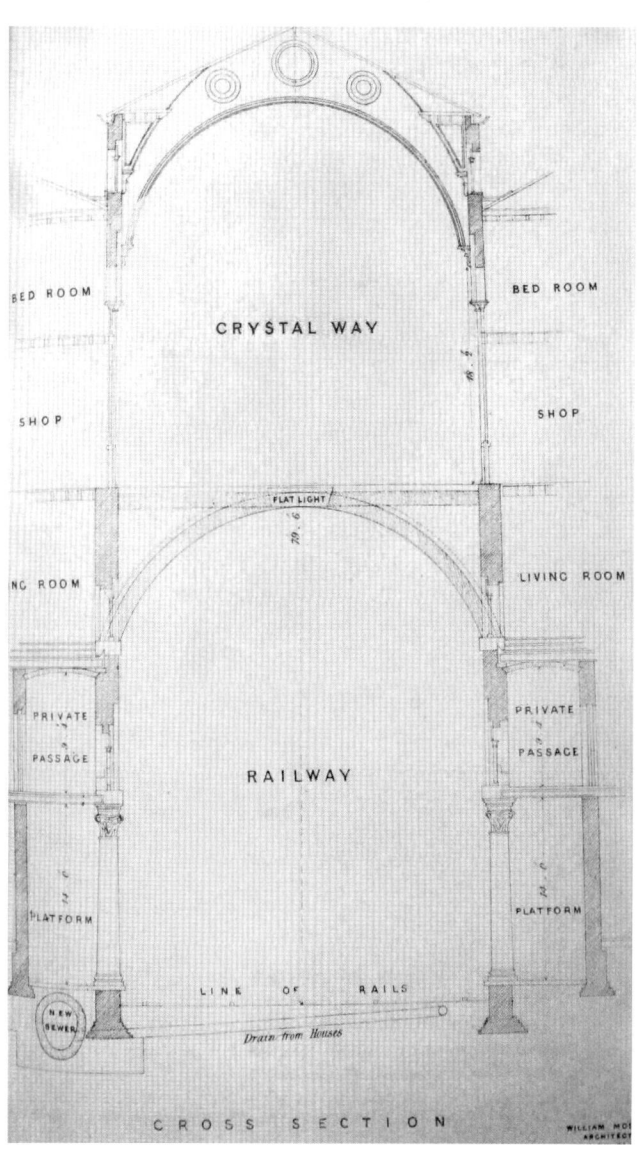

people found it quicker to walk from the railway terminus to their place of work than to take a cab or an omnibus, while others opted for economy and convenience by travelling in their own vehicle, without realising that, in fact, they were only increasing the road congestion.

As the years went by, the situation worsened and a solution to solve the problem was desperately needed. Following reports on London's traffic problems, by a Royal Commission in 1844-51 and a Select Committee in 1854-55, a Metropolitan Board of Works was established in 1855 in the hope of, inter alia, relieving congestion by improving the city's street pattern. It proceeded to do this, vigorously, until it was succeeded in 1888 by the new County Council, which implemented some of the later schemes initiated by the Board. Roads regulations were then established: drivers were required to keep to the left, and buses to pick up passengers at the nearside kerb rather than in the middle of the carriageway. And it was in such matters that the police became involved in traffic supervision. The removal of bridge tolls was suggested, as well as the linking of the main railway stations.

By 1845 only five radial main-line railways served the capital, with short suburban routes to Blackwall and Greenwich. Fifteen years later, four major routes had been added, with several branches and the North London line to serve the docks, but a recommendation of the 1846 Royal Commission

London Bridge was the first of London's railway termini to be opened, in 1836 by the London & Greenwich Railway, terminating outside the City of London, south of the River Thames. By the next decade, it was already inadequate for the needs of passengers as the station was shared by the London & Croydon Railway, the London & Brighton Railway and the South Eastern Railway and the original station would have to be rebuilt. *From Bell's Life in London*

Euston station was opened the following year to London Bridge, by the London & Birmingham Railway in 1837. Passengers, with their luggage, would have to cross London on foot or by horse-drawn vehicles until Pearson's vision of an underground railway for London came to fruition three decades later. From the London & Birmingham Railway, *Thomas Roscoe*

on Metropolitan Termini was still preventing the intrusion of railways into the central area of town, thus causing a problem since, with the rapid growth of the railway network, some link between the lines running north and south of the Thames was becoming necessary. Before 1863 various schemes for establishing a physical connection between the termini and bringing the country lines into close contact with the heart of the city, were started: one suggested draining the Regent's Canal and transforming it into a railway with wide extensions; or a scheme for an overhead railway on arches; or a scheme for a 72-foot-wide Crystal Way, all round London, to be covered with glass and lined with Staffordshire tiles, with a four-track railway line at street level and a boulevard bordered with shops on the first floor; or the bold scheme of four double lines under new thoroughfares, also known as London's venture underground and defended by Mr Charles Pearson. The last-mentioned was the one that was chosen, and it became the nucleus not only of the Metropolitan Railway but also the first underground railway in the world.

However, before the Government authorised the project, it took Charles Pearson a lot of patience, perseverance and effort to make himself heard by his contemporaries and convince them that it was the best solution to their problems.

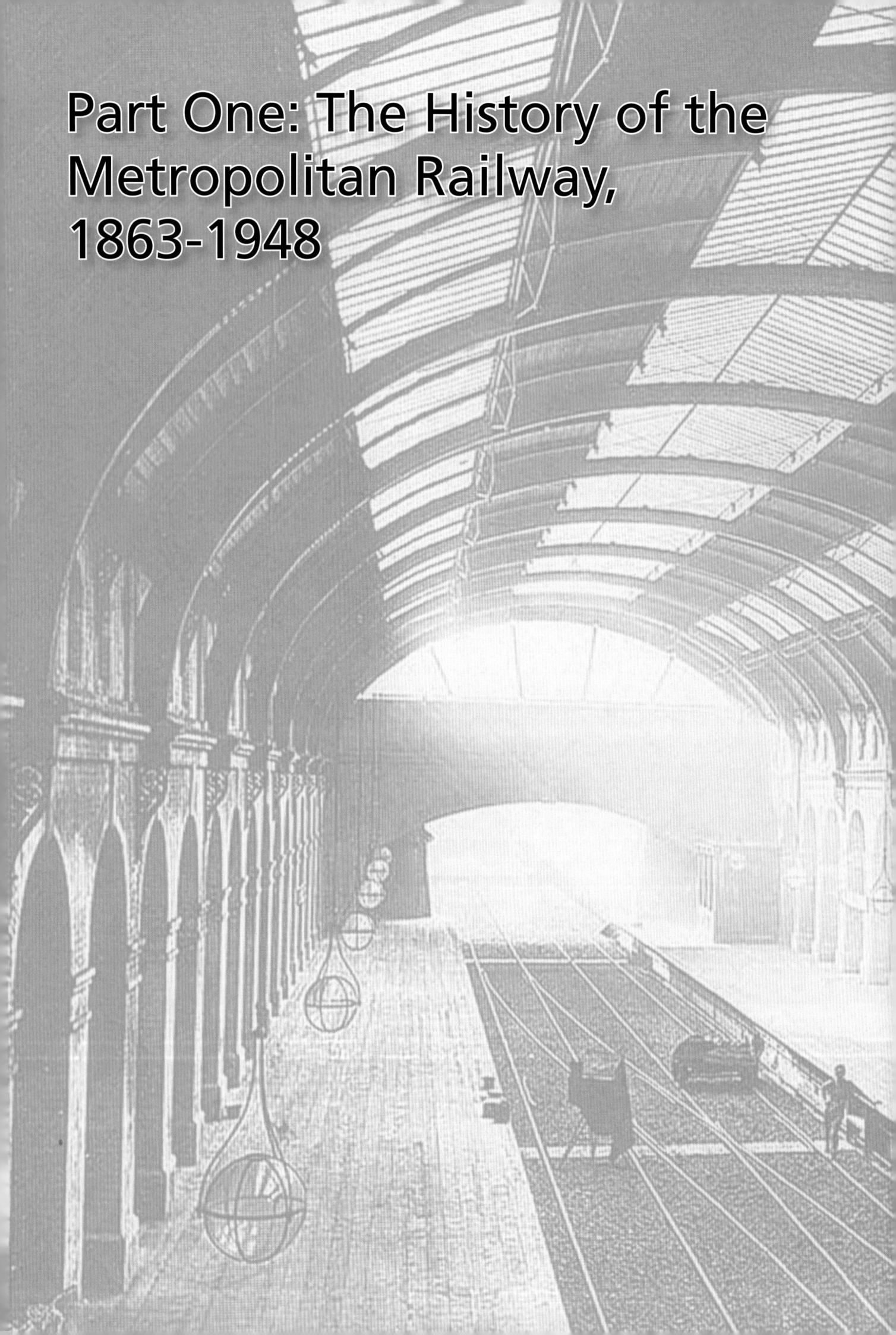

Part One: The History of the Metropolitan Railway, 1863-1948

1

The Underground Project

London's main traffic problem in the 19th century lay in the fact that railway lines were not allowed inside the town; they all terminated on the outskirts. None of the big companies had the courage to venture into the centre, not just because of people's opposition, but also because they could not afford it, for once inside the town it would mean pulling down buildings that they would, by law, have to buy first at a very high price. (Around St Paul's, for instance, a small plot of land cost about £66,000 in the 1850s.) This is why the promoters started to think of building lines underground, but this time under roads or open spaces so as to keep the cost down. Robert Stephenson, for instance, thought in the 1830s of extending the future London & Birmingham Railway to the Thames by means of a line running under Gower Street and down to the north end of Waterloo Bridge; but building so close to expensive properties was too risky, for the slightest subsidence could lead to high compensation claims, and Stephenson was not prepared to take the risk. In the meantime another underground scheme was put forward, which was to run from King's Cross down the valley of the River Fleet to Snow Hill, but this project was also abandoned.

The railway network in London in 1855, showing that none of the railways penetrated into central London.

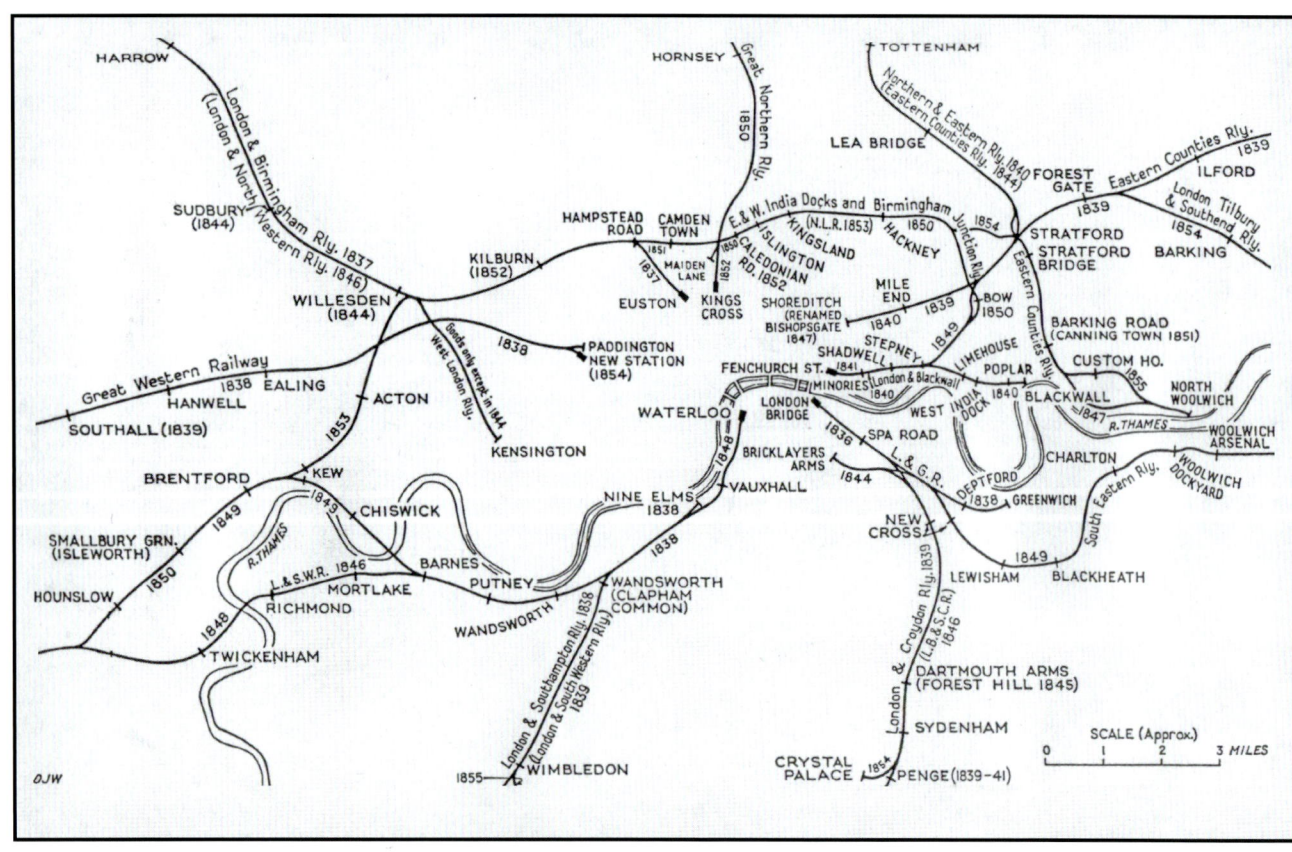

12

Charles Pearson, progressive campaigner, reformer and politician, who first put forward detailed proposals for an underground railway into central London in the 1830s and later was instrumental in the building of the Metropolitan Railway.

However, these schemes made an impression on Charles Pearson, who was born on 4 October 1793 in the City of London. His father, Thomas Pearson, was a feather merchant and upholsterer. After he completed his education in Eastbourne, Charles studied law and became a solicitor. In 1817 he married Mary Dutton. Between 1831 and 1820 and then between 1830 and 1836 he served as a Common Councilman for the ward of Bishopsgate and he was also the chairman of the City Board of Health 1831–33. In 1839 he was appointed City Solicitor and Solicitor to the Irish Society and he held both posts until his death in 1862. Between 1857 and 1850 he was an MP for Lambeth. From 1859 till his death he also served as Solicitor to the Commissioners of Sewers. During his life he campaigned against corruption in jury selection and against the death penalty. He was instrumental in the removal from the Monument of the inscription blaming the Catholics for the Great Fire of London and he fought for the rights of Jews to be brokers in the City, for penal reforms and universal suffrage.

Now, Charles Pearson is mainly remembered as the man who thought out a plan for a railway line into the heart of the City, not just to relieve traffic congestion but also to allow the businessman to get to his office quickly and to enable the poor people to live in healthy surroundings outside London by means of cheap railway travel. Pearson had put forward a plan for the construction of underground railways lines between Battle Bridge, near King's Cross, and Farringdon Street where he wanted to build a central railway terminus which would be shared with several railway companies.

Unfortunately, the Court of Common Council was then rejecting any attempt to enter the city by railways, and was backed by the people, who at the time did not trust underground railways because of the noise, the dirt or the damage they might cause. People were indeed frightened that trains would crash into their houses, or that the vibrations might cause them to collapse, or that they would be asphyxiated by the fumes of the trains passing underneath. The idea of an underground train was soon turned into a joke, and everyone laughed at the thought of it – ministers, back benchers, comedians, street people, newspapers. *Punch* called it the Sewer Railway. In other words, everyone except Pearson, who was a born pioneer and not the type to abandon a well-thought-out scheme, however strong the opposition might be, and who 'set out with his superabundance of energy and determination to make his cherished idea a reality'[3]. But what really gave Pearson the courage to persist in his enterprise was the success of Marc Isambard Brunel's tunnel under the Thames, which demonstrated the possibility of underground transportation in London.

This tunnel, built under the Thames between Wapping and Rotherhithe between the years 1825 and 1843, is the real forerunner of not only the Metropolitan Railway but of London's Underground system. Two previous attempts to bore under the Thames in 1799 and 1804 had ended in disaster. Brunel's shield-driven tunnel was inspired by the boring activities of a shipworm called 'teredo navalis', and followed the example of the mollusc burrowing its way into the wood by means of a round shell scored with parallel rows of small teeth resembling the cutting edge of a file and leaving behind a tunnel lined with a shell-like substance. Brunel's shield was a cast-iron casing 37 feet wide, 22 feet high and 8 feet deep, with a series of projecting cutters, and was divided into 36 compartments, in each of which worked a miner or a bricklayer. When the earth in front of the cell was excavated to a certain depth; the cavity was secured by poling boards and struts, then lined with brickwork.

The work was arduous and long, and Brunel and his team had to face many obstacles and quite a few accidents, but finally the river was conquered and the tunnel finished; it was opened with great ceremony on 25 March 1843. For a long time it remained a pedestrian subway, as the intended approaches to it for vehicular traffic were never built. We have to wait until 1869 to see it used as a railway tunnel by the East London Railway.

Thus Brunel's success encouraged Pearson to fight

for his idea of a railway under the street surfaces and also helped him to gather some supporters. He called meeting after meeting, explained, cajoled and harangued continuously. He begged the railway companies to forget their differences and unite in order to obtain a central terminus. Meanwhile the situation above ground was gradually worsening and the authorities soon realised that Pearson's idea was probably not as mad as it might have seemed, and could indeed be one way to alleviate the increasing confusion and congestion in the city; it could in fact improve the town, especially in the Fleet valley area, which was one of the worst slums in London.

In 1846 a Royal Commission was set up to investigate the numerous projects to extend the railways into London. Pearson tried very hard to convince them and to gain supporters. He produced drawings, models, explained that the line and the new properties built along its course would bring a lot of profit to its builders, that the new road built on top of the line would open up communications across the squalid Fleet valley and would help to wipe out its slummy habitations, and the existing canal could also be used for the transport of goods from the railway to the port. Pearson also intended to build a suburban village of 10,000 cottages for the poor, 6 or 7 miles from London, with easy access to the city. Unfortunately, the time was not ripe, and all the plans presented to the Commission were rejected.

Pearson therefore let his plan lie dormant from 1846 to the summer of 1850. By then he had prepared more plans and models, and in late 1851 he asked for his plan, to build two lines, one from King's Cross to Holborn Bridge and another from King's Cross to Edgware Road, to be referred to a committee. The Council appointed the Fleet Valley Improvement Committee, which, after having studied the plan, approved it on 15 January 1852. Yet Pearson was not the only one fighting for an underground railway. His efforts were indeed being supplemented by those of the Bayswater, Paddington & Holborn Bridge Railway, whose plan was to build an underground line from Paddington to King's Cross and there join the one proposed by Pearson's City Terminus Company. The Bayswater, Paddington & Holborn Bridge Railway's scheme was cheaper, for it intended to build its line under an existing wide road, 'The New Road' (later the Marylebone/Euston Roads), avoiding the need to pull down many properties and thus cutting the expense by half.

This scheme gained a lot of support, and the Bill presented in Parliament was not opposed. At the end of August 1853 the company was authorised by an

Marc Isambard Brunel's tunnel under the Thames, completed in 1843, demonstrated that it was possible to build a railway underground in London. *London Transport Museum*

Inside Brunel's tunnel under the Thames, which was used as a pedestrian walkway until bought by the East London Railway Company in 1865. *From a contemporary illustration*

Act of Parliament to build a line between Paddington and King's Cross; the company was then renamed the North Metropolitan. Pearson was not as successful, but the directors of the North Metropolitan could not let Pearson's plan die, so they took over the City Terminus's scheme and began to amend it. They were more interested in short-distance traffic than providing the main lines with a route into the city. Thus in order to save money and to spike the guns of those who were against the penetration of the city by the main lines, they dropped the idea of a big city terminus. The route of the line was also changed to allow it to serve the General Post Office and thus gain GPO support. There was opposition in Parliament, but the Post Office and respected engineers like Brunel and Hawkshaw supported the scheme; and William Malins, one of the promoters of the project, pleaded the case so well before the Committee that an Act was passed in 1854 and the company was renamed the Metropolitan Railway Company.

The next step was to raise some money, which was rather difficult, for with the Crimean War in progress money was short. After a few unsuccessful attempts by the Metropolitan Company, Pearson came back on the scene; although he had given up the chance of forming his own company, he had not given up the plan, and continued his vigorous campaign, this time in favour of the Metropolitan Company, and set out to unite all the different interests that might together build the line. He also advised the company to buy the site of the Metropolitan Cattle Market at Smithfield, which was being moved to Copenhagen Fields (north of King's Cross), for it would provide a suitable railway terminus. Finally, after a lot of struggle and effort, more money was found; the City Corporation agreed to subscribe for shares and the Metropolitan agreed to cut the cost of the line by not building the section from Cowcross Street to the Post Office and to build a line from the Great Northern, so that the cattle slaughtered at Copenhagen Cattle Market could be brought by railway to Smithfield to be sold. Money was also to come from the Great Western Railway, in return for connecting it with the underground line and building it to the broad gauge. Banks also gave their support by lowering their rates to 2½ per cent.

2
The construction of the first underground railway

By the second half of 1859 sufficient capital had been raised to start on the line, and in October John Parson was put in charge of the building operations. In December the contract for the construction of the line went to Mr Jay; the western section from Euston Square to Paddington was given to Smith & Knight after Brotherhood had withdrawn his tender. By March 1860 the contractors were ready to start on the building, and shafts were sunk at several places along the line.

In his book *Our Iron Roads* (5th edition, 1884), Frederick S. Williams gave a graphic description of the start of the work:

'A few wooden houses on wheels first made their appearance, and planted themselves by the gutter; then came some wagons loaded with timber and accompanied by sundry gravelled coloured men with picks and shovels. A day or two afterwards a few hundred yards of roadway were enclosed, the

Excavating in Praed Street near Paddington station in 1866. *London Transport Museum*

Work in progress on the Metropolitan Railway at King's Cross. *London Transport Museum*

The tunnel at King's Cross. *London Transport Museum*

In June 1862 the Fleet Sewer burst and flooded the first tunnel under London, delaying the opening of the Metropolitan Railway. *London Transport Museum*

ordinary traffic being, of course, driven into the side streets; then followed troops of navvies, horses and engines arrived, who soon disappeared within the enclosure and down the shafts. The exact operation could be but dimly seen or heard from the street by the curious observer who gazed between the tall boards that shut him out; but paterfamilias, from his house hard by, could look down on an infinite chaos of timber, shaft holes, ascending and descending chains and iron buckets which brought rubbish from below to be carted away; or perhaps one morning he found workmen had been kindly shoring up his family abode with huge timber to make it safer. A wet week comes, and the gravel in his front garden turns to clay; the tradespeople tread it backwards and forwards to and from the street door; he can hardly get to business or home to supper without slipping and he strongly objects to a temporary way of wet planks, erected for his use and the use of passers-by, over a yawning cavern underneath the pavement…'[4]

The form of construction used was mainly cut-and-cover: the surface of the street was taken up, and a trench was dug out and lined with bricks. As the railway had to accommodate double tracks of mixed gauge (standard gauge of 4ft 8in and broad gauge of 7ft 0¼in), most of the covered way consisted of a brick arch of a 28ft 6in span made of six elliptical rings standing above vertical side walls which were three bricks thick and 11ft high. It was built with ordinary stock bricks and blue lias or greystone. Cast iron girders were used for the roof. Where there was insufficient depth for the arched way, they built recesses and concrete side walls in 8ft bays of piers. Then after arches or girder supports had been put in at the top, the roadway was rebuilt over the trench.

The section between King's Cross and Farringdon Street included the Clerkenwell Tunnel which was 728 yards long and built between November 1860 and May 1862. It was also the only true tunnel on the original line.

Digging through London clay was not an easy task and many obstacles had to be overcome. All the water and gas pipes had to be moved, rivers and sewers had to be diverted, claims for compensation from various members of the public had to be settled, and the construction was not without accidents. The first happened on 30 May 1860, when a train, whose guard was too drunk to apply the brakes, overshot the platform at King's Cross (Great Northern Railway station) and drove straight through the enclosing wall into the Metropolitan diggings. Several people were injured, but no one was killed. On 1 November the firebox of an engine drawing wagons of dirt exploded at the mouth of the tunnel connecting the Metropolitan Railway with the Great Northern, killing two people and injuring others. On another occasion, a big water pipe in the vicinity of Clerkenwell burst, causing some damage. In May 1861 the collapse of the earthworks in Euston Road, near Tunbridge Place, hampered the progress of the work for a few weeks. The original contract stipulated that the line should be completed within 21 months and opened for the 1862 Exhibition.

Trial trips were made on 28 November 1861 and 24 May 1862, and it was hoped that the line could be opened in July 1862, but on 18 June the works were once more delayed by the bursting of the Fleet Ditch Sewer into the works in Farringdon Street, where the tunnel was flooded to a depth of 10 feet as far as King's Cross. By August the damage had been repaired and opening on 1 October was expected. Unfortunately, due to some signalling problems and requirements for a few modifications, the line was not ready for the final check by the Board of Trade until December. The final inspection took place on 3 January 1863 and thence until 8 January a service of empty trains was run to test the signalling and train staff. Finally, on Friday 9 January 1863, the line, which had five intermediate stations – Edgware Road, Baker Street, Portland Road, Gower Street (renamed Euston Square on 1 November 1909), and King's Cross – was officially opened. A party of officials and guests travelled the whole length of the line and banqueted at Farringdon Street in a specially built

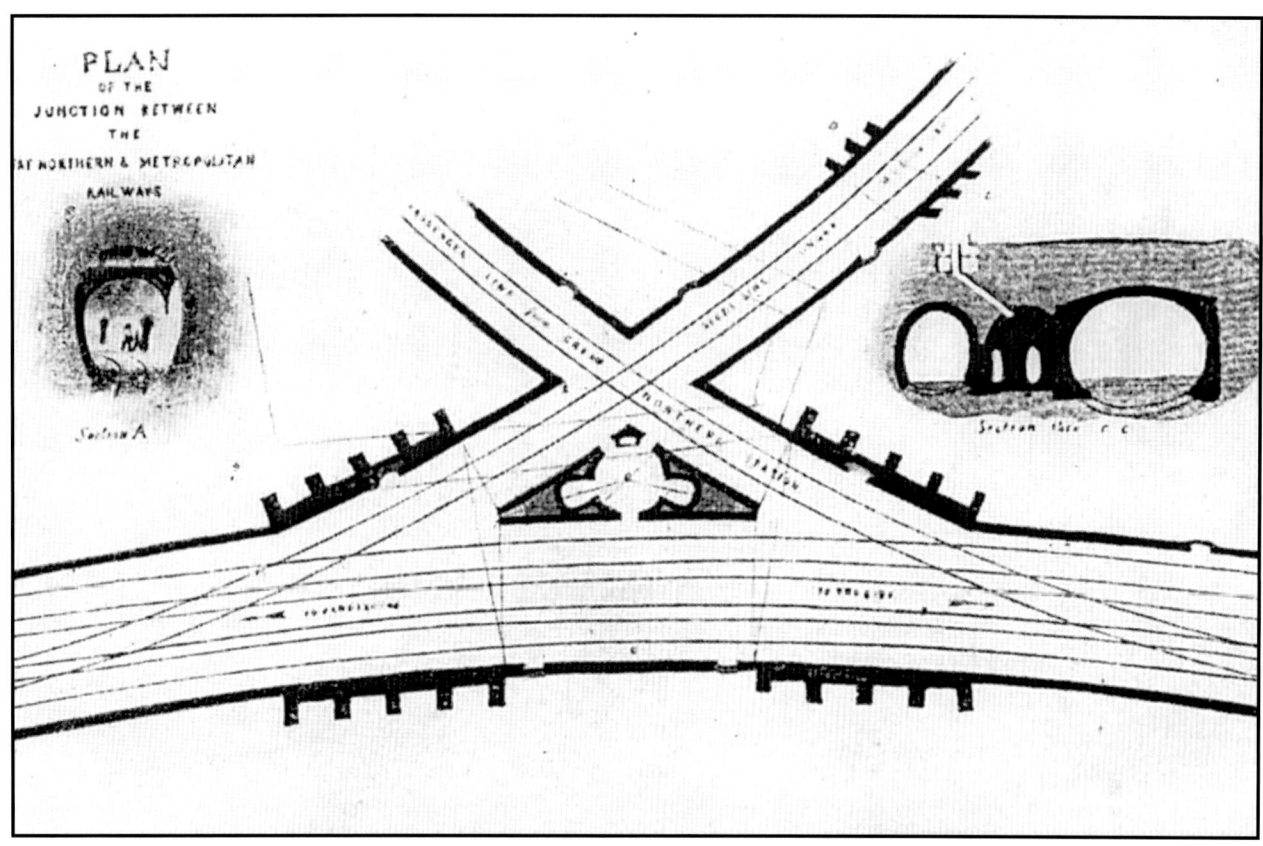

Above: Contemporary plan of the Great Northern and Metropolitan Junction at King's Cross.

Below: Two views of the trial trip at Edgware Road on 24 May 1862. Fowler's prototype fireless locomotive, nicknamed 'Fowler's Ghost', can be seen at the head of the train. *Crecy Heritage Library*

The inaugural banquet in Farringdon Street station, January 1863. *London Transport Museum*

temporary hall 250 feet long and 50 feet wide, and many speeches were delivered. On 10 January the long-awaited public opening brought great numbers of people, eager to experience their first trip down the 'Drain'. The *Daily Telegraph*'s report, printed on the following Monday, gave a vivid picture of the excitement of that memorable day:

'On Saturday, from as early an hour as six o'clock in the morning until late at night, trains filled with people were running at short intervals of time between Paddington and Farringdon Street. It soon became apparent that the locomotive power and rolling stock at the disposal of the company was by no means in proportion to the requirements of the opening day. From eight o'clock every station became crowded with intending travellers, who were admitted in sections, but poor were the chances of a place to those who ventured to take their tickets at any mid-way station, the occupants being, with but very rare exceptions, long distance or terminus passengers. However, the crowding at King's Cross was immense.

This station is certainly the finest on the line, throwing even the termini into shade. Here the constant cry as the trains arrived, of 'No room!' appeared to have a very depressing effect upon those assembled. Between eleven and twelve at this station, and continuously for the space of an hour and a half, the moneytakers refused to take money for passengers between King's Cross and Farringdon Street, but they issued tickets between that station and Paddington, and many whose destination was Cityward, determined to ride on the railway on its first day of opening, took tickets for the opposite direction in order to secure places for the return journey.

At twelve o'clock the clerks informed the public who were certainly then assembled to the number of five or six hundred at King's Cross that there were enough people at Paddington to fill four trains in succession; and that therefore their instructions were to issue no Farringdon Street tickets for an hour. This announcement had the effect of getting rid of very large numbers. Whilst, however, all the tendency of the traffic was towards the Farringdon Street terminus during the morning, the public were enabled to proceed westwards with but little inconvenience. Towards afternoon, however, the tide set in the other way, and the approaches to the trains

Opposite: A collage from a contemporary newspaper showing the Metropolitan Railway's stations as originally built.

at Victoria Street can be compared to nothing else than the crush at the doors of a theatre on the first night of a pantomime. Between one and two o'clock thousands of anxious travellers by the new route were collected outside the Victoria Street terminus, and when the outer doors were opened, which was only at intervals, the rush was tremendous and on reaching the ticket office the task of exchanging the cash for a ticket was an extremely difficult one. The platform gained, the next grand struggle was for a seat in the incoming and presently outgoing train. Classification was quite lost sight of, and prudent persons took 3rd Class tickets, whatever kind of carriage they hoped to travel by. Hundreds on each occasion, however, had to be left behind to take their chance of the next train. The timetables indicate that twenty-one minutes will be occupied in each run; but a much longer space of time was found necessary on the opening day, in consequence of the delay at every station. For instance, a train which left Farringdon Street at 2.15 reached King's Cross Station at 2.18 – a little over a mile – bringing up at the platform in three minutes. Gower Street was reached at 2.25, Portland Road at 2.30, Baker Street at 2.36, Edgware Road at 2.42, and the terminus in 33 minutes. There were other journeys performed which were longer, reaching over 40 minutes, but the time above specified may be taken as about the average throughout the day. The endeavours of persistent people to get places, and the running about of officials at every station, to see if there was a seat for one here, or two there, took up more than twice the time which will be needed for stoppages on ordinary occasions.'[5]

The only person missing on that big occasion, among all these rejoicements, was Charles Pearson, who had died on 14 September 1862; however, he was not forgotten, since he was spoken of and much praised by various officials in the speeches delivered at the opening banquet. On the first day the company collected about £850 in fares and during the first six months they transported an average of 26,500 passengers a day.[6]

Originally there were 67 trains running each way on weekdays and 48 on Sundays. They stopped at all the stations, and it took them 18 minutes to cover 3¾ miles. The frequency of the service was 15 minutes between 8am and 8pm, and 20 minutes between 6am and 8am and between 8pm and 12pm on weekdays and between 8pm and 10.40pm on Sundays. Trains did not run during church hours on Sunday mornings, and this customary suspension of service was respected on the Metropolitan Line until 30 October 1909.

Though a lot of effort had been put into the building of the line, much thought also had to be put into the working of it. At the time steam was the only form of reliable traction, but the exhausting of steam and smoke would present a problem underground. Therefore John Fowler, the company engineer, came forward with the idea of the 'hot-brick engine' – in other words a locomotive without fire. In order to achieve this, he used a cylindrical egg-ended boiler which was to be charged at each end of line with superheated water under pressure coming from a stationary boiler. The boiler had a firebox which was connected to a big combustion chamber which contained storing energy fire bricks. A set of short firetubes connected the firebox to the combustion chamber, allowing the exhaust steam to be re-condensed and fed back to the boiler instead of escaping. This would allow the dampers to be shut when the train was in a tunnel and steam

Farringdon Street station, 1863. *London Transport Museum*

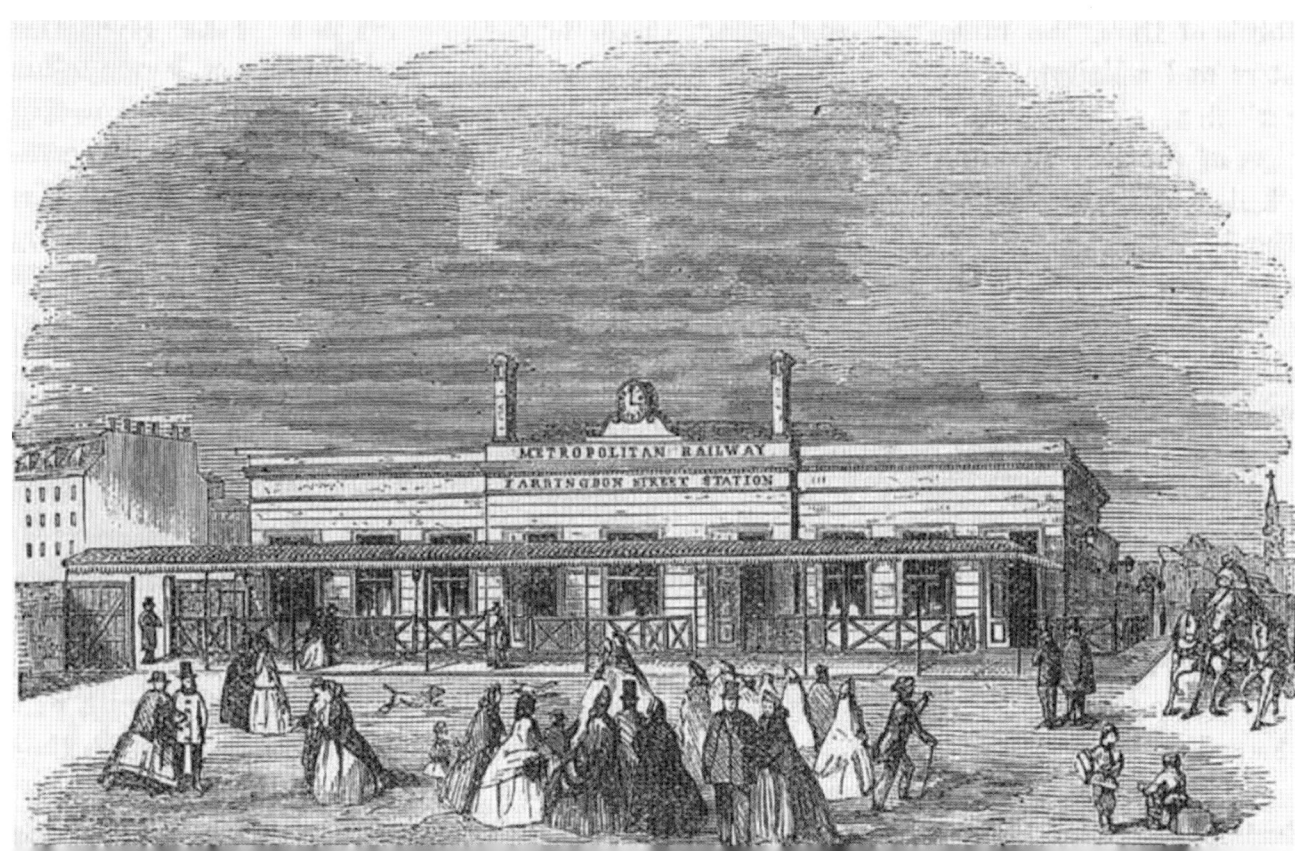

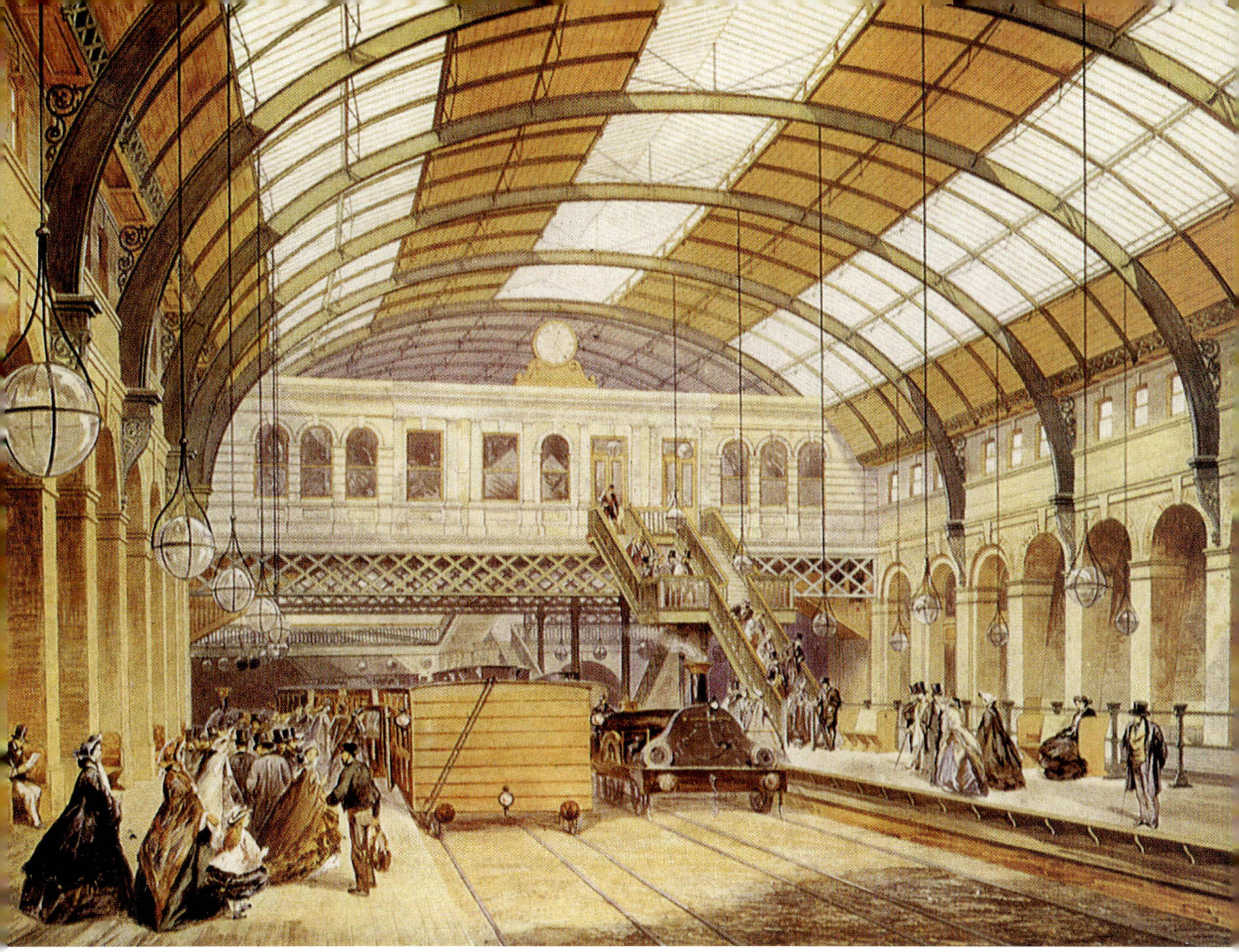

King's Cross station, c1863, showing the mixed gauge tracks and a broad gauge Great Western Railway trains. *London Transport Museum*

would be generated by using the heat stored in the firebricks.

He was supported in his venture by Isambard Brunel. Fowler went ahead with his plan, and Robert Stephenson & Co of Newcastle were asked in 1860 to build a prototype. But Fowler's fireless locomotive, nicknamed 'Fowler's Ghost', was not successful and had to be dropped. Daniel Gooch, locomotive superintendent of the Great Western Railway, was given the task to design a locomotive for the Metropolitan, and he came up with a 2-4-0 tank with 6-foot coupled wheels and outside cylinders measuring 16 by 24 inches. The heating surface of the firebox was 125 square feet and of the tubes 615 square feet; the grate area was 18.5 square feet, and the capacity of the normal feed tank was 420 gallons. It was tried in October 1862 with a 36-ton train between Farringdon Street and Paddington and the journey took 20 minutes. It was more successful than Fowler's engine.

Meanwhile, it was decided that the

Sir John Fowler, the Metropolitan Railway's chief engineer who supervised the construction of the railway.

'Fowler's Ghost', his prototype fireless locomotive, on a trial trip at Stafford Street Bridge near Edgware Road station. *Crecy Heritage Library*

new line was to be worked by the Great Western Railway, thus turning the Metropolitan Railway into a broad gauge line. At the time the signalling commonly used was the mechanical type, but the Metropolitan was the first railway to use throughout its system the absolute block system where all points and signals were interlocked.

Though the venture was successful and the company was making a good profit, it still had to face some big problems, the main one being disagreement between itself and the Great Western Railway, which arose because the GWR was interested in through trains only, whereas the Metropolitan wanted more than four local trains an hour, thus leaving little room or none at all for the Great Western's through trains. The GWR was also dissatisfied because no provision had been made, as yet, for freight trains. Moreover, John Parson, the Deputy Chairman of the Metropolitan, and Charles Saunders, Secretary of the Great Western, did not get on well. Things between the two companies became worse in July, when a junction with the Great Northern was about to be opened. The Great Western, which knew that the Metropolitan had no coaches or locomotives of

Scale drawing of Fowler's broad gauge 0-6-0T locomotive built for the Metropolitan.

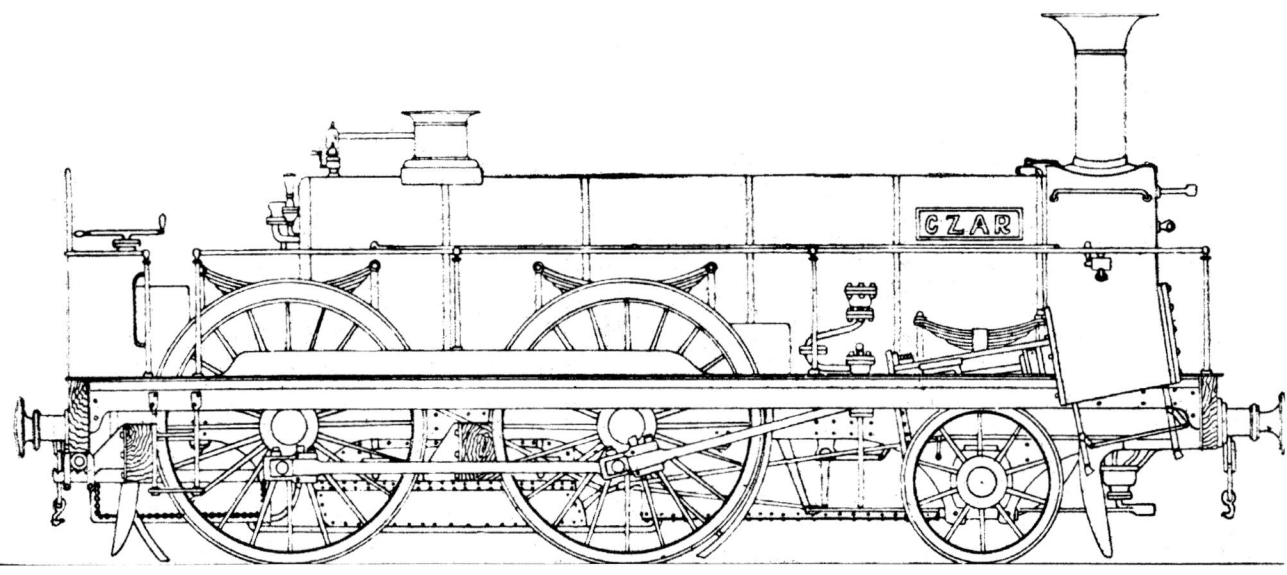

Daniel Gooch's 2-4-0T GWR 'Metropolitan' class broad gauge locomotive, *Czar*, built 1862 and withdrawn 1871.

its own, informed its neighbour of its intention to withdraw all its rolling stock after 30 September, and not to sell it to the Metropolitan. The aim was to make an impression on the smaller company and obtain from it what it wanted, but the threat failed to produce the expected panic; in retaliation the GWR decided to advance the date of withdrawal to 11 August.

The Metropolitan Railway therefore asked the Great Northern Railway to help it out, which it did by letting the Metropolitan use the four- and six-coupled tender engines that the GNR had ready for its through-city service, and by converting some other stock it possessed. However, since the GNR stock was not broad gauge and the middle rail on the Metropolitan Line had not been used before, all did not run smoothly at first and the traffic declined. There were also complaints from the staff about the smoke in the tunnels, which was heavier than before since the Great Northern stock was not built to run in tunnels for such long periods of time; consequently the staff requested permission to grow beards in order to protect themselves.

Meanwhile the Metropolitan Railway Company had placed an order for carriages with the Ashbury Railway Carriage & Iron Company of Manchester, and with Beyer, Peacock & Company, also of Manchester, for locomotives, which became known as the 'A' class. The first carriages were ready in October 1863, but the company had to wait until July 1864 to get the first locomotives, which then allowed it to run a more frequent service.

By 1863 the Great Western and Metropolitan had reconciled their differences, allowing co-operative working arrangements to be resumed.

In the early days there were a lot of complaints about the lack of ventilation in the tunnels, where the sulphurous fumes emitted by the engines were

GNR 0-6-0 standard gauge locomotive No 138 (No 155), which operated on the Metropolitan Railway.

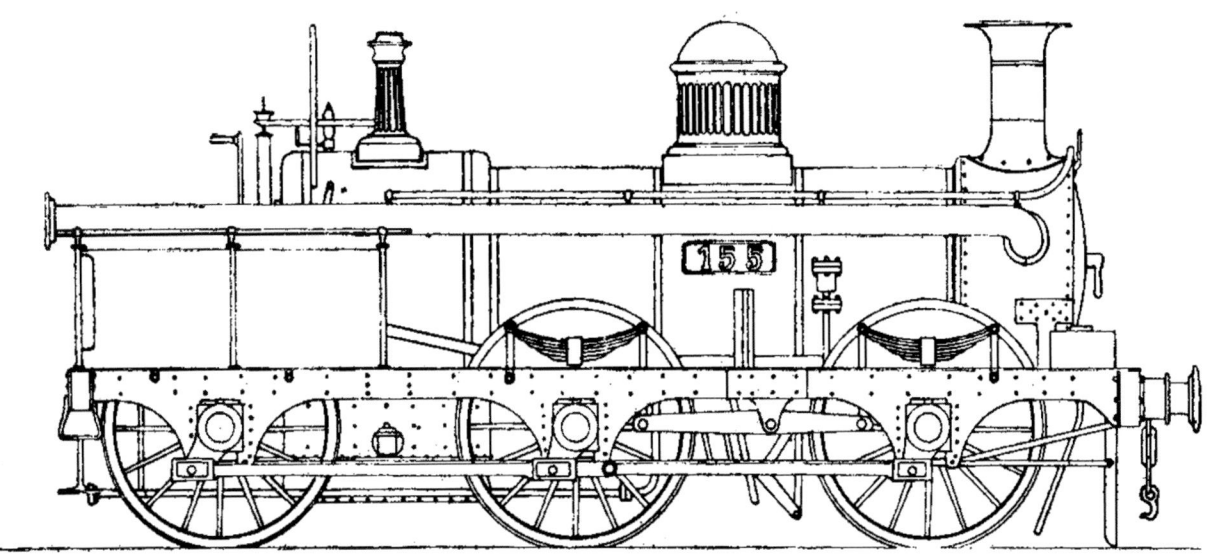

Class A Metropolitan Railway 4-4-0T locomotive No 4. The initial order of 18 were delivered from Beyer Peacock in Manchester in 1864, and in all 40 were built. *Crecy Heritage Library*

abundant, even though some doctors maintained that they were especially beneficial for asthmatic people. Still, the company tried its best to improve the situation by building ventilation shafts, and removing the glass from the windows of some stations to increase the circulation of air. In 1871-72 condensing 'blow holes' were made in the tunnel roof to the road above on the section between Edgware Road and King's Cross. The company tried to refill them completely with fresh water regularly, but with the increasing traffic mostly all they had time to do was to top it up, which of course made the condensers less effective. The Metropolitan also started to use coal instead of coke, as it was discovered that it polluted the atmosphere less.

The first carriages were similar to those of the Great Western, except of course that they were standard gauge rather than broad gauge. Gas bags used for lighting were kept in the roofs, which were quite high. The 39ft 6in teak body was mounted on an angle-iron frame 6 inches shorter than the body itself. In a standard-length train there were 1st Class

Class A 4-4-0T with original boiler fittings but cab added (after 1895).

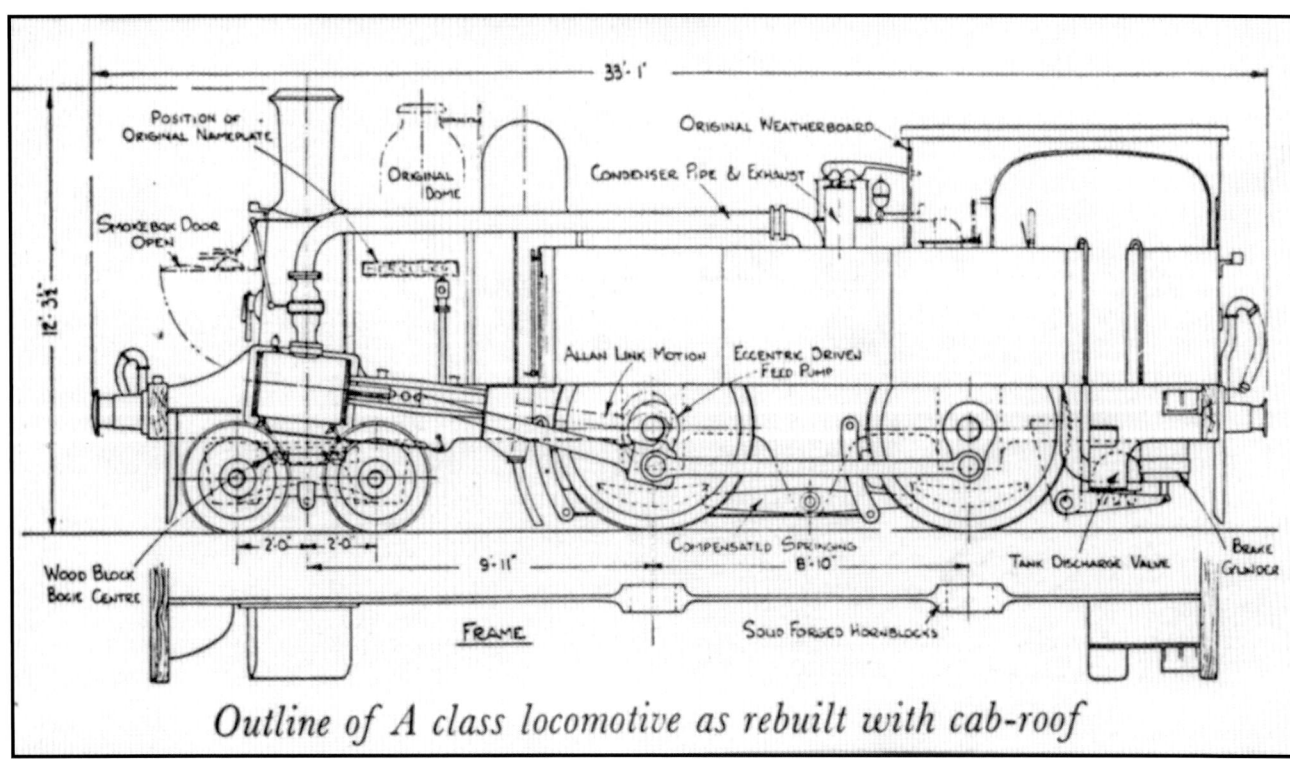

Outline of A class locomotive as rebuilt with cab-roof

Period	Passengers	Receipts
10 January- 30 June 1863	4,823,437	£53,058
1 July-31 December 1863	4,631,731	£48,649
1 January-30 June 1864	5,207,335	£54,740
1 July-31 December 1864	6,614,554	£61,749[7]

coaches with six compartments, 2nd and 3rd Class coaches with eight compartments, and composite coaches with seven compartments, the three in the middle being 3rd Class. Smoking was not allowed in any of them until 1 September 1874. Inside, they were all quite comfortable, with carpets, mirrors and good upholstery. At first the carriage doors were square, but later on the tops were rounded off so as to give them better protection in the event of accidental opening in the tunnels. The first carriages had a length over buffers of 42 feet, and were not carried on bogies but on four axles grouped in pairs. Flexibility on curves was assured by a translation movement of the central axlebox connected to the mainframes with links hanging from the end of the springs at about 30-degree angles, but in fact since the outer wheels of each pair were more than 6 feet from the ends of the carriage, the wheelbase of the vehicle was practically rigid. However, this arrangement varied from batch to batch and was finally changed when the automatic vacuum brake was introduced. The previous brake system had been Newall's hand brake, which was placed in the guard's compartment and applied wooden brake blocks to the four wheels of the coach. Then came the Wilkins & Clark chain brake, later improved by Francis Webb, which consisted of a cord passing over the carriage roofs, capable of releasing weights that then operated the handbrake lever in the guard's compartment of each carriage.

In 1870 the company started to buy from the Oldbury Carriage Company some vehicles that were four-wheeled and close-coupled in pairs; each pair was 43ft 8in long. The body of each vehicle was 20 feet long and contained either three 1st Class compartments or four 2nd and 3rd Class compartments. In the 1st Class compartments four passengers could be seated side-by-side with armrests between them; lighting was provided by two gas lamps, and the partitions between the compartments were full height. In the 3rd Class compartments there were wooden bench seats, only one lamp and the partitions between the compartments were only waist-high. One striking characteristic of this stock was the provision in each compartment of small windows above the main ones.

Despite a few problems and a few accidents, the line was on the whole a success and the number of passengers and receipts grew rapidly: the number of passengers carried and receipts earned by the Metropolitan in 1863-64 were as in the table above.

During the first year's working the company paid to its shareholders a 5 per cent dividend, and for the first half of the second year, and the second half of that year, 7 per cent. This success encouraged the directors to strike while the iron was hot, and they wasted no time in appealing for more capital in order to carry out the extensions they had planned.

Metropolitan Railway Class A locomotive No 22. One of the second batch of the class to be built in 1866 by Beyer Peacock, these condensing steam locomotives were intended to minimise smoke in the confined underground tunnels.

3
The first extensions

Extension to Moorgate

Before the first stretch of the line was finished, the Metropolitan Railway Company received Parliamentary sanction for its first extension. By an Act of 6 August 1861 the company was authorised to extend its railway to Moorgate Street and to build a terminus there. And following the successful opening of the original line money was raised for the purchase of property. The works started in March 1864, 'narrow' (standard) gauge trains started to run on 23 December 1865, and broad gauge trains on 1 July 1866. The junction with the Great Northern had been completed on 10 October 1863, so the GNR started to run trains to Farringdon Street.

The Hammersmith & City Line

Meanwhile, westward, a line to Hammersmith (using the Great Western Railway between Bishops Road and Westbourne Park), backed by the Metropolitan Railway and the GWR and engineered by Fowler, was promoted by a separate company known as the Hammersmith & City Railway. It was promoted not only as a feeder to the Metropolitan Line, but also because in the late 1850s Hammersmith, which had a population of about 24,500, was without an effective rail link to the City. The new line ran from the Great Western main line at Green Lane (now Great Western Road), about a mile out of Paddington, and described a quarter-circle round the suburbs to a terminus near the north side of Hammersmith Broadway. There were intermediate stations at Notting Hill (now Ladbroke Grove) and Shepherd's Bush (not the present station).

A branch left the main line at Latimer Road (the station of that name did not open until December 1868) and ran to Kensington Addison Road (now Olympia). The main line opened on 13 June 1864, and the branch, which formed a junction with the West London Railway at Uxbridge Road Junction, on 1 July. The West London Railway, which had opened on 27 May 1844, was never successful, but its link with the Hammersmith & City Line allowed passenger trains to be run from Kensington onto the Underground.

At the beginning the line was worked with broad gauge stock by the Great Western, which used it for urban passenger traffic, for goods traffic to and from Paddington and Smithfield, and also for some main-line trains. Then on 1 April 1865 Metropolitan trains with standard gauge stock started to run to Hammersmith. The track was mixed gauge but, because of delays on the Great Western section, two extra tracks were laid and opened in May 1867. After that the Hammersmith & City Line

The Metropolitan Railway in 1863.

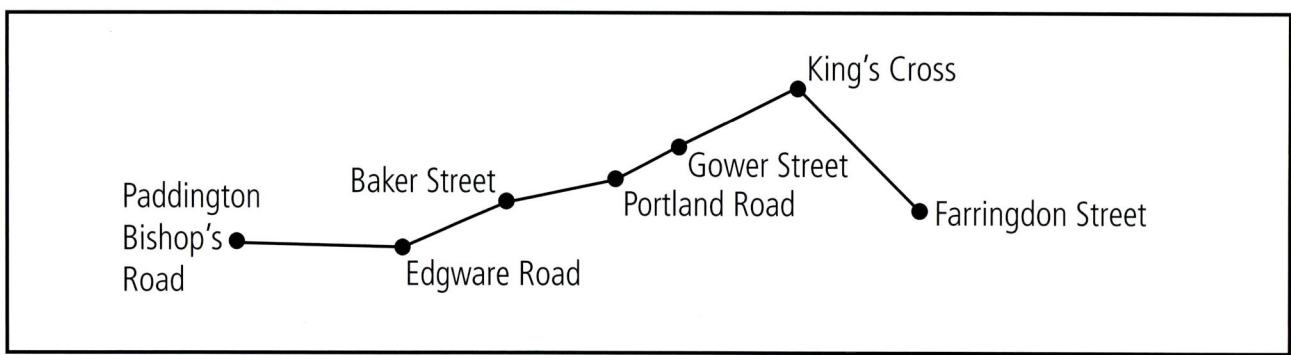

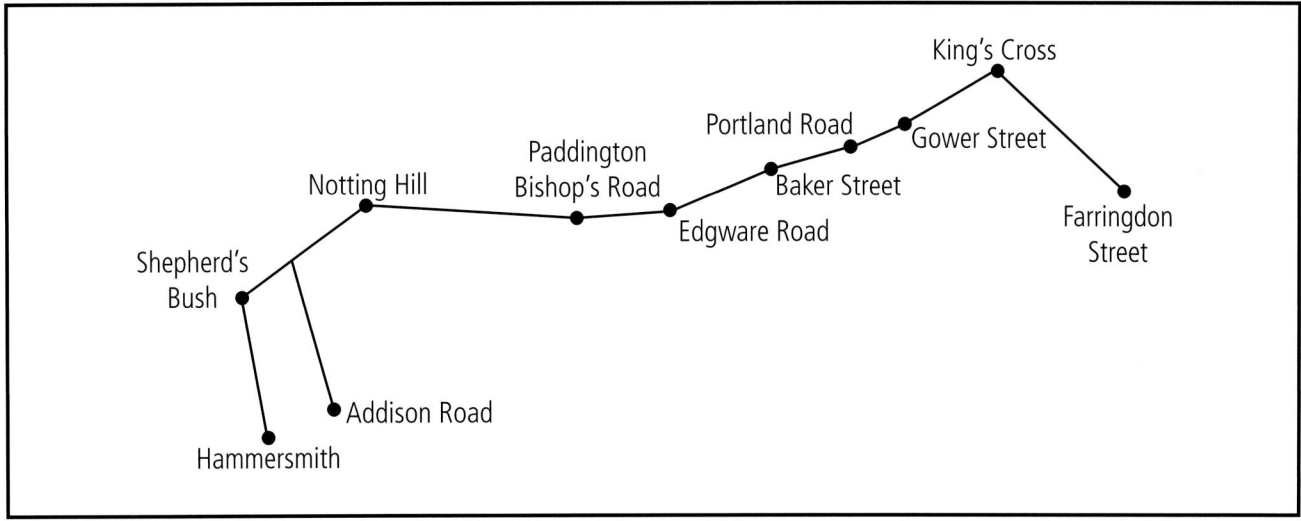

The Metropolitan Railway in 1864.

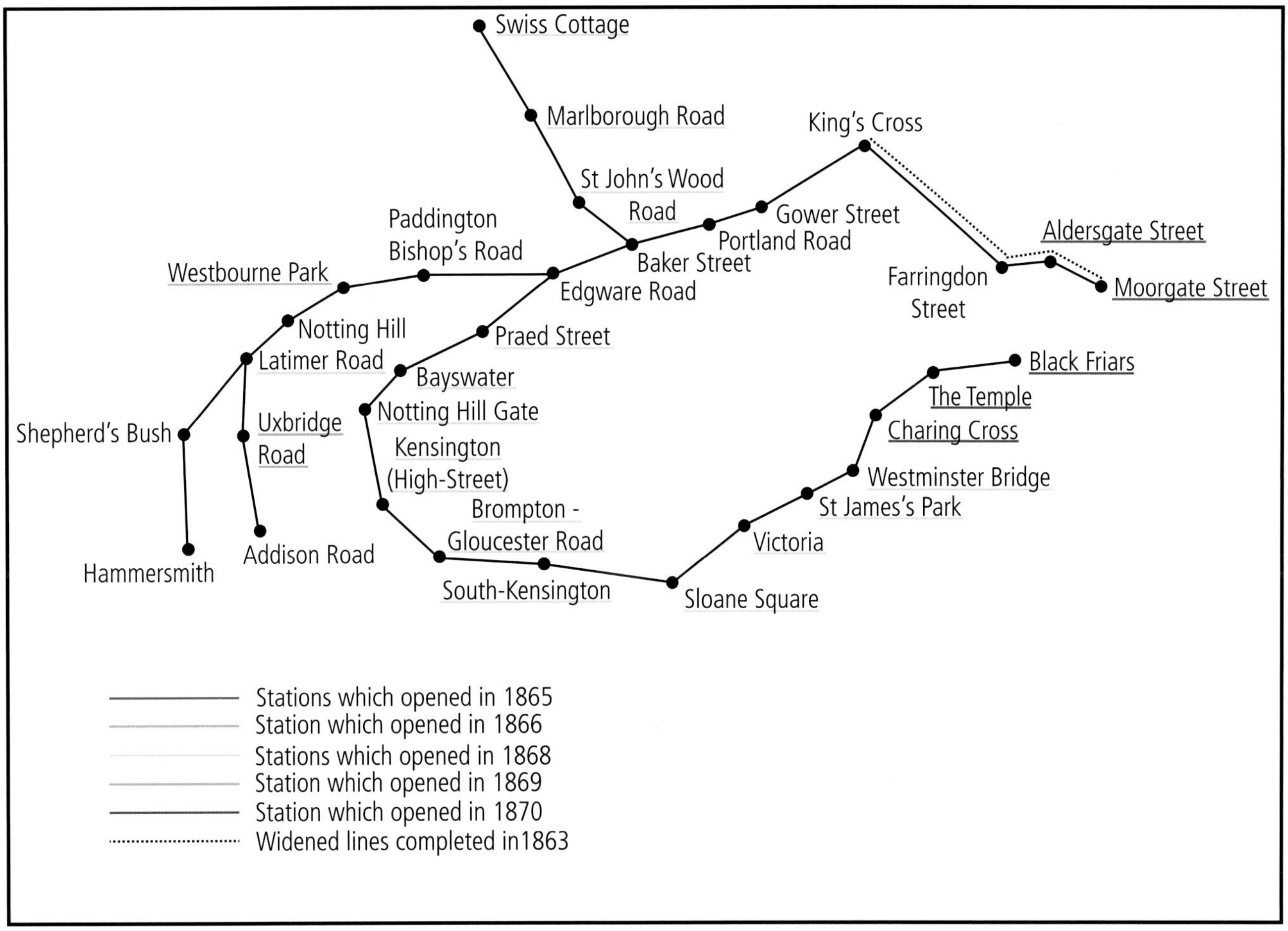

The Metropolitan Railway in 1870.

was vested in the Great Western and Metropolitan jointly by an Act of 15 July 1867. The passenger traffic grew rapidly, and at Westbourne Park, where the line crossed the Great Western Railway main line, there was often some congestion, so in 1878 a subway was built to take the Hammersmith & City Line under the Great Western. Some of the Great Western and Metropolitan trains used to run through to Richmond; they left the main line just before Hammersmith and headed towards Grove Road, there they continued towards Turnham Green, Kew Gardens and Richmond via the London & South Western Railway (LSWR). However, the loss of traffic on that section due to competition from other routes, together with the fact that the Hammersmith & City Line was going to be electrified while the LSWR was going to remain steam-worked, caused the Metropolitan Railway to withdraw its trains from that section in 1905. In 1875 the trains ran mainly between Hammersmith

The City Line and the Widened Lines (right) north of Farringdon Street Station. *Crecy Heritage Library*

and Liverpool Street, but later that year the service was extended first to Bishopsgate, then to Aldgate in 1876 and to New Cross, via the East London Railway, in 1884. There was also a shuttle service between Addison Road and Edgware Road, but the traffic over that section (which catered for visitors to exhibitions at Olympia) varied a great deal.

The Widened Lines

Charles Pearson's idea of a big central terminus for main-line trains was never pursued, but more and more suburban trains of different railways were using some portion of the Metropolitan to reach a City terminus, since the line had links with most of the main lines: at Paddington with the Great Western Railway, at King's Cross with the Great Northern Railway (whose increasing suburban traffic presented a problem), with the London, Chatham & Dover Railway (LCDR) at Farringdon Street, at King's Cross with the Midland Railway (which ran trains to Moorgate from 13 July 1868, before St Pancras was opened on 1 October 1868), and in 1880 with the South Eastern Railway. In order to meet the needs of these 'foreign' railways, the Metropolitan had to build at great expense a second pair of tracks, known as the Widened Lines, from King's Cross to Moorgate Street, which became the largest station on the Metropolitan Line after a few more platforms were added to bring the total to eight. The Metropolitan Railway kept its original line for its own trains, while the new line was used by the GNR, the Midland Railway and the LCDR for passenger and freight traffic. The new line was opened on 1 March 1866 between Aldersgate Street and Farringdon Street, and on 1 July of that year between Aldersgate Street and Moorgate Street. The remaining section, between King's Cross and Farringdon Street, was completed only in May 1867, as it involved heavier work.

A 733-yard-long widening tunnel, parallel with the Clerkenwell Tunnel, had to be dug. From King's Cross the new tracks ran to the north of the original line, then passed under it by a skew bridge near Farringdon Street, known as the 'Ray Street Gridiron'. This section of the line was opened on 27 January 1868 for goods traffic and 17 February 1868 for passengers. This enabled the Midland Railway to establish a local passenger service between Bedford and Moorgate Street from 13 July 1868. The connection with Smithfield Market was opened in November 1868 and started to be served by trains on 3 May 1869. In 1871 the Metropolitan Railway opened between Moorgate Street and Snow Hill, where there was a new connection with the London, Chatham & Dover Railway, which agreed to run 80 trains a day over that section from its line to Moorgate Street. Unfortunately the passenger traffic was never as lucrative as the freight traffic, and in 1916 the South Eastern & Chatham Railway

The burrowing junction on the Widened Lines just to the west of Farringdon Road, with a westbound train going into the original tunnel, and an eastbound train, on the Widened Lines, emerging from the deeper-level tunnel. The 'Gridiron' allowed Widened Lines trains to pass under the Metropolitan line near Farringdon Street.

(SECR, successor to the South Eastern and London, Chatham & Dover companies) decided to stop the running of trains to Moorgate Street; this did not please the Metropolitan, which was receiving a proportion of the fares (1d per passenger, which in fact was not much). As the SECR refused to restore the service, the Metropolitan took successful legal action against it in 1923, but the passenger traffic was not resumed. However, the number of freight trains exchanged between the southern and northern railways remained important. More connections were planned, but did not materialise, including one with the London & North Western Railway (LNWR) at Euston, and a branch line that was to run directly to the General Post Office.

In 1926 the Metropolitan Railway, which till then had never used the Widened Lines, started using them to run trains to Moorgate. In order to do so the upper part of the line west of King's Cross was linked to a section of the unused Euston tunnel and electrified. Unfortunately, this new link was not very successful and the running of trains over that section was later suspended.

The Metropolitan & St John's Wood Railway

This next step towards expansion was later to become an important one. The Metropolitan & St John's Wood Railway, an underground railway promoted by an independent company, whose engineer was also Fowler, was incorporated in 1864, and was to run from Baker Street to meet the Hampstead Junction Railway near the latter's Finchley Road station. When the company started to run into great financial difficulties, the Metropolitan Railway came to the rescue and, with its help, the new company managed to open its line on 13 April 1868. It consisted of a single-track line that left the Metropolitan by a junction at Baker Street and ended at Swiss Cottage. It ran just under

Metropolitan Railway Class B No 58 is seen at West Hampstead station on the St John's Wood branch.

the ground level in tunnels (one for the up line and one for the down line), ventilated by many gaps and openings. In the stations the lines merged and were partly open to daylight. On the platforms the retaining walls were faced with bricks, and offered waiting rooms and other passenger facilities.

At first a through service was run from Swiss Cottage to Moorgate Street, but in March 1869, when the company proposed to double the frequency of the service, the Metropolitan closed the junction, refusing to allow through trains, and passengers were made to walk along communicating galleries to the Metropolitan platforms at Baker Street. On 30 June 1879 the line was extended to West Hampstead and on 24 November 1879 to Willesden Green. It was intended to make a connection by tunnel with the Hampstead Junction Railway, but the work was never completed. However, a connection was made for the transfer of freight with the Midland Railway on 1 October 1880, and a goods yard was laid by the Metropolitan Railway at Finchley Road on a site near the passenger station and the Midland depot. Finally, the company was vested in the Metropolitan Railway Company on 1 January 1883 by an Act of 3 July 1882.

The running of the line was not easy, as the track was not level; indeed, there were a number of steep gradients, especially the hump over the Regent's Canal, and to face these difficulties it was at first thought that some specially powerful locomotives should be built to work the line. An order for five 0-6-0 tank locomotives, numbered 34 to 38, was placed with the Worcester Engine Company. The new engines were put into service in 1868, but it was soon found that they were too powerful and that standard 4-4-0 tank locomotives could cope perfectly well. Consequently they were sold.

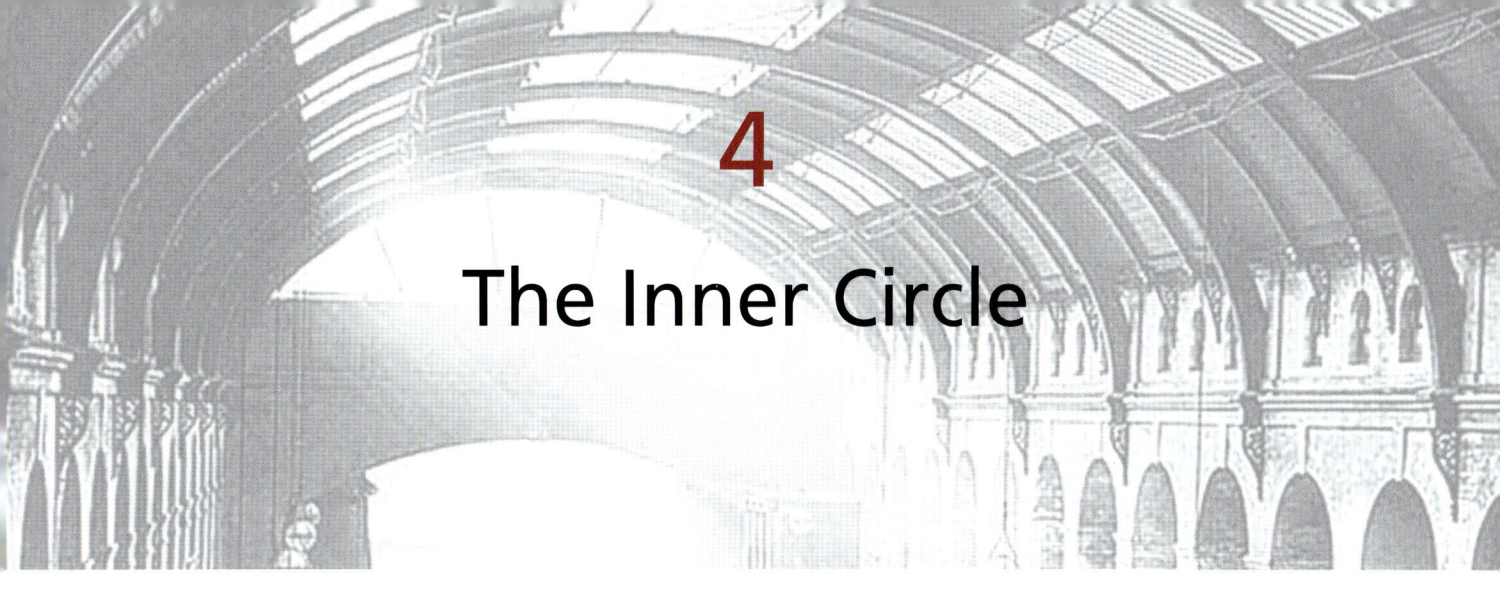

4

The Inner Circle

As the leader writer of *The Times* commented at the time

'It is characteristic of Englishmen that they are slow to adopt a principle, but when they are once converted to it, they give it an impulsive and boisterous welcome that goes far beyond the calmer acquiescence of their neighbours. Now that one or two companies have set the example of coming right into London, Metropolitan Railways are quite a rage.'[8]

This proved to be quite accurate since, very soon after the opening of the Metropolitan Railway, Parliament was confronted with many competing schemes for building railways within central London itself. The project that was recommended, having been proposed by John Fowler, was the extension of the existing underground railways to form an inner circuit, in order to link the new main-line termini. The building of a new road along the north side of the River Thames to relieve the traffic on the Strand was also suggested. The Metropolitan Railway applied for permission to build from Moorgate to Trinity Square (Tower Hill) and also from Paddington to Notting Hill Gate, Kensington and Brompton. This was authorised by the Metropolitan Railway (Notting Hill and Brompton Extension) Act and the Metropolitan Railway (Tower Hill Extension) Act, which received the Royal Assent on 29 July 1864.

Such an undertaking was going to be very costly, and the Metropolitan could not afford the building of the whole circle on its own. Thus the intermediate section, from Brompton (South Kensington) to Trinity Square (Tower Hill) via Westminster was handed to a new company, the Metropolitan District Railway Company, which was incorporated by an Act of 29 July 1864. This new company was at the beginning a very close associate of the Metropolitan Railway; it had in fact been promoted as a stop-gap to meet the financial needs of the time, and it was intended at first that the two companies should merge their interests as soon as it was financially possible.

Fowler was appointed engineer in chief, and W. A. Wilkinson, Chairman of the Metropolitan Railway Company, and three other directors were appointed to the Board of the Metropolitan District Railway Company. The new company was also authorised to build alongside the Metropolitan line from

Building the Metropolitan Railway under Leinster Gardens, Bayswater, c1866. *London Transport Museum*

The dummy houses, 23 and 24 Leinster Gardens, above the railway today.

South Kensington to Gloucester Road and continue through Earl's Court to a junction with the West London Extension Railway at West Brompton, and to build a line from Kensington High Street, also through Earl's Court to join the West London Railway near Addison Road. Both companies started to work simultaneously at different points on the 'circle'.

However, the venture soon became a very costly one, since the line was to cross residential areas, which implied that quite a lot of money had to be spent on compensation to property owners. In Leinster Gardens, for instance, the Metropolitan Railway had to build false-fronted houses where the line ran under the road, in order to conceal the railway. (These false houses, Nos 23 and 24, still exist and have been the subject of many practical jokes.) As to the Metropolitan District Company, besides carrying its line through residential districts or areas of historical interest like Westminster Abbey, it became involved with the widening of Tothill Street and a slum clearance.

The stretch from Paddington to Brompton (Gloucester Road) was opened on 1 October 1868, and that to South Kensington on 24 December. The section from Brompton to West Brompton was opened on 12 April 1869, and worked by a shuttle service until 1 August 1870, when the link with South Kensington came into use. The Kensington High Street stretch was finished by 7 September 1869, but the authorised junction with the West London Railway at West Brompton was never built. The Cromwell Curve, put in on the night of 3 July 1871, provided a through route between Kensington High Street and Gloucester Road by District rails.

From 1870 Westminster station had a subway to the nearby Houses of Parliament. Unfortunately the Metropolitan District Railway Company soon ran into trouble, and arguments began to arise between the two companies. It seemed that the Board of the Metropolitan Railway was taking some liberties with the company's capital. Between 1864 and 1868 the Metropolitan was paying shareholders good dividends, up to 7 per cent, and the shareholders were not very willing to subsidise a less profitable

Notting Hill Gate station in 1868. *London Transport Museum*

Bayswater station interior, 1868. *London Transport Museum*

Contemporary cartoon of Sir Edward Watkin, appointed Chairman of the Metropolitan Railway in 1872.

undertaking like the Metropolitan District. The latter route's mileage, at the time, was only 5.7, the traffic was only passenger, and the line was isolated and had no direct connection with a main-line railway. At the beginning, being worked by the Metropolitan, the Metropolitan District was keeping 45 per cent of the gross receipts from through and local traffic, but soon it was only receiving 38 per cent because it had to pay more for the extra trains it required. Moreover, some investigation showed that the books of the Metropolitan Railway Company had not been kept satisfactorily, that there had been a lot of waste in stores and engineering departments, and that some members of the company had filled their pockets nicely. So it seems that if the company had been able to dispose of all of its authorised capital, it would not have encountered such great financial difficulties.

Soon the Metropolitan District became fed up with being the Metropolitan Railway's poor relation, and thought it could do better on its own, so decided to inform the Metropolitan on 3 January 1871 of its intention to terminate the working agreement, which was due to expire on 3 July. In the meantime the Metropolitan's directors on the board of the Metropolitan District had to resign, and a Managing Director, in the person of James Staats Forbes (1823-1904) was appointed in 1871; in 1872 he became Chairman. Forbes had a strong personality. He had trained under Saunders on the Great Western, had been general manager of a railway company in the Netherlands, and at the time was General Manager of the London, Chatham & Dover Railway, which he helped out of a catastrophic financial collapse. He was a forceful and dynamic character and had a genius for the propagation of railways, and for scenting new avenues for connections and train services. In other words he was a good match for the Metropolitan Railway Company's new head, Edward Watkin, who had been since 1866 Chairman of the LCDR's greatest rival, the South Eastern Railway. As we shall see later, Watkin also had a great personality.

The District now purchased its own rolling stock and built its own depot at Lillie Bridge. So far the Metropolitan had been avoiding the construction of its section east of Moorgate Street; but the new board appointed in 1872 and under the leadership of Watkin raised some money and pressed on with the building of that extension. The stretch to Liverpool Street, where the Metropolitan's line could link with the Great Eastern Railway, was opened on 1 February 1875, and the stretch to the Metropolitan Railway's own station at Bishopsgate on 12 July 1875. On 18 November 1876 the line was extended to Aldgate. At that time the terminus of the Metropolitan District Railway was at the corner of Queen Victoria Street and Cannon Street (Mansion House). The proposed circuit was not yet completed, and the Metropolitan District Railway was still in financial difficulties and could not embark unaided on the completion of the Inner Circle. The Metropolitan was not prepared at the time to spend any money to help, but a link between the two lines was desperately needed as traffic congestion to the east of Cannon Street had become heavy. Consequently, a company called the Inner Circle Completion Company decided to come to the rescue.

This company won the support of the Metropolitan Board of Works and in 1874 secured Parliamentary sanction. However, when it started to raise money in 1877, the Metropolitan Railway Company suddenly changed its mind and proposed that the Metropolitan and Metropolitan District Railway companies should finish the line themselves. The main reason for this change of attitude was in fact quite selfish, since what the Metropolitan had in mind was the possibility of later building a branch (the Whitechapel branch) from the Circle to join the East London Railway, so as to have an extension into the eastern suburbs and a link with the main-line railways south of the river. The Metropolitan already had a junction with the Great Eastern Railway (GER) at Liverpool Street, but only until it had its own station at Bishopsgate, and through trains were never run because the two companies could not agree on the fares. In 1878 the GER accepted the proposal to reopen the junction, but would not let the Metropolitan Railway link with the East London Railway, which was the main reason why the former had become interested in the Inner Circle again, all the more so as Watkin had helped the East London Railway out of its financial problems by becoming its Chairman.

The Metropolitan & District Railways (City Lines and Extensions) Act became law on 11 August 1879, but the works could not be started straight away since the former company, which offered to finish the Inner Circle, had to be compensated. The various organisations involved in the financing of the operation also had to be convinced to transfer their grants to the new route and to increase them, and land also had to be purchased.

Finally, the first stretch between Aldgate and Trinity Square (known as Tower of London) was opened on 25 September 1882, and the remaining stretch on 6 October 1884. So, after 20 years of fighting and arguing, the Inner Circle line was at long last opened – but ironically it initially brought more problems and appeared to be a complete failure. The first problem arose from the attempt to increase the frequency of trains from six to eight per hour in each direction, and at the same time to feed into the system the existing trains from the branches and extra ones from the District section and the East London Railway. The situation was sometimes so bad that traffic came to a standstill and angry passengers were known to have got out of the train in the tunnel and walked to the next station. This chaotic state of affairs was partly due to the companies' dislike for each another, their lack of confidence in each other, and the fact that each was only concerned with its own interests. They went as far as stealing each other's passengers – they were not able to choose their own way, but were sent on the longest route over the line owned by the company issuing the tickets. At joint stations the companies had separate booking offices and, with a vast advertising campaign, were hoping to attract one another's passengers. And on one occasion, because of a dispute over the rights to a siding, the District went as far as to run a Metropolitan train into a siding and chain it to the spot.

However, the problems did not arise only from the ill-will and the rivalry between the two companies – there were also some technical problems. The trains needed to be gassed (the gas containers for the carriage lighting had to be constantly refilled), watered (the water in the locomotives' condensing tanks had to be changed often, so as not to fill the tunnels with steam and fumes), and checked regularly. Before the Inner Circle was completed, this servicing could easily be done at the termini, but now that there were no termini, it had to be done on the line or in a siding, which created numerous delays. Finally, a solution was found: the trains were stopped at Aldgate for the change of water, and fuller servicing took place at Kensington. It was also decided that the Metropolitan trains would travel on the outer track and the District trains on the inner track. A journalist travelling round the Inner Circle on the footplate of a locomotive in 1893 described his journey as follows:

'[At first] the sensation altogether was much like the inhalation of gas preparatory to having a tooth drawn. I would have given a good deal to have waited just a minute or so longer. Visions of accidents, collisions and crumbling tunnels floated through my mind; a fierce wind took away my breath, and innumerable blacks filled my eyes, I crouched low and held on like grim death to a little rail near me... Before and behind and on either side was blackness, heavy, dense and impenetrable... Westminster Bridge, Charing Cross, and the Temple were passed before I could think of anything but holding on to that rolling, rushing engine... [At Aldgate] the fireman at once jumped off the engine and made the necessary arrangements for filling our water tanks. So quickly was this done that probably none of the passengers noticed any difference in the length of the stoppage... From Farringdon Street to King's Cross is the longest stretch without a station, and the driver here gave us an exhibition of full speed, and No 18 came into King's Cross at the rate of some 40mph. The average speed of trains between one

Contemporary painting of James Staats Forbes who became Chairman of the Metropolitan District Railway in 1872.

station and another is from 20 to 25mph. The road now begun uphill, and at the same time the air grew more foul. From King's Cross to Edgware Road the ventilation is defective, and the atmosphere on a par xwith the "tween decks forrud' of a modern ironclad in bad weather, and this is saying a good deal. By the time we reached Gower Street I was coughing and spluttering like a boy with his first cigar. "It is a little unpleasant when you ain't use to it," said the driver with the composure born of long usage, "but you ought to come on a hot summer day to get the real thing!" Fog on the underground appears to cause less inconvenience than do the sultry days of July; then the atmosphere is killing. With the exception of this one section (between King's Cross and Edgware Road) I found the air far purer than I had expected, and the bad air so much complained of by the 'sewer-rats' – as those who habitually use this circle are called in 'the City' – is due in great measure to their almost universal habit of keeping all the windows and ventilators closed…

At High Street Kensington, engines are changed so we jumped off. Engine No 18 went off into a shed to rest a while, and No 7, a precisely similar one, backed onto the train in her place. This resting of engines is rendered a frequent necessity from the strain caused by the numerous stoppages; incessant running in one direction has also been found bad for them as it wears the wheels on one side sooner than on the other. To remedy this, the engines half their time run 'backwards forwards'… Off again, and this time downhill. We dashed rapidly through the grass embankments outside Gloucester Road, past some men posting bills on the advertisement hoardings that border the line below South Kensington, now deep into a tunnel, now traversing a cutting open to the sky, until we shot once more into St James Park 70 minutes after leaving it.'[9]

The misplaced hopes of a large increase in traffic from railways south of the river, and the competition due to omnibus services, contributed to the failure of the Inner Circle line, which cost £2,500 to complete. There were two other circles: the Middle Circle and the Outer Circle. These were called circles, but in reality they were more horseshoe-shaped. The Middle Circle was worked by the Great Western Railway. It ran from Paddington to Westbourne Park, thence over the Hammersmith & City Line to Latimer Road Junction; the trains then took the branch to Uxbridge Road Junction, on the West London Railway, stopping at Addison Road, and joined the Metropolitan District Railway at Warwick Road Junction, continuing thence to Mansion House. The Outer Circle was worked by the London & North Western Railway. It started at Broad Street (the North London Railway's terminus) and went via Dalston, Camden Town, Hampstead Heath and Kensal Rise to Willesden Junction, thence over the West London Railway to Addison Road; it then took the same route as the Middle Circle to Mansion House. Both 'Circles' provided a half-hourly service. However, over the years, these services gradually disappeared, leaving only the exhibition services between Olympia and Earl's Court.

The Metropolitan Railway and part of the Metropolitan District Railway in 1880.

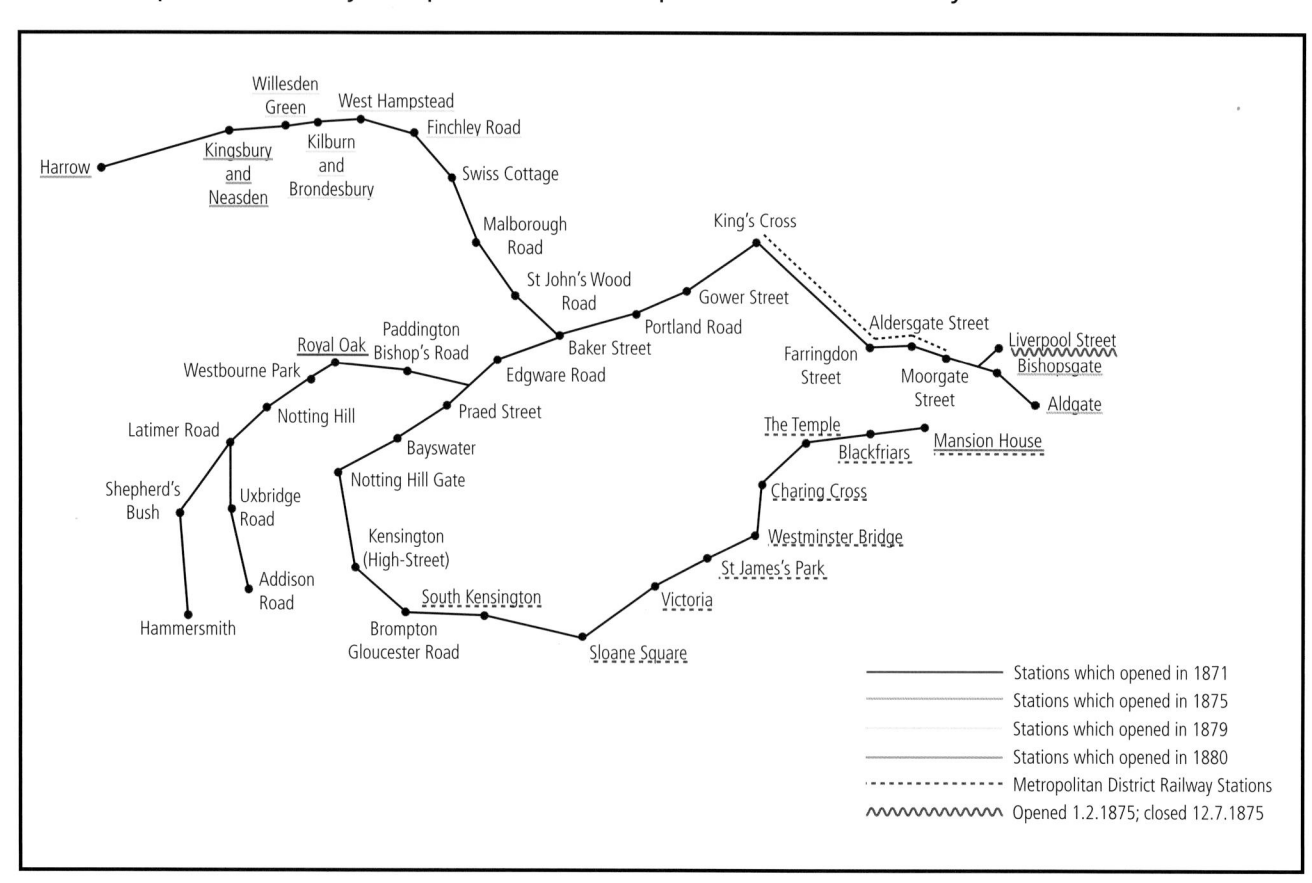

5

The East London Railway

Before going on to the Metropolitan Railway Company's extensions into suburbia, let us first turn towards another railway line, coveted by the Metropolitan – the East London Railway (ELR) – which we have mentioned briefly in the previous chapter.

The company was incorporated by an Act of 26 May 1865, and was granted powers to build below London Bridge a line that would connect all the railways entering London from both sides of the Thames. The plan was to build a line from Old Kent Road on the South London Railway and from junctions at New Cross with the London, Brighton & South Coast Railway (LBSCR) and the South Eastern Railway (SER) to Liverpool Street. The new line was to be carried through Deptford Road, Rotherhithe and Wapping (situated at each end of the Thames Tunnel), Shadwell, Whitechapel and Shoreditch. Its purpose was also to give access to the Great Northern and Midland companies.

On 25 September 1865 the company bought the famous Thames Tunnel between Rotherhithe and Wapping. On 7 December 1869 the section between Wapping and Shadwell station, and a temporary station at New Cross, were opened to the public. The intermediate stations were then Rotherhithe and Deptford Road. The service was run by the LBSCR with its own rolling stock. On 13 March 1871 the section between Deptford Road Junction and Old Kent Road was opened. The northern section of the line, between Wapping and Bishopsgate, 1 mile 55 chains long, took longer to build because it involved more work as the railway had to pass under the London Docks. This final section was opened to the public on 10 April 1876 with intermediate stations at Shoreditch, Whitechapel and Shadwell. Southward extensions were also undertaken; one of them was a branch from Deptford Road Junction to a point on the up side of the LBSCR at New Cross (renamed New Cross Gate on 9 July 1923), and the other was in fact two junctions, one up and one down, with the South Eastern Railway at the latter's New Cross station. The LBSCR started to run trains from Liverpool Street in June 1876, and from New Croydon on 1 July. On 1 November of that year the East London Railway's station at New Cross was closed. On 1 August 1877 the ELR trains were projected southwards from Old Kent Road to terminate at Peckham Rye (the LBSCR station).

The East London Railway and connections.

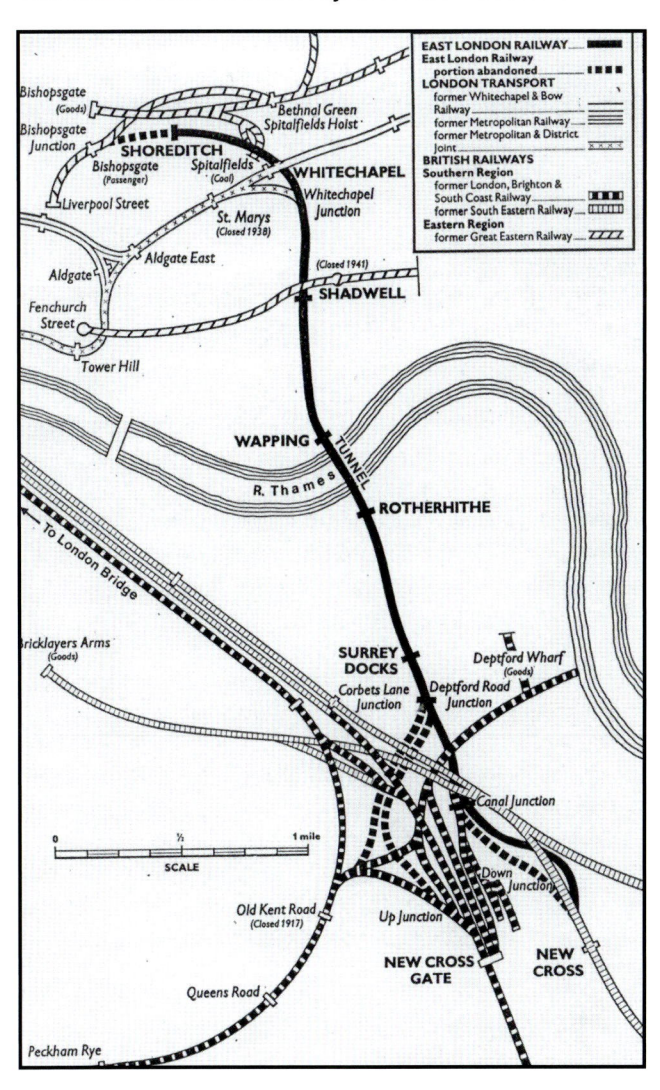

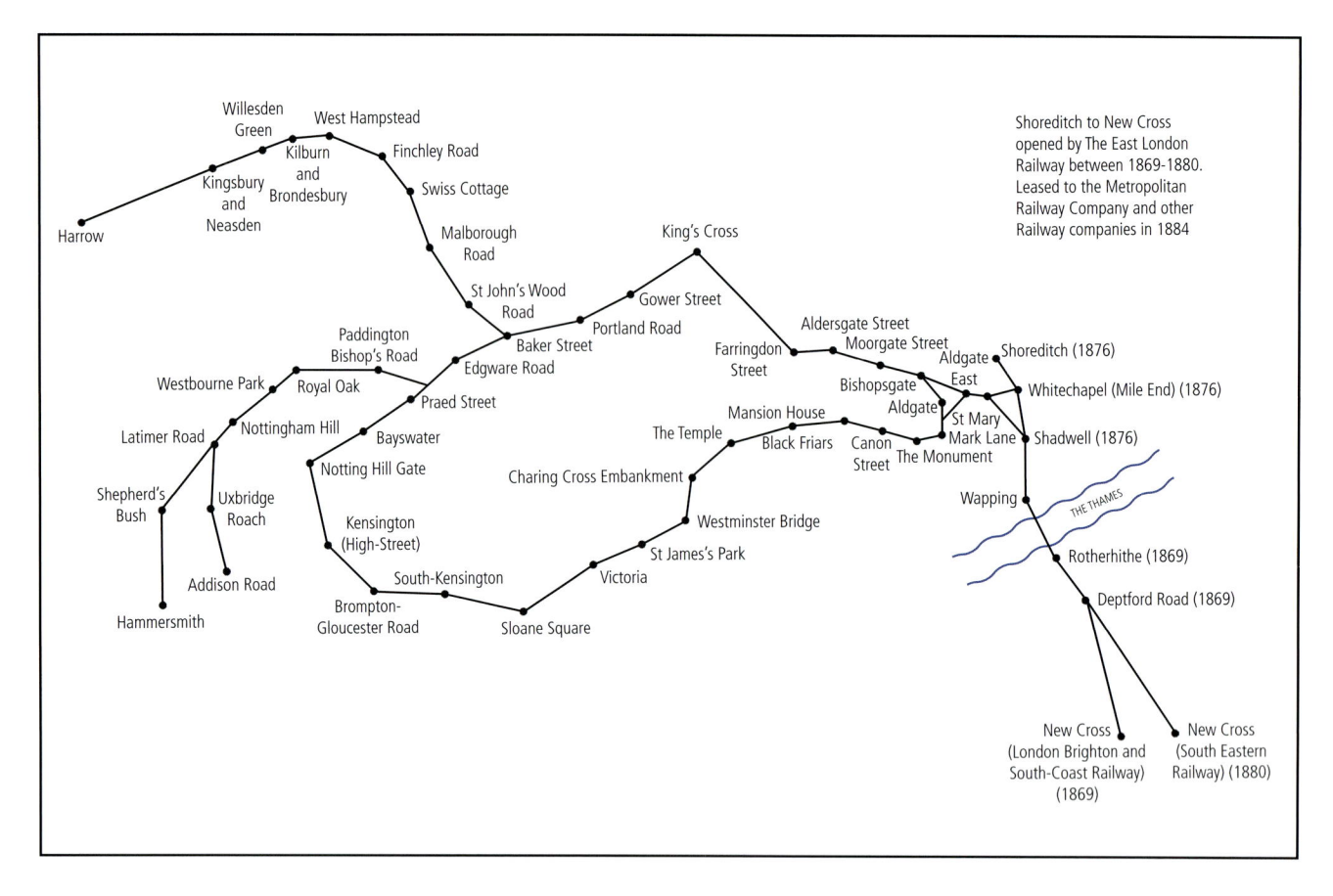

Metropolitan Railway and Connections in 1884.

Unfortunately the company soon came into great financial difficulties, and Sir Edward Watkin, who came to the rescue, became the new Chairman in May 1878. As we have already pointed out, his gesture was quite selfish since his intentions were in fact to connect the ELR line with the Metropolitan line by building a link between Aldgate and Whitechapel, and to authorise at last the junction built a few years previously with the SER at New Cross, which he had opposed till then.

The Metropolitan and Metropolitan District companies were authorised by the Metropolitan & District (City Lines and Extensions) Act of 11 August 1879 to build jointly a link between Aldgate and Mansion House, and to extend the line from the vicinity of Aldgate to Whitechapel, where it was to connect with the East London. However, the original plan was slightly altered, since the connection was not made at Whitechapel, where the Metropolitan District Railway had built a terminal station, but at a higher level. Between Tower Hill and Whitechapel the Metropolitan District Railway had two intermediate stations: Aldgate East and St Mary's. In 1882 the ELR was granted powers under an Act of 10 August to build a curve called the Whitechapel Junction Railway, from a point south of its Whitechapel station to the newly built St Mary's station. Work started in August 1882 and the junction was opened to the public in March 1884, and the SER diverted its Addiscombe Road trains to St Mary's station instead of Liverpool Street.

Also in 1882 the East London Joint Committee was formed, and its members (the London, Brighton & South Coast Railway, South Eastern Railway, London, Chatham & Dover Railway, Metropolitan Railway and Metropolitan District Railway) agreed to lease the East London Railway in perpetuity. In 1885 they were joined by the Great Eastern Railway. At first the LBSCR was put in charge of the maintenance and staffing, but in 1885 the SER took over the maintenance work. On 1 October 1884 the lease came into effect, and the Metropolitan and Metropolitan District railways both started to run local services to New Cross, the former to the SER station and the latter to the ELR station. The latter station had been closed since 1876 and had therefore to be temporarily opened. From 31 August 1886 the trains were transferred to the nearby LBSCR station. On 1 October 1884 the Metropolitan & District Joint Committee acquired the Whitechapel Junction Railway. In December of that year the LBSCR stopped running trains through to Liverpool Street and all terminated at Shoreditch. On 1 January 1886 GER trains started to run between Liverpool Street and the LBSCR station at New Cross, and on 1 February 1887 some trains started to run to Croydon on weekdays.

It is also important to note that on 6 October 1884 the last link in the Inner Circle and the extension to Whitechapel were opened to the public. This allowed the Metropolitan Railway to run trains between Hammersmith (Hammersmith & City Line station) and New Cross (SER station) via the northern part of the Inner Circle; the Metropolitan District Railway also started to run trains between its own station at Hammersmith and the LBSCR station at New Cross, via the southern part of the Inner Circle.

Unfortunately more problems arose again, since most of the railways with which the ELR was linked were beginning to electrify their lines and the company was not wealthy enough to raise the necessary money to electrify its own; consequently a few stations were closed, and many disagreements arose between the railway companies. Hence the Metropolitan Railway stopped running trains between 1906 (the date of the electrification of the Inner Circle and of the Hammersmith & City line) and 1913, when the ELR line was finally electrified with the help of the GWR, SER, Metropolitan and Metropolitan District companies at a cost of £77,591.

Thus on 31 March 1913 the Metropolitan Railway started to run a full service of electric trains from South Kensington to New Cross via the northern part of the Inner Circle, and from Hammersmith (Hammersmith & City line station) in February 1914.

On behalf of the Joint Committee, the Metropolitan Railway Company was entrusted with the management of the line from 1 July 1921, and with its maintenance from 1 January 1924. In 1925 the ownership of the line was vested in the Southern Railway (successor to the LBSCR and SER companies), but it did not affect the running of the line, since the Joint Committee continued to function as before. Finally, the Joint Committee was dissolved on 2 April 1949, after the nationalisation of the railways on 1 January 1948, and the East London Railway became part of the London Underground system, managed by London Transport.

St Mary's station (Whitechapel), opened by the Metropolitan and Metropolitan & District Joint Railway in 1888. *London Transport Museum*

6

The Metropolitan tries to become a main-line railway

Sir Edward Watkin

As already mentioned in a previous chapter, everything was not going well for the Metropolitan Railway in the late 1860s and early 1870s, and the company was in poor shape. The sudden drop in dividends in the course of 1871 alarmed the proprietors, who ordered an investigation. Messrs H. D. Pochin and Benjamin Whitworth were elected to the board in order to investigate the problem. By August 1872 their report was ready and revealed that figures had been made to lie for years and concealed mismanagement and dishonesty. It was also proved that there had been much slackness and waste in the stores and engineering department, that the books and ledgers had been badly kept, and contained many fictitious and false entries. They also uncovered a serious error in the last balance sheet. Thus, with the company on the verge of bankruptcy, the chief shareholders decided to meet the board on 31 July 1872.

They had to find someone of Forbes's calibre to save the company from financial ruin. They found such a man in the person of Sir Edward Watkin, who was not only Forbes's equal but his rival. On 7 August he agreed to become the company's new Chairman, but in order to make way for him one of the directors had to retire, and after a ballot the lot fell on John Parson (who was apportioned a large part of the blame for the mismanagement of the company's affairs and who even told the committee of the inquiry that he did not understand the figures).

Watkin was one of the great railway tycoons of the 19th century, and was said to be a walking encyclopaedia of railway knowledge and experience. Watkin was born in Salford in 1819. He was the son of an important cotton merchant and it was in his father's office that he started his career. He then became the director of the Manchester Athenaeum and started the Saturday half-holiday movement. He made his debut in the railway world in 1845, as secretary of a scheme that became the Trent Valley Railway. From then on he became involved in many railway projects and undertakings. At different times he was either director, chairman, president or board member of various railway companies such as the Great Western, the Boston, Sleaford & Midland Counties (worked by the Great Northern), the Grand Trunk of Canada, the Aylesbury & Buckingham, the East London, the Blackpool, the New York, Lake Erie & Western, the South Eastern, the Cheshire Midland, and others. He also had a political career, and was Member of Parliament for Stockport between 1864 and 1868, for Hythe between 1874 and 1885, both times as a Liberal, and between 1886 and 1895 as Unionist Member of Parliament for Hythe.

So, on 7 August 1872 Watkin, then Chairman of the South Eastern Railway and of the Manchester, Sheffield & Lincolnshire Railway, was appointed Chairman of the Metropolitan Railway Company, mainly for his great knowledge and experience, but also because many of the shareholders knew him well since they had some interest in Manchester (for example, Pochin was a chemical manufacturer there, and Whitworth was in cotton), it was thus not surprising that they called on their Manchester friend to help them. And they chose well, at the time, for Watkin quickly put the company back on its feet. However, in the long run the choice was not so good, because during the 22 years that he controlled the company's destiny, his only aim was to make of the Metropolitan a main-line railway by extending it into the country.

Watkin was indeed a very ambitious man: his dream was to link the Metropolitan Railway with the Manchester, Sheffield & Lincolnshire Railway by constructing a new trunk line to London that would carry the coal of South Yorkshire, the merchandise of Lancashire and the passengers from the North of England straight through to Dover by means of the Metropolitan and South Eastern companies, and to Paris by means of a tunnel under the Channel. Not only did he intend to carry goods and passengers to the continent, but he also wanted to make of Baker

Street a great terminus. And his line thus crossing Britain would then become a sort of backbone for the commerce and industry of the country. He negotiated the building of a tunnel under the Channel with both British and French Governments, and in 1881 excavations started on both sides. But in 1882 digging was stopped on the English side by the Board of Trade, for public opinion thought the tunnel to be a national danger.

Extension to Harrow

In spite of the failure of his most cherished plan, Watkin did not give up the idea of turning the Metropolitan into a main line. And he did not waste any time, for in 1873 the St John's Wood line obtained powers to extend to Kingsbury (known as Neasden). The outward extension of the route was opened to West Hampstead on 30 June 1879 and to Willesden Green in November of that year (the initial section of the line was doubled from Baker Street to Swiss Cottage on 10 July 1882, and the new track ran in a separate tunnel alongside the old one).

Harrow-on-the-Hill became the next target. The powers for an extension from Willesden to Harrow had already been granted by an Act of 1874, and the Kingsbury & Harrow Joint Committee (comprising the Metropolitan Railway and the Metropolitan & St John's Wood Railway) was incorporated to carry out the extension and build an intermediate station, called Kingsbury & Neasden. The section to Harrow-on-the-Hill was opened on 2 August 1880, and a transfer yard for exchange of freight traffic with the Midland Railway was also opened at Finchley Road.

The whole line to Harrow involved few engineering works apart from culverts and a girder bridge over the LNWR at Kenton, but the permanent way is worthy of mention. The chairs and the bullhead rails, weighing 86lb per yard, were of the type generally adopted by the Metropolitan after the City line broad-gauge track was removed, but the Committee experimented with steel sleepers and special fishplates. The former were of an inverted channel section, and the fishplates, which were deeper than the normal type, gripped the lower flange of the rail. The steel sleepers were relatively short-lived, but the fishplates became standard and spread over the whole system.

The most distinguished feature of the extension was undoubtedly Harrow-on-the-Hill station. The architecture of all Metropolitan buildings was taken seriously, and the earliest examples received favourable comments from the critics of the day; it was natural for the latest station to have character and dignity in keeping with the town and its associations. Contemporary writers regarded it as an attempt to show that architecture and engineering could go hand in hand, and there was nothing but praise for the modified Queen Anne style that was said to predominate. Booking offices and waiting rooms were adorned with stained glass windows, painted dados, and coloured walls faced with enamelled bricks. The opening on 2 August 1880 was celebrated with the customary speechmaking between railway and civic officials, in this case augmented by celebrities of Harrow School, and held at the well-known King's Head inn; free trips were granted over the railway to

Electric locomotive No 7 with Class E No 78 at Harrow-on-the-Hill, 2 October 1920. *A. W. Croughton/Stephenson Locomotive Society*

The official opening of the Chesham Branch on 8 July 1889. *Stephenson Locomotive Society*

Another view of Chesham, this time in 1935 with Class E No 80 on the 6.12pm to Chalfont. *A. W. Croughton/Stephenson Locomotive Society*

Willesden Green. The service consisted of 36 trains to and from Baker Street on weekdays and a good number on Sundays, although in common with the whole system there was the customary church interval in the morning.[10]

The Metropolitan Railway now extended 9½ miles from Baker Street, and was no longer crossing suburban areas but serving small rural villages. However, Watkin was not going to stop there, for he had already made plans go further, though the objective remained a close secret at the time.

Extension to Aylesbury

This next step forward was to be carried out by the Harrow & Rickmansworth Railway, which was incorporated in 1874. (As we have already seen, the Metropolitan Railway Company's extensions were often carried out first by a separate company set up for the purpose and later absorbed by the parent company.) The responsibility for further construction was vested in the Metropolitan Company directly, and under the powers it had been granted in 1880 it carried the line through Pinner, which opened on 25 May 1885, to Northwood and Rickmansworth, both of which opened on 1 September 1887. One might wonder what the possible object was of carrying a line through areas consisting only of fields and farms. Watkin was determined to carry out his dream, and his immediate object was to reach Aylesbury; however, as the company was short of money at the time, it tried to interest the landowners along the route in the project by offering them shares, as a means of raising finance, but as these would have produced no return unless the company's earnings exceeded 5 per cent, the landowners naturally showed little interest in such an offer.

The Metropolitan board offered as a first stage a line from Rickmansworth to Chesham through Chorley Wood and Chalfont Road (renamed Chalfont and Latimer in 1915). The building of the line to Amersham and Aylesbury was authorised by the Aylesbury & Rickmansworth Railway Act of 1885, and the Chesham branch by the Metropolitan Railway Act of 1885; the branch was to diverge from the main line at a point three-quarters of a mile from Chalfont & Latimer, and was to be 2½ miles long. The branch was built first, and opened on 8 July 1889. Most of the land for this section was bought from the Duke of Bedford and Lord Chesham, but the land for the building of the last section was given by the town's inhabitants, to make sure that the station would be built in the centre of the town, and not on the outskirts as planned by the company, for they realised that they needed good railway connections. Subsequently the Metropolitan Railway bought more strips of land, extending almost 1½ miles north of the station in the direction of Berkhamsted, but the branch was never extended beyond Chesham. The section from Rickmansworth to Chalfont Road was double track, but the branch section to Chesham was single track, as it was intended to be a branch line only. However, according to C. Baker, a good service was provided:

Metropolitan Class H locomotive No 107 is seen at Aylesbury in 1925. *A. W. Croughton/Stephenson Locomotive Society Collection*

Aylesbury in 1933, with Class G No 87 on the 1.37pm to Baker Street. *A. W. Croughton/ Stephenson Locomotive Society*

'Chesham was the starting place of various "long distance" excursions to other companies' lines and, in the first week of operation, "specials" worked to the Crystal Palace. In addition to through trains, a shuttle service has always been maintained to Chalfont Road to meet main-line trains. Chesham had an excellent service of trains and some of those to Baker Street took only fifty minutes.'[11]

To thank the people of Chesham for their generosity, the Metropolitan Railway Company invited them, on 15 May 1889, to inspect the branch, then almost completed, and entertained them to a banquet afterwards. Finally, on 8 July, the line from Rickmansworth to Chesham was opened to traffic, and Chesham became for a while the northern terminus of the Metropolitan Railway. It is also interesting

Quainton Road is seen here on 25 November 1935, after the Metropolitan Railway was taken over by the London Passenger Transport Board, with Class A locomotive No 41 and a single carriage. *A. W. Camwell/Stephenson Locomotive Society*

A busy scene at Verney Junction in the LPTB period, in 1940, as a Class H tank is ready to depart. *Crecy Heritage Library*

to note that before the line reached the town, the Metropolitan was running a special omnibus service between there and Rickmansworth.

It was only three years later, on 1 September 1892, that the Metropolitan Railway reached Aylesbury, with stations at Amersham, Great Missenden, Wendover and Stoke Mandeville.

Edward Watkin had been interested in various railway activities in Buckinghamshire as early as the 1870s, because they fitted in well with his ideas of a through route, and the St John's Wood and Metropolitan companies joined with a group led by the Duke of Buckingham, a wealthy local landowner, to obtain powers to complete the London & Aylesbury Railway. This had been incorporated in 1871 with powers to build a line south-eastwards from Aylesbury to Rickmansworth, where it was to connect with the London & North Western Railway, which ran from Watford Junction, but without a direct facing connection to London. According to Michael Robbins:

The Aveling & Porter Wotton Tramway locomotive of 1872. *London Transport Museum*

Manning Wardle 0-6-0ST No 2 Wotton in the branch platform at Quainton Road station. *Stephenson Locomotive Society*

Waddesdon Road station on the Brill Branch. *Stephenson Locomotive Society*

'In the Metropolitan collection in the British Transport Commission archives is an important letter which shows that the Duke of Buckingham had his own ideas about a route to the Midlands at this time. The letter, quoted in full by Mr Harold Pollins in the November 1959 issue of the Journal *Transport History*, is headed 'Through Route' and is dated 20 September 1873. In it the Duke proposed a combination of the London & Aylesbury, Aylesbury & Buckingham, Princes Risborough & Watlington, Wotton Tramway, Banbury & Towcester (i.e. Northampton & Banbury Junction), and East & West Junction (Towcester to Stratford-on-Avon via Fenny Compton) railways, with various short connecting links, to give new routes from London to Aylesbury, Oxford, Buckingham, Northampton, Banbury, Stratford-on-Avon, and to Birmingham via the Midland from Alcester (as I read the letter 'Worcester' is printed). In other words, the North Western is no longer the protector of the Aylesbury line; the newcomer wants to carve out a wedge of territory for itself.

The letter suggested the formation of a small syndicate to make an agreement with the lines concerned and to promote the missing links. The syndicate would then control 120 miles of connecting lines having the shortest route from London to Aylesbury, Oxford, Winslow, Buckingham and Stratford-on-Avon, and a good route to Northampton and Banbury. It would also ultimately command a probable route via Fenny Compton and a new line to Birmingham equal in distance to that of the London & North Western Railway (113 miles). It was also pointed out that the Watlington & Princes Risborough, although not leading directly to any large town, would be an important lever in dealing with the Great Western, since it would threaten Reading, only 13 miles away. This is a rich specimen of the kind of thinking that lay behind a good deal of branch promotion in the High Railway Age.

Whether Watkin had any part in helping to form the Duke's ideas cannot be known; but in November 1874 an agreement was signed between the East & West Junction Railway and the Duke of Buckingham, Sir Edward Watkin, Alexander Young, and Francis Rummens. This agreement referred to the formation of a new railway from the Midlands and the North entering London via the Metropolitan Railway. The agreement provided for exchange of running powers between the East & West Junction (later the Stratford-upon-Avon & Midland Junction) line and a suggested new railway system that had an interesting origin. A group that did not include the East & West Junction was trying to obtain powers to build a line from near Verney Junction to a point near Wappenharn or Towcester, and also to bring together the various railways lying between the East & West Junction and the Metropolitan, which was to be included in the combination of railways. As the Buckinghamshire and Northamptonshire Railways Union Railway Bill, this scheme went before Parliament in 1875, but it was rejected by a committee of the House of Commons.'[12]

When the Metropolitan Railway arrived at Aylesbury, two other railways, the Great Western and the London & North Western, already served the town. The GWR ran to Aylesbury through the countryside by a line acquired from the Wycombe Railway, which started

Quainton Road station in 1935. *Crecy Heritage Library*

Metropolitan Railway Class A locomotive No 23 at Westcott station. *Crecy Heritage Library*

at Princes Risborough. As to the line from Aylesbury to Cheddington on the LNWR main line, it was promoted by the Aylesbury Railway Company (incorporated on 19 May 1836) and opened to traffic on 15 June 1839; in 1846 it was merged with the LNWR.

Extensions to Verney Junction and Brill

There was also the Aylesbury & Buckingham Railway, which we are now going to study more closely, as it was to become part of Watkin's dominion. By an Act of Parliament of 1847 the Buckingham & Brackley Railway and the Oxford & Bletchley Railway were amalgamated to become the Buckinghamshire Railway Company and were given powers to extend northwards from Brackley to Banbury and southwards from Claydon to Aylesbury. The Duke of Buckingham was appointed a director of the new company and a friend of his, Sir Harry Verney, was appointed Chairman. The Bletchley-Claydon-Buckingham-Banbury section was opened on 1 May 1850, and from Claydon to Oxford on 20 May 1851. In July 1851 the LNWR, which had been supporting this undertaking from the start, obtained a 999-year lease on the lines, and in 1879 completely absorbed the smaller company.

Consequently, the project to link Claydon with Aylesbury was abandoned. However, a few years later the project to build that section was revived and put forward to the Duke of Buckingham, who liked the idea but could not support the line unless it was diverted to bring it near the villages of Quainton and Waddesdon. Only then would he be prepared to support the project financially. This was agreed, and on 6 August 1860 the Aylesbury & Buckingham Railway was incorporated and was granted powers to build a line from Aylesbury to Claydon via Quainton. The Duke of Buckingham (at that time Chairman of the LNWR) was appointed Chairman, and Sir Harry Verney Deputy Chairman. The line started at Aylesbury from a junction situated close to where the Wycombe Railway had arrived in October 1863. It went northwards to Quainton Road, Grandborough Road, Winslow Road and finally Claydon, which was renamed Verney Junction in honour of Sir Harry Verney on whose land it was built.

Unfortunately, all did not go well, and the company was faced with several difficulties that delayed the opening of the line. The Duke of Buckingham resigned from the Board of the London & North Western Railway, causing the latter to withdraw from its agreement with the Aylesbury & Buckingham Railway Company, which was then left without any rolling stock and in great financial difficulties. It was helped out by the Great Western Railway, which had taken over on 1 February 1867 the Wycombe Railway, including the section to Aylesbury from Princes Risborough.

Consequently, the Aylesbury & Buckingham Railway line, instead of terminating at a junction with the LNWR, terminated at the end of the Princes

The Brill Branch near Wood Siding. *Stephenson Locomotive Society* (both)

Class H No 103 at Verney Junction on the 6.20pm to Baker Street, 6 June 1936. *A. W. Croughton/ Stephenson Locomotive Society*

Risborough-Aylesbury branch line, where the GWR and the Aylesbury & Buckingham built a joint station, sharing the cost equally. The line was finally opened to traffic on 23 September 1868 with three trains running daily in each direction. It had cost a lot of money, and despite the financial losses the Duke of Buckingham had to bear he embarked on a new project – he intended to link his estate at Wotton with the Aylesbury & Buckingham Railway at Quainton Road.

He had been delaying this project for some years because of the construction of the Aylesbury & Buckingham Railway, but when the latter was finished construction work started on 8 September 1870, using workers from his estate. Since there were no earthworks involved and the line was almost entirely on the Duke's land, no Act of Parliament was required. The 6½-mile line, built to standard gauge and laid on longitudinal sleepers, was opened to Wotton on 1 April 1871, with stopping places at Waddesdon, Westcott, Wotton, Church Siding and Wood Siding; an extension to a brickworks near Brill was completed by November of that year, although evidence suggests that certain sections of the line had been opened before that date. The three-quarter-mile section to Brill was opened during the summer 1872. The original purpose of the tramway-type light railway was to carry agricultural produce and minerals to and from the Duke's estates, but because of public demand, in particular from residents of Brill, passenger traffic commenced in January 1872. At first horse power was used, but the horses could not cope with the gradient between Church Siding and Brill, so it was decided to buy an engine; consequently a four-wheeled geared traction locomotive built by Aveling & Porter together with a borrowed carriage were put into service in January 1872.

The railway was initially known as the Wotton Tramway and was under the control of R. A. Jones, one of the Duke's personal assistants. In 1873 the Duke tried to have his tramway authorised as a railway, but was unsuccessful, as it did not comply with the railway regulations of the time. However, in 1883 the Duke and Sir Harry Verney joined forces to promote the Oxford, Aylesbury & Metropolitan Junction Railway Company, which was to extend the Wotton Tramway to Oxford, but the project, though authorised by an Act of Parliament, never materialised through lack of financial support, and the powers were allowed to lapse.

Despite the failure, the Duke did not give up, and in 1888 a new Bill was passed, setting up the Oxford & Aylesbury Tramroad, with similar powers to take over and extend the Wotton Tramway to Oxford. Even though all the advantages and proposals were valid ones, nothing was done, the powers granted by the Act were not exercised, and the extension of the line to Oxford was never constructed. The failure of the extension scheme was mainly due to a lack of financial support and the death of the Duke on 26 March 1889. No significant changes took place until 1 December of that year, when the Metropolitan Railway Company took over the lease of the tramway, for the working of which it acquired in 1894 two locomotives, built by Manning, Wardle & Co and named *Huddersfield* and *Brill*. In 1899 *Huddersfield* was removed and replaced by a third similar locomotive named *Wotton*. They were all of the 0-6-0 saddle tank type with 12-inch-diameter inside cylinders. Later the Metropolitan transferred locomotives Nos 23 and 41 of the 'A' class to work the line, which they did in turns.

In 1874 the Great Western Railway had the chance to absorb the Aylesbury & Buckingham Railway, but the opportunity was missed and the local company remained in private ownership until later approached and absorbed by the Metropolitan Railway Company on 1 July 1891, vesting powers having been obtained by an Act of 25 July 1890. The Metropolitan section to Aylesbury was not opened until 1 September 1892, and a public luncheon was then held at the Town Hall to celebrate the occasion. At the time, only a temporary station was provided, in Brook Street, until a junction could be installed by the GWR to enable Metropolitan trains to run into the main station. The GWR and Aylesbury & Buckingham station in Aylesbury was a joint one, but when the Wycombe Railway extension from Princes Risborough was being surveyed, the GWR had intended to open its own station in Aylesbury closer to the town centre. However, this would have prevented the Aylesbury & Buckingham from either completing a junction with the Aylesbury Railway or extending southwards along the Missenden valley, as had been planned by the company. The Aylesbury & Buckingham Railway subsequently objected to the GWR's proposals, but an agreement was later reached between the two companies.

When the Metropolitan absorbed the Aylesbury & Buckingham company, it negotiated new agreements with the Great Western and modified the joint station to accommodate extra services. The present station was opened on 1 January 1894. Soon after taking over the Aylesbury & Buckingham Railway, the Metropolitan commenced doubling the track in preparation for through services from the City to Verney Junction, in the heart of Buckinghamshire 50½ miles from its headquarters at Baker Street, and through trains started to run in 1897. The Metropolitan also replaced all the level crossings between Aylesbury and Verney Junction by bridges, and rebuilt all the old stations. It also established a direct connection with the Wotton Tramway, which cost it £623; it rebuilt the station at Quainton Road on a different site and replaced the level crossing by a bridge.

In 1897 a new station was built on the line at Waddesdon Manor (changed to just Waddesdon in 1923), at the request of Baron Ferdinand Rothschild, who wanted a station near to his estate at Waddesdon Manor, which he had had built in 1880.

On 1 December 1899 the Metropolitan Railway Company also started to work the Oxford & Aylesbury Tramroad. The company intended to obtain Parliamentary sanction to purchase the tramroad, but in a letter to Earl Temple, John Bell, General Manager of the Metropolitan Railway Company at the time, said that the company would temporarily rent the line at a cost of £600 per annum, and would maintain the line, stocks, stations and signals in good working order, and would indemnify the company from all liability regarding accidents, loss, damages to goods, passengers, etc. Ultimately the Metropolitan never applied for Parliamentary sanction and the line was worked according to the terms stated in John Bell's letter, as the parties were finding that agreement satisfactory. Later, the company tried unsuccessfully to sell off the line to various other companies.

The Metropolitan Railway Company also became involved in other railway schemes, such as the Aylesbury & Buckingham Railway's line to Towcester in 1885, which did not obtain parliamentary authorisation, and the Worcester & Broom Railway, which was authorised in 1885 and obtained permission to extend the East & West Junction Railway 17 miles westwards, but again these powers were never used.

The Metropolitan Railway Attempts to Advance North

In 1888, the Manchester, Sheffield & Lincolnshire Railway wanted to break out of the West Riding in the direction of Nottingham by promoting a line southwards from Beighton to Chesterfield, but it was unsuccessful.

The following year, the Metropolitan actively supported the bill to extend the powers of the Worcester & Broom Railway Company and to produce a line from the East & West Junction Railway at Morton Pinkney to join the Aylesbury & Buckingham at Quainton Road. In the same year, the Welsh Railways Union Bill authorised the various Welsh railways from Swansea to the Dee to make working arrangements with each other and to connect with the Manchester, Sheffield & Lincolnshire Railway. In 1889, Watkin was also appointed Chairman of one of the Welsh companies involved, the Neath & Brecon Railway. The success of the Worcester & Broom's proposal would enable the Metropolitan to connect with Worcester which was 60 miles away from Watkin's empire.

Harrow-on-the-Hill station, 1933. *London Transport Museum*

A 1st Class Metropolitan Railway 'Jubilee' stock coach. *London Transport Museum*

In 1889, the Manchester, Sheffield & Lincolnshire Railway Company was granted permission to build a short line southwards to Annesley, for local purposes only, to gain access to coalfields in Derbyshire and Nottinghamshire. Although its General Manager assured the Great Northern Railway that they would not apply for powers to build south of Annesley, he was not believed. For them, the Worcester & Broom scheme for the Quainton Road–Morton Pinkney line confirmed their fears about Watkin's activities. In the end, the Manchester, Sheffield & Lincolnshire Railway Company was granted permission to build through to Annesley, with working powers over the Great Northern into Nottingham in exchange for similar powers to the Great Northern to run into Sheffield by the new route from Nottingham, but the Worcester & Broom project failed due to the opposition of the London & North Western and the Great Western companies

The Metropolitan tried again, in the 1890 session, to obtain powers for through traffic between London and Worcester. It also sought permission for the Manchester, Sheffield & Lincolnshire Railway to reach Ellesmere from Chester via Wrexham and for filling the gap between there and Worcester by the Birmingham, Kidderminster & Stoke Railway. But all that was granted to them was the powers to take over and double-track the Aylesbury & Buckingham Railway.

However, the reason behind this northward advance of the Metropolitan Railway became public when in 1890 Watkin presented to the Metropolitan's shareholders a railway map on which he had drawn a railway line showing his proposed trunk line from Manchester southwards. He explained that Parliament had agreed to the Manchester, Sheffield & Lincolnshire extension to Annesley and, by running powers over the Great Northern, to Nottingham, Parliament had also authorised the Metropolitan extension to Aylesbury; he also told them that the Board had entered into an agreement with the Aylesbury & Buckingham company to take their line further north and he invited the shareholders to accept an agreement with the Manchester, Sheffield & Lincolnshire Railway, which would give them running powers over the Metropolitan between Quainton Road and Baker Street; one third of receipts would go to the Manchester, Sheffield & Lincolnshire Railway and two thirds to the Metropolitan. If the scheme had succeeded Baker Street station could have become a big London through station. But things did not go according to plan as, in 1891, the application to build a line from Annesley to Quainton Road had been rejected by a committee of the House of Commons.

After the failure of the first Bill, the negotiations were left to John Bell, who, before Watkin's retirement in 1894 had been given the task to carry through the management policies. While Bell was an apprentice on the Manchester, Sheffield & Lincolnshire Railway, he came into contact with William Pollitt, who later on became General Manager of the Manchester, Sheffield & Lincolnshire Railway Company. The animosity which developed between the two men may have had an influence on the events that followed.

The Manchester, Sheffield & Lincolnshire Railway Company obtained several Acts of Parliament in connection with the London extension which did not meet the approval of the Metropolitan Railway company. Later on, the Manchester, Sheffield & Lincolnshire Railway Company tried to override the 1890 through running agreement. They did not succeed, but they continued their attack by saying that the Metropolitan was not capable of carrying it out, due to the congestion on the Metropolitan Line caused by the popularity of the partially built Watkin Tower at Wembley Park and they demanded an independent running line between London and Wembley Park. As John Bell was a strong supporter of the tower, this was probably aimed at discrediting him and Watkin and at attacking the 1890 agreement. In the end, in 1892, the Manchester, Sheffield & Lincolnshire Railway Company managed to have the 1890 agreement modified and it was given permission to build a line of its own through St John's Wood to Marylebone.

However, due to some political changes, the Royal Assent was only given in March 1893. The Manchester, Sheffield & Lincolnshire Railway, which was extending the area of its influence in the Midlands and in the North, and which had been anxious to reach London for a long time, could finally do so. Through services to King's Cross started to be operated over the Great Northern Railway, and an express service from Manchester to London was inaugurated; unfortunately, the company's hopes of amalgamating with the GNR never materialised, hence the company's decision to build its own line, and in 1893 work began. The Manchester, Sheffield & Lincolnshire Railway Company (called the Great Central Railway [GCR] from 1897) was granted running powers over the Metropolitan tracks between Quainton Road and Harrow-on-the-Hill. Between Harrow and Finchley Road (or more exactly, between a point south of Harrow-on-the-Hill station called Harrow South Junction and a point opposite Finchley Road station called Canfield Place), the Metropolitan Railway Company built for the Great Central Railway Company two more tracks on the down side. The rest of the line between Canfield Place and Marylebone was built by the Great Central Railway itself. Marylebone was the last railway terminus to be built in London. Finally, the Great Central extension to London was opened to coal traffic in 1898 and to passenger and goods traffic the following year.

However, everything was not going well between the GCR and the Metropolitan. Friction arose from time to time, and as a result of one incident between the two companies the GCR looked towards the Great Western Railway for assistance. Consequently, by a joint Act of Parliament of 1 August 1899, the GWR and GCR promoted a line from Grendon Underwood, about 3 miles north of Quainton Road station, to Ashendon and Princes Risborough, giving the Great Central access to either Marylebone or Paddington. A large proportion of the GCR's traffic was subsequently diverted onto the alternative route over the joint line, which lost Aylesbury the opportunity of having a more intensive main-line service to London.

From 2 April 1906 all Metropolitan services north of Harrow South Junction to Verney Junction, including the Chesham and Brill branches, came under the auspices of the Metropolitan & Great Central Joint Committee, set up under an Act of 1905 to manage the joint lines of the two companies. The Metropolitan leased the line from Harrow to Verney Junction (the Chesham branch included) for 999 years at a cost of £44,000 a year, while the Great Central leased, also for 999 years, the line used by its trains from Harrow South Junction to Canfield Place, at a cost of £22,000 a year. In the agreement the Metropolitan also stipulated that, in order to safeguard its suburban traffic, the GCR's first station outside London should be situated to the west of the River Brent (which was further out than the first stations of any other railway line with a London terminus). The chosen stations were Harrow-on-the-Hill on the Aylesbury line and Wembley Hill when the Neasden-High Wycombe section was opened in 1906 (which was part of a grander scheme not only to give the Great Central independent access to London but also to contemplate a direct line for the Great Western from London to Birmingham). The running of the joint line was undertaken by the Metropolitan & Great Central Joint Committee, and every five years each company became alternately responsible for the entire maintenance of the joint line.

So, Watkin's dream nearly came true. Had he lived longer, an amalgamation between the Metropolitan Railway Company and the Great Central Railway Company might have materialised, but after Watkin's retirement and death the two companies went their own ways, not only because of personal differences between Bell and Pollitt (Watkin's successors), but also because their interests became incompatible: the Metropolitan was essentially a short-distance passenger business, no longer interested in becoming a long-distance railway line, whereas the Great Central was hoping to become an important long-distance passenger and freight traffic line.

As R. W. Perks, Chairman of the Metropolitan District Railway, said while giving evidence before the 1903-06 Royal Commission on London traffic:

'The policy of the late Sir Edward Watkin has been subsequently justified by the success of the extension to Harrow, Rickmansworth and Aylesbury. His project of making a through railway from the north of England to the south by a continuation of the Manchester, Sheffield & Lincolnshire; the South Eastern, and Metropolitan Railways, of which he was Chairman, was frustrated partly by a controversy between the Manchester and Metropolitan Railways, after his death and … by a change of policy of the South Eastern as to its connections with the Northern Lines via the Metropolitan.'[13]

Rolling stock

With all these new extensions being opened, more adequate rolling stock was required, and during the period 1891-1901 the 'C', 'D', 'E' and 'F' classes of locomotives were brought into service – see the Appendix for further details on these locomotives.

As far as carriages were concerned, that period saw the introduction of what is remembered as the 'Jubilee' stock, since it was introduced during the celebrations of Queen Victoria's Jubilee in 1887. Three trains of nine carriages were initially built by Craven Brothers of Sheffield. The vehicles were four wheeled and 27ft 6in long over the ends with a wheelbase of 14 feet. In a nine-car train, there were two 1st Class and two 2nd Class coaches, all fitted with Smith's simple vacuum brakes. The 1st Class cars had four compartments, whereas the other classes had five. Each of these trains had two brake carriages, a 3rd Class at one end, which consisted of three compartments and a luggage compartment, while at the other end there was a 2nd Class brake with five compartments, one of them being occupied by a guard and also offering seats for five passengers. Later they were all fitted with steam heating coils. The lighting inside was provided by Pintsch high-pressure gas.

In 1892 four more trains of that stock were bought for the Aylesbury line. They came in sets of eight coaches, which were in fact two four-coach portions, as the train had to be split at Chalfont Road to allow one section to go to Chesham while the other proceeded to Aylesbury. They had long buffers and screw couplings at the outer ends of each four-coach set. This arrangement did not last, and soon the inner brake cars were converted to standard types, but the trains kept their eight-coach formation. Many of these coaches were discarded when the line was electrified, but some were eventually rescued and converted to be used with electric locomotives. They were finally taken out of service in 1912.

Between 1898 and 1900 the 'Bogie Stock', also known as the 'Ashbury Stock', came into service. These were the first six-coach trains with bogies on the Metropolitan Railway. The Ashbury Railway Carriage & Iron Company made the first six, which were put into service in 1898 on the extension lines from Baker Street. The dimensions of the coach bodies were length 39ft 6in, overall length over buffers 42ft 4¼in, width of the frame 8ft 3in plus another 5 inches over the outside grab rails, and height above rail level 11ft 7in plus another 6 inches to clear the top of the 'torpedo'-type ventilators. All three classes were represented on each train, and in each compartment there were ten seats. In the 1st Class carriages there were six compartments fitted with comfortable upholstery; in the 2nd and 3rd Class carriages there were seven compartments, and in the brake carriages there were five compartments and a luggage compartment; in the 1st/3rd composite carriages there were six compartments. All the coaches were supplied with blinds, steam heating, floors lined with felt to reduce the noise, and electric lighting. A train was usually 252 feet long and was arranged as follows: 2nd Class Brake/2nd Class coach/1st Class coach/3rd Class coach/3rd Class Brake. The coaches were equipped with pressed steel bogies at 25-foot centres, the wheelbase of each bogie was 7 feet, and each wheel was fitted with two cast-iron brake shoes linked by a rigging system of wires to the vacuum brake cylinder. Altogether the Ashbury Railway Carriage & Iron Company built eight sets, one set was built by the Metropolitan Railway Company and two by Cravens Brothers of Sheffield.

With the electrification of the line, most of these carriages (some being converted for electric working) and all the rigid-wheelbase stock were made redundant.

7
The Metropolitan Railway's last extensions

Uxbridge branch

After Watkin's death, no one was interested in his dream, and the Metropolitan Railway Company's last extensions were suburban ones. The first was the Uxbridge branch.

At the end of the 19th century Uxbridge was quite an important town in Middlesex on the Oxford Road, in the Colne Valley, with corn mills, wharves, timber mills, breweries and an iron foundry. Since 1794 it had been served by the Grand Junction Canal, on which boats transported freight to Brentford and London in one direction, and to the Midlands in the other. West Drayton on the Great Western line was the nearest railway station from 1838 until 8 September 1856, when a branch line from West Drayton north to Uxbridge was opened, and a station was built in Vine Street, close to the town centre. Some trains ran through to Paddington. T. B. Peacock says that the station was

'…built of local yellow brick … amply furnished to deal with all classes of traffic… The branch was initiated by the Great Western & Uxbridge Railway Company, for which an Act was passed in 1846, reviving the project which had been abandoned a year or so before; an Act of 1853 enabled the Great Western to complete the line. It was opened as single broad gauge in 1856 from a junction with the old line at West Drayton. The branch was converted to standard gauge in 1871 and doubled in 1880…'[14]

Though Uxbridge was now served by a railway line, it was not on a main line, which was a disadvantage, therefore much encouragement was given by the town to any scheme that would

Diagram of the Metropolitan Railway in the 1930s and of its connections with other railways.

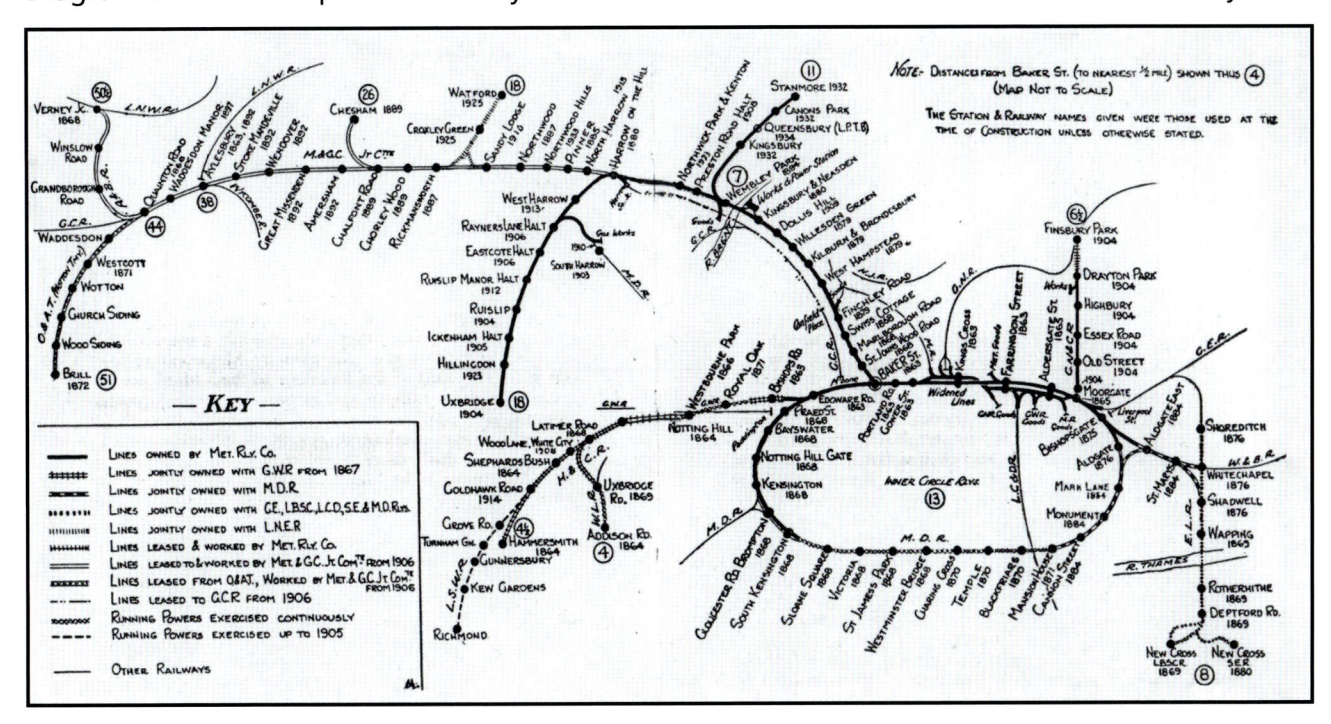

give it a position on a main line, or at least a direct communication with London. Many schemes were proposed to crack the Great Western Railway's monopoly in the town, but the Metropolitan District Railway took the lead. In July 1879 its line had reached Ealing and was contemplating heading to the north (Harrow) and to the north-west (Uxbridge and High Wycombe). However, the Great Western disapproved of the Metropolitan District Railway's intrusion into its territories and strongly opposed any Bill put forward by that company to extend to Uxbridge. In the meantime, the Metropolitan District was trying to reach Harrow. In 1893 it put forward an Ealing & South Harrow Railway Bill, which obtained Royal Assent on 25 August 1894; the line opened on 28 June 1903, but the company still had its eyes on Uxbridge and High Wycombe. In 1896 it promoted through a nominally independent company an extension of the Ealing & South Harrow Railway through Ruislip, Ickenham and Uxbridge, where the line would link with the proposed Uxbridge & Rickmansworth Railway. In February 1897, with local support, the company presented the High Wycombe Bill, which included an extension from Uxbridge to High Wycombe. Unfortunately, due to further strong opposition from the GWR, the Uxbridge-High Wycombe section of the Bill was deleted. The remainder, the section from South Harrow to Uxbridge, was authorised as the Harrow & Uxbridge Railway Act of 6 August 1897. Thus the Metropolitan District finally won the battle – it was going to reach Uxbridge at last, at least on paper.

Indeed, when it came to raising the money, the company met with great difficulties, as it was already facing the high costs of the Ealing & South Harrow Railway and the Whitechapel and Bow extension. So if Uxbridge wanted a railway, it would have to look for a saviour, and to the disappointment of Forbes, Chairman of the Metropolitan District Railway, the town turned to the Metropolitan Railway Company, which promoted a Bill in 1899 in order to obtain powers to link its railway at Harrow with the Harrow & Uxbridge at Rayners Lane, with a curve at that point so as to allow the through running of trains between South Harrow and Harrow-on-the-Hill, and a flyover at the junction point with the Metropolitan Railway. Forbes objected to the project at first, since he would have liked the undertaking to be a joint one, but he soon realised that his company would not be able to raise half of the required capital and he had to let the Metropolitan company go ahead. The latter was put in charge of the working and management of the line.

This is how *The Uxbridge Gazette* in the special edition of 30 June 1904 related the construction of the line:

The inaugural train of the Uxbridge branch at Ruislip on 4 July 1904. *Stephenson Locomotive Society*

'The contractors began their work in September, 1901, and the line they have laid is, from the junction with the Metropolitan at Harrow to Uxbridge, six and a quarter miles in length and at Rayners Lane there is a junction, from which point another one and a quarter miles of line joins it to the South Harrow station of the Ealing and South Harrow line, thus bringing it into connection with the District line. Rayners Lane is on the Harrow side of the Ruislip station. One of the constructional features of the new railway is a viaduct half a mile long, on the branch from South Harrow station to the Rayners Lane Junction. This viaduct has seventy-one arches. The works have also included 28 bridges, the largest of which is the four-span brick one at Park Road, Uxbridge. Other interesting particulars are that there have been three steam navvies employed and thirteen locomotives, and the whole of the ballast has been obtained locally being taken from the vicinity of the Hundred Acres, Denham, by a steam 'grab' on a floating pontoon and conveyed along a specially constructed line over a mile in length to its destination.'[15]

The Harrow & Uxbridge line opened to the public on 4 July 1904. It was laid out for electric traction, but as the Metropolitan Railway's new power station at Neasden was not ready, for the first months the line was run by steam trains. The line was formally opened on 30 June 1904, and on that day a six-bogie train hauled by 0-4-4 tank locomotive No 1, suitably bedecked for the occasion, left Harrow-on-the Hill for Uxbridge, where all the guests, who were invited to a luncheon in a marquee, alighted. At first there were only two stations, at Uxbridge and Ruislip (the latter situated half way between Rayners Lane and Uxbridge).

This was how the local newspaper described the new station at Uxbridge:

'The building comprises a booking hall, which divides the imposing structure with a gable, and has on the far side a gentlemen's waiting room, a ladies waiting room, porters' room, store room, and the other usual appointments of a railway station, and on the near side the ticket office, the station master's room, the parcel office, and first at hand, but not to be reached without coming on the platform, the refreshment rooms. The whole is built with stock bricks with red band courses pointed in black. The roof is covered with ornamental red tiles, and the chimneys are elaborated into something of the minaret shape, giving altogether a good artistic effect. The platform runs on the left hand side of the block, and is covered with glass in its entirety, and on the other side of the line also, there will be a sheltered platform. There will be two approaches to the station; the general one at the junction of Belmont Road with York Road, and the other for goods, some half way along York Road. This will give ready access to the weight office and the goods shed. The shed has room for six trucks. There is also, convenient to the station platform and the main approach, provision for loading stock. Ruislip station, which is near Thomas Collins' Farm, is planned on similar lines, with the exception that it has no goods shed and no refreshment rooms, and is on a smaller scale than the Uxbridge. Both stations are wired for the electric light. (At present, however, they are being lit with oil, the electric connection not yet being made.)'[16]

The other stations on the line as we know them now did not open immediately. The next to open were in fact halts, coming into use at Ickenham on 25 September 1905, at Eastcote on 26 May 1906, at Rayners Lane on 26 May 1906, at Ruislip Manor on 5 August 1912, at West Harrow on 17 November 1913, and finally at Hillingdon on 10 December 1923.

The traffic on the line was at first disappointing, since urban development was initially quite slow, but very soon, as we will see in another chapter, this branch of the Metropolitan Railway became the most successful.

Watford branch

The next suburban branch to be built was that to Watford. At the beginning of the 19th century, Watford Junction station on the London & North Western Railway served the north-east of the town, but Watford was growing in all directions and the inhabitants felt that they needed more and better rail facilities. They therefore made a request to the Metropolitan Railway Company, as early as 1892, to construct a branch from Wembley Park to Watford, via Bushey, Stanmore and Edgware. This was planned, but it never materialised. As nothing had been done by 1904, a petition was organised, and as soon as the LNWR heard about it, it planned its Croxley Green branch and after, obtaining powers, built it. The first train ran on 15 June 1912.

In 1913, the Metropolitan Railway, with its partner the Great Central Railway, formed the Watford Joint Railway Committee, and the Metropolitan prepared a plan with a terminus in the middle of the town, but as it included an embankment across Cassiobury Park it was opposed by Watford Corporation. Then came the war, and a few years elapsed before the project was taken up again; but then the plans had to be modified so as to avoid any more opposition, and a shorter route was chosen, with the station near the park instead of the High Street as planned originally. (However, the station in the High Street had been built before the line, and when the plans were changed it was destined never to be used and became successively a restaurant, a furniture shop, a clothes shop and a hamburger restaurant.)

Parliamentary approval was obtained in 1922 for a branch to Watford based on plans drawn up by E. A. Wilson, Civil Engineer to the Metropolitan Railway Company. In 1922, under the Metropolitan's supervision, work began on the 2½ miles from the site of the proposed junction north of Moor Park (then called Sandy Lodge) to the terminus near Cassiobury Park, in Cassiobury Avenue. The contractors, Logan & Hemingway of Doncaster, found the work difficult as it involved the laying out of goods yards, the construction of ten bridges (two of which crossed over the Grand Union Canal and the River Gade), the construction of heavy embankments, and difficult cuttings entailing the excavation of about half a million cubic yards of gravel and chalk. Consequently the undertaking became quite expensive for the railway company, costing about £300,000).

There was one intermediate station at Croxley Green and a goods yard at Watford. The station buildings were both two storeys high and built of red brick. A north curve was also put in between Croxley Green and Rickmansworth, to enable Watford trains to work northwards without having to reverse, and a shuttle service of electric trains was also run between Rickmansworth and Watford (this link ceased to be used regularly after 21 January 1934). The line was officially opened on 31 October 1925 by Lord Faringdon, Deputy Chairman of the London & North Eastern Railway (LNER, successor to the Great Central) and Lord Aberconway, Chairman of the Metropolitan Railway Company, but public services only began on 2 November. In all, 140 trains ran daily and, since the line was shared equally by the Metropolitan and the LNER, 70 trains composed of electric multiple-unit stock went to Baker Street and beyond, and 70 steam-hauled trains went to Marylebone. However, after the General Strike of 1926, the LNER steam train service was never resumed.

The new Metropolitan Railway station in Watford lay in the quiet western part of the town, which made the company soon realise that a direct connection to the centre of the town was needed, and on 2 November 1927 it started to run a bus service between its Watford terminus and the High Street. All the buses connected with the trains and ran via Cassiobury Road, Merton Road, High Street, Church Street, Vicarage Street and Queen's Avenue, and the fare was 1d. The fleet consisted of four 28-seater Albion buses finished in standard Metropolitan livery; however, the company had no Parliamentary powers to operate buses and failed to obtain them when they were granted to the four main-line companies in 1928. Henceforth, the buses had to be transferred to a subsidiary company, called the North West Land & Transport Company Limited. After a year this amalgamated with the Watford omnibus undertaking of Mr Frederick Lewis to become the Lewis Omnibus Company Limited, which operated until absorbed into the London Passenger Transport Board in 1933. Unfortunately, this branch of the Metropolitan Railway Company never was a success.

After the opening of the Watford branch it was decided to build a burrowing junction 1,200 feet long at Harrow, which would facilitate the handling of the additional traffic, since the existing flat junction

Work on constructing the Watford Branch south of Croxley Green, which opened in 1925.

was the cause of many delays, especially during rush hours. A tunnel was cut under the existing Harrow and Aylesbury line, and the Uxbridge line was graded to a low level to enable the trains to cross under and enter or leave Harrow station in either direction without having to conflict with the traffic on the Aylesbury line. The line was then widened between the station and the junction over a distance of about half a mile; 50,000 cubic yards of earth were removed, 12,000 cubic yards of concrete and brickwork were used for the retaining walls, heavy steel girders were put into place, and 2,300 yards of new permanent way were laid down. This was a difficult task, but it was completed successfully without causing any delay or disturbance to the passing trains, and thus increasing the traffic capacity of the station. The traffic was also improved by the electrification of the line as far as Rickmansworth on 5 January 1925.

Great Northern & City Railway

Before going on to the Metropolitan Railway Company's last suburban extension, we must go back to the City, where in 1913 the company bought another railway company in difficulty, acquiring cheaply the Great Northern & City Line from Moorgate to Finsbury Park. This company had been incorporated in 1892 and intended to build a tube railway from the Great Northern Railway to the City. The Great Northern & City tube was wider than any other London tube, as it was meant to accommodate main-line trains. The 3-mile-long line started from a tunnel below the GNR station at Finsbury Park, then ran partly in the open to Drayton Park and finally in a tunnel again, through Highbury, Essex Road and Old Street stations, to Moorgate Street station, its City terminus. This was situated near the Metropolitan Railway station but at a lower level, and the two stations were connected by lifts. The promoters probably intended to establish a physical link with the GNR and to extend the line beyond the City to link it with railways south of the Thames, thus providing a through link between the northern and southern companies.

The line was electrified using the multiple-unit system (instead of having a locomotive hauling the train, the motors were dispersed along the train, and simultaneously controlled from one point). The power was supplied by a power station situated in Poole Street. The line was intended for intensive traffic, fast running and short station stops. Although the undertaking may have seemed successful at first, it was not profitable as the company had to face strong competition, and no extension was made. Hence it had no alternative but to amalgamate with another company.

The initiative was taken by the Metropolitan Railway, which with the intention of extending the line secured powers, in an Act of 1913, to acquire it and extend it southwards to Lothbury; however, powers to connect the line with the Waterloo & City Line and with the Metropolitan's own line near Liverpool Street were not granted. The following year the Metropolitan and the GNR companies tried to promote a Bill transferring the line to a joint committee of the two railways; they also sought to build an exchange station with the Waterloo & City Line, rather than a junction as suggested earlier, and to establish a direct connection with the GNR and a link with the Metropolitan near Aldgate. The project never materialised as it encountered the strong opposition of the North London company, which saw its interests threatened; hence the Metropolitan Railway was left alone to make the best it could of this isolated line.

First, it improved the service by reducing the journey time to 10½ minutes (9½ for semi-fast trains), and increasing the rush hour service to a 2-minute interval in the morning and evening, instead of the 4-minute interval during slack hours. Then, on 24 September 1914, the Metropolitan closed Poole Street power station and supplied the line from Neasden power station with a substation at Drayton Park, which contributed to make a great economy. On 15 February 1915, when the Metropolitan introduced 1st Class accommodation in order to attract the GNR's season ticket holders, the Great Northern & City Railway became the first and only tube railway with more than one class of accommodation. The rolling stock, apart from adopting Metropolitan livery, remained unchanged. Finally, in October 1934, the railway was transferred to the Northern Line of the Underground system; it was closed between Finsbury Park and Drayton Park on 4 October 1964, between Moorgate and Old Street on 7 September 1975, and between Old Street and Drayton Park on 5 October 1975, being subsequently reopened by British Rail on 16 August 1976, apart from Old Street to Moorgate, which reopened on 8 November.

Improvements to the Finchley Road-Wembley Park section

The increasing residential traffic between Baker Street and Harrow soon made the quadrupling of that section of the line necessary. In 1914-15 the first part to be quadrupled was that between Finchley Road and Wembley Park, where new up and down fast roads were laid on the up side of the two original tracks, while at Willesden Green, Neasden and Wembley Park stations extra platforms were provided for the fast line. After the First World War it was the turn of the section between Wembley Park and Harrow to be quadrupled; there, the fast roads were laid on the down side of the two original tracks and the crossover between the two sections was included in the layout at Wembley Park. Preston Road station (first opened as a halt in 1908) and Northwick Park & Kenton station (opened in 1923) were the two stations on that section of the line.

The Metropolitan Railway also undertook the linking up and utilisation of an old tunnel running parallel with the Metropolitan line between Euston Square and St Pancras, so that Metropolitan trains could be switched onto the Widened Lines, thus providing an alternative route to Moorgate and having the effect of doubling the most important section of the Inner Circle, so that more through trains could be run between 'Metro-land' and the City. The work was carried out by the cut-and-cover method and was not easy since it had to be done without interfering with the passing traffic, and many obstacles had to be overcome, such as the removal of a big portion of the tunnel wall, the construction of a new single tunnel about 700 feet long and the provision of a junction at the eastern end of the old tunnel so as to reach the Widened Lines. These engineering operations also made it possible to bring electric traction to the Widened Lines extending from King's Cross to Moorgate, over which were running steam trains of the Great Northern section of the LNER as well as the London Midland & Scottish Railway.

Relief line project

Soon the Metropolitan Railway Company became so successful that it faced serious congestion problems at the northern approaches to Baker Street. As we have seen, the section between Wembley Park and Finchley Road had become four-tracked in 1914-15, but to put additional tracks, parallel to the existing ones, in the tunnel section between Finchley Road and Baker Street and the rebuilding of Baker Street station to accommodate more platforms would be very complex and very costly. So in the autumn of 1925 the Metropolitan deposited a Bill for an avoiding line 3 miles 7.9 chains long and costing £2.05 million, which would leave the existing line south of Willesden Green and at Mapesbury Park would burrow under the existing tracks and enter deep-level tunnels with an internal diameter of 15ft 6in to accommodate Metropolitan Railway rolling stock and locomotives, running thence under Kilburn High Road, Maida Vale and Edgware Road to finally meet, with a curve, the Circle Line, by means of a 200-yard cut-and-cover section ending a few yards west of Edgware Road Metropolitan Railway station. Three intermediate stations were to be built at Quex Road, Kilburn Priory and near the Regent's Canal. Edgware Road station was also to be rebuilt with four eight-car platforms to accommodate the new trains. Royal Assent was given on 4 August 1926, but nothing ever materialised except the rebuilding of Edgware Road station where *The Uxbridge Gazette* reported

'...the two original platforms were replaced by two island platforms with four through roads; the outer for Inner Circle and Hammersmith and City traffic, and the inner ones intended for trains from Aylesbury

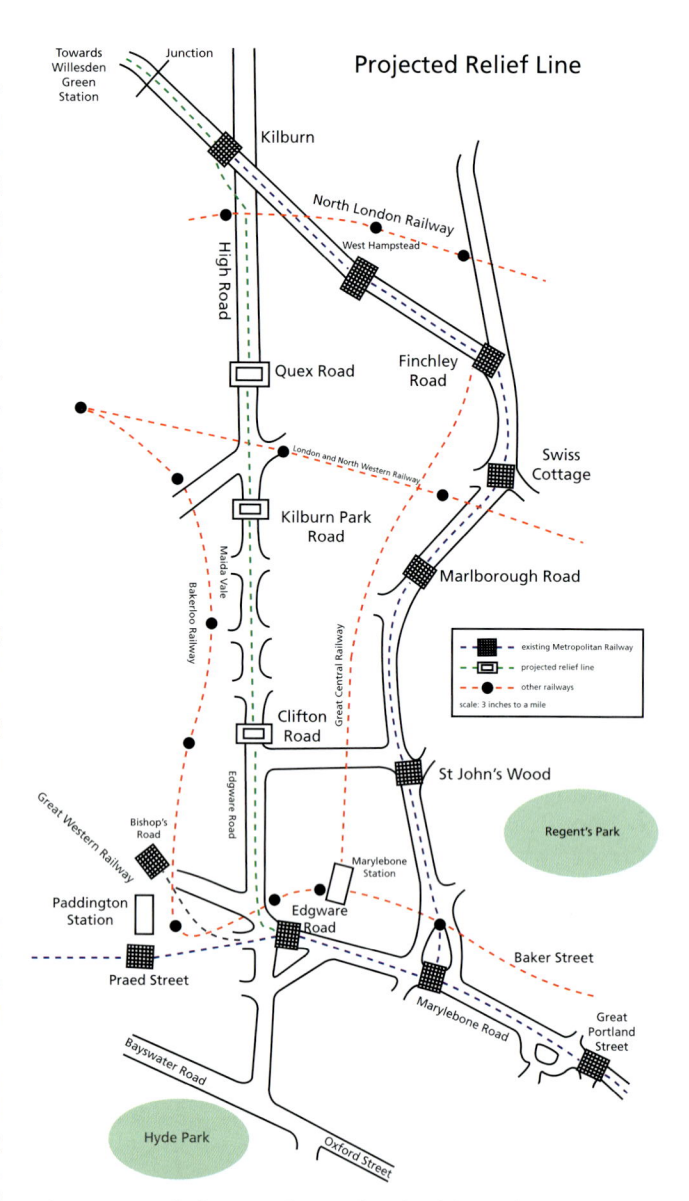

Diagram of the projected relief line from Willesden Green to Edgware proposed in a Bill in 1925 to ease congestion on the northern approaches to Baker Street.

and the Addison Road lines. They could be used for traffic from either direction terminating at Edgware Road, or for the through running of trains from the main line to South Kensington. Sidings were also laid down for the reception of rolling stock. The station was well provided with train departure indicators, and it is interesting to record that they were equipped to advise passengers that the next train was destined for Aylesbury and Verney Junction before a yard of the proposed tube railway to take it there was cut.'

In the meantime, congestion on the Finchley Road-Baker Street section was gradually growing worse. The company tried to solve the problem but not very successfully.

For instance, it tried to close St John's Wood and Marlborough Road stations during part of the rush hours to allow the operation of more trains during that period, but because of protest from local residents the two stations had to be reopened.

Stanmore branch

Having to face so many problems, one may wonder why the Metropolitan Railway Company continued to extend its country lines and why in fact it built another branch.

'The first idea, of 1923-24, was to go into the territory between the main line and the Uxbridge branch by means of a new line from Eastcote by Harefield to Chalfont St Giles. At a public inquiry into a proposed independent light railway from Harefield to Uxbridge, the Metropolitan had promised to do something about this area, but by 1928 it was clear that the scheme was dead.'[17]

But when in 1929, under the Development (Loan Guarantees & Grants) Act, a prospect of guaranteed interest on new expenditure was offered, the Metropolitan Railway Company quickly came forward with a new project: the construction of a 4-mile-long branch from Wembley Park to Stanmore.

'At the annual general meeting in February 1930, Lord Aberconway explained that the Stanmore catchment area was being rapidly developed for housing, and that he looked upon it as the legitimate territory of the Metropolitan. To the very pertinent question put by a shareholder – How would they handle the additional traffic south of Finchley Road? – his Lordship gave a soothing answer that they were building many additional coaches of an improved type and lengthening trains.'[18]

The Bill was not opposed on the grounds that the project would contribute to relieve unemployment, and it obtained Royal Assent on 4 June 1930; Treasury approval for a grant under the 1929 Development (Loan Guarantees & Grants) Act followed a month later.

Going to Stanmore was not a new project for the Metropolitan Railway Company. As early as 1902-03 there had been plans for an extension from Wembley to Watford via Stanmore. The idea came up again in 1908, when the Watford and Edgware interest saw it as a means of getting its line built. In 1911 Bushey residents tried to revive the project, but nothing materialised until 1929, when the Metropolitan Railway, attracted by the urban development of Stanmore, a promise of Government help and the prospect of getting a substantial parcel of land free or cheap from All Souls' College, decided to consider a possible extension in that direction. As there was no opposition from the landowners and only a few houses to demolish, the company decided to go ahead with the project. The only company that did not really approve of the project was the London Midland & Scottish Railway (LMS), which already had a station in Stanmore and therefore disapproved of the competition, but the Metropolitan Railway pointed out to the LMS that it intended to serve a different district and that its facilities would offer greater convenience to Stanmore travellers.

The works started early in 1931, under the Metropolitan Railway's Chief Engineer, E. A. Wilson. About half a million cubic yards of earth were removed, the Wealdstone Brook, which crossed the route of the line five times, had to be diverted, which necessitated the building of concrete channels and large culverts to carry the water from the west side to the east and back again, and six important bridges were also erected.

The new line being equipped for electric traction, additional substations had also to be built. Finally, the branch was officially opened by the Minister of Transport, Mr P. J. Pybus, on 9 December 1932, and public services started to run the next day. There were 140 trains a day, and the fastest did the journey from Stanmore to Baker Street (11½ miles) in 20 minutes, but in normal hours a shuttle service was run between Stanmore and Wembley Park, forcing passengers to change train at the latter station. The service was also reduced on Sundays.

The double-track branch left the main line by a 15-chain curve at a junction situated 7 miles from Baker Street to run north-east on an embankment, twice crossed the Wealdstone Brook and reached the first station at Kingsbury by entering a deep and wide cutting, passing below the Kingsbury-Kenton Road.

Kingsbury '…should have been called Kingsbury Green, as that place was but half a mile east of the line, whereas Kingsbury itself was well over a mile away, close to Neasden station, which was called Neasden and Kingsbury until the new station was opened. The entrance block, on the south side of the road bridge, was in the centre of three cottage-style red brick and tile two-storey blocks of shops, with flats above. There were five shops in each of the side blocks and three each side of the main entrance. From the entrance hall with its Passimeter ticket office, covered stairs led down to the platforms either side of the cutting, each platform with a short canopied red-brick building containing a waiting room with tiled fireplace and wooden bench seats along the walls. Electric lamps held in pretty iron scroll work lit the platforms at night. When the station was opened there were no significant population centres nearby other than the small settlement at Kingsbury Green and, a little to the north, Roe Green, the interesting World War I garden village for workers in adjacent aviation factories.'[19]

The line then crossed some open land and continued on embankment to its next station, Canons Park.

'At street level each side of the northern abutment of the bridges was a canopied entrance to a booking hall beneath the first arch of the six-span masonry viaduct supporting the platforms. Either side of the entrances were small two-storey blocks of shops

The opening of the Stanmore branch. *London Transport Museum*

with flats over. Platform structures were similar to those at Kingsbury.'[20]

Finally, the line turned slightly north-west to enter, in a cutting (as it encountered the upward slope of the Elstree Ridge) its terminus, the summit of the line, which was scooped out of the side of the hill. The main station building was situated on the south side of the London Road and about half a mile east of Stanmore village centre. At Stanmore station:

'The terminal platform was an island protected by a canopy which also covered the waiting room, staff accommodation and the lower landing of the covered staircase to the roadside building, a large three-storey block with its first floor at ground level. East of the platform was the only goods siding on the branch, together with two stabling roads... The roadside buildings at Kingsbury and Stanmore were executed in a domestic style of pleasing and unassuming simplicity by the company's architect, Charles W. Clark... Stanmore, with its handsome hipped roof, four chimneys and Georgian windows would not have looked out of place on a country gentleman's estate. Both buildings were in red multi-coloured bricks set on a few courses of dark brindled bricks which formed a mock plinth. Their long red tiled roofs were broken by dormer windows, which lit the entrance hall. These halls were tiled in khaki tone below plaster friezes, whilst the doors, clock and other features were elegantly framed in hardwood. Canons Park was less impressive; here the roadside buildings were flat-roofed, the horizontal motif of bridge and roof emphasised by the pattern of brickwork and the dark granite plinth. All three stations had platform buildings in matching red brick with workmanlike glass and steel canopies valanced in metal.'[21]

A fourth station was later added at Queensbury. This first opened as a wooden halt on 16 December 1934, then in 1936, as the population in the area started to grow, a proper station with a spacious entrance hall was built.

Stanmore terminus had been built so that it would require little alteration if the line was ever to be extended towards Elstree or St Albans, but tunnelling through the Elstree Ridge would be an expensive business, which is why the project never materialised. The signalling was of the conventional type with three-aspect coloured lights fitted with train stops, but what was unique at the time was that the whole branch was controlled from the Wembley Park signal box, where a comprehensive illuminated diagram showed the position of every train on the line. This Westinghouse centralised traffic control system was used here for the first time in Great Britain, and in the world, for purely suburban traffic. The power was supplied from Neasden at 11,000 volts three phase AC and was converted to traction voltage in the two new rotary substations at Preston Road (3 x 1,500kW) and Canons Park (2 x 1,500kW).

The traffic on the line developed slowly, for the fares were not cheap and there was a competitor – the Edgware tube – situated a mile east of Queensbury or Canons Park, which was served by many buses and which offered cheaper fares. The branch was therefore not a success for it only contributed to push more traffic into the already congested area between Finchley Road and Baker Street. This problem was not solved by the Metropolitan Railway Company, but was handed over to the London Passenger Transport Board in 1933 (when all the London local railway companies came under one ownership), which decided to link the branch with the Bakerloo Line by building a 2½-mile tube link between Baker Street and Finchley Road, rearranging the Metropolitan tracks between Finchley Road and Wembley Park, building a burrowing junction at Wembley Park, and also rebuilding Wembley Park station. This new tube was opened on 20 November 1939, and the Stanmore branch was then turned over to Bakerloo operation until 30 April 1979, when it became part of the Jubilee Line, following the official opening of the new 2.75-mile section between Charing Cross and Baker Street.

The Stanmore branch was a typical example of the lack of coordination between the various passenger transport operators in London at the time, and the failure of the line a sign of decline for the Metropolitan Railway Company, whose railway would have probably become unworkable if it had remained independent much longer. However, before relating this last chapter in the history of the Metropolitan Railway Company, let us study more closely the improvement that, at the beginning of the century, turned the company into a successful suburban railway company and prevented it from sinking into bankruptcy: electrification.

8

Electrification

The Metropolitan Railway Company had thought of electrifying its line in the early 1880s, and in order to demonstrate that electric traction was possible on a commercial scale, it carried out some experiments in Wembley Park, and in 1882 even obtained Parliamentary sanction to electrify the whole line. Unfortunately, the project did not materialise immediately for it was not an easy task to build a new electric railway line, and it was also quite a costly business to electrify an existing line. However, as the years went by the company realised that it would have either to electrify or die, as competition from buses, trams and especially the new electric lines like the City & South London Railway and the Central London Railway (the latter running very close to the Metropolitan Railway) was increasingly becoming a threat; passengers also kept on complaining about the insalubrious atmosphere in the tunnels, and the price of the high-quality coal the company had to use was continuously rising. In those circumstances, the Metropolitan and Metropolitan District companies decided in 1899 to get together and finally agreed to try, at a cost of £10,000 each, a full-scale experiment, which consisted of electrifying the section between Kensington High Street and Earl's Court, the power being provided by a third rail.

On 21 May 1900 that section was opened to the public, who could travel on it at a special fare of 1 shilling, which was quite costly considering that for the past ten years people had been travelling on the electric trains of the City & South London for just 2 pennies. However, after six months the two companies considered the experiment a success and decided to go ahead with the project. They formed an Electric Traction Joint Committee, but all did not go smoothly, because the two companies did not agree on the system to use. The Metropolitan District favoured the one proposed by the British Westinghouse Company, which offered a low-tension direct current supply, whereas the Metropolitan wanted to adopt the cheaper proposition made by the Hungarian company Ganz & Company, which consisted of electrifying the line with 3,000-volt three-phase alternating current using overhead copper wire conductors. This was favoured by the Metropolitan because the installation and operation of the system was simple, no substations would be needed, and overhead wires would be cheaper than conductor rails – in other words, mainly because the system was all round less expensive.

The Metropolitan District company did not like the system, not only because it had not been tried anywhere under commercial conditions, but also because it thought that the overhead wires would be difficult to install in the tunnels and might even be a hazard to the passengers; also, since alternating current motors had a poorer starting torque, it would become a disadvantage to trains that had to stop frequently. The Metropolitan had nearly convinced the Metropolitan District, which did not really have much choice since it was on the point of bankruptcy, when a rich American tycoon named Charles Tyson Yerkes, an expert in railway electrification, came to the rescue and assumed full control of the Metropolitan District Railway Company. This was of course unfortunate for the Metropolitan Railway Company, since Mr Yerkes was in favour of the direct current traction that was already in use successfully in America. In order to settle the dispute, Yerkes offered to assume responsibility for the electrification of both lines in return for either a payment of 3 farthings per passenger carried or a lease of the whole line for which he would guarantee an interest of 3½ per cent. The Metropolitan refused, thus starting a new battle between the two companies. Finally, after vehement arguments from both sides, the dispute had to go to arbitration, and Yerkes won the fight. Direct current traction at 600 volts and a four-rail system was adopted.

The Metropolitan District Railway built its power station at Lots Road, Chelsea, and designed it so that it could supply electricity to more than one railway line, but the Metropolitan Railway refused to share with its enemy and built its own power station at Neasden on the east bank of the River Brent. The erection of the buildings was carried out by the company's architects, and the equipment was supplied by the British Westinghouse Electric & Manufacturing Company. The work started in 1902, and the station was opened on 1 December 1904. The electric service on the Baker Street-Uxbridge section started on 1 January 1905, on the Aldgate-Whitechapel section on 1 July 1905, and on the Inner Circle on 24 September 1905. The line between Edgware Road and Hammersmith and the branch between Latimer Road and Addison Road were electrified from 5 November 1906. Electric trains started to run on the East London Railway on 31 March 1913, and on the section between Harrow and Rickmansworth on 5 January 1925.

Substations, the function of which was to convert high-tension current by static transformers and rotary converters to low-voltage current, then to distribute it to the sections within their zone, were also initially built along the line at Baker Street, Neasden, Harrow-on-the-Hill, Ruislip, Farringdon Road and Gloucester Road, and later on at Bouverie Street, Euston Road, Moorgate, Willesden Green and Drayton Park.

Originally, the Neasden power station covered an area of 3,660 square yards and was equipped with four 3,500kW alternators that each generated a three-phase current at 11,000 volts, $33^1/_3$ periods, but only three of them were used to start with. The output of the station was increased to 25,000kW in 1910, and to 87,000kW in 1937. However, when the Metropolitan became part of the London Passenger Transport Board in 1933, the station was linked with the two other principal ones, at Lots Road and Greenwich. Finally, on 21 July 1968 Neasden station was closed.

Meanwhile, electrification and an improved signalling system brought new life to the Metropolitan Railway, which was now able to provide its passengers with a better service as more trains could be run and journey times could be cut; a trip round the Inner Circle, for instance, which took 70 minutes by steam train, was cut down to 60 in 1905 and 50 in 1907. Electrification of the main line also made possible the running of through trains to the City without the necessity of changing at Baker Street, and from 1 July 1909 there were 12 through trains a day running from Aylesbury. With such improved means of transport, people stopped complaining about fumes and dirt and started to

Neasden Power Station was built 1902-4 to enable the Metropolitan Railway to convert from steam-powered to electrified services. Coal for the power station was delivered by rail. 'A' class locomotive No L.45 was the last of its class to survive, undertaking service duties at Neasden in its latter years before withdrawal in 1948 and subsequent preservation. *Stephenson Locomotive Society*

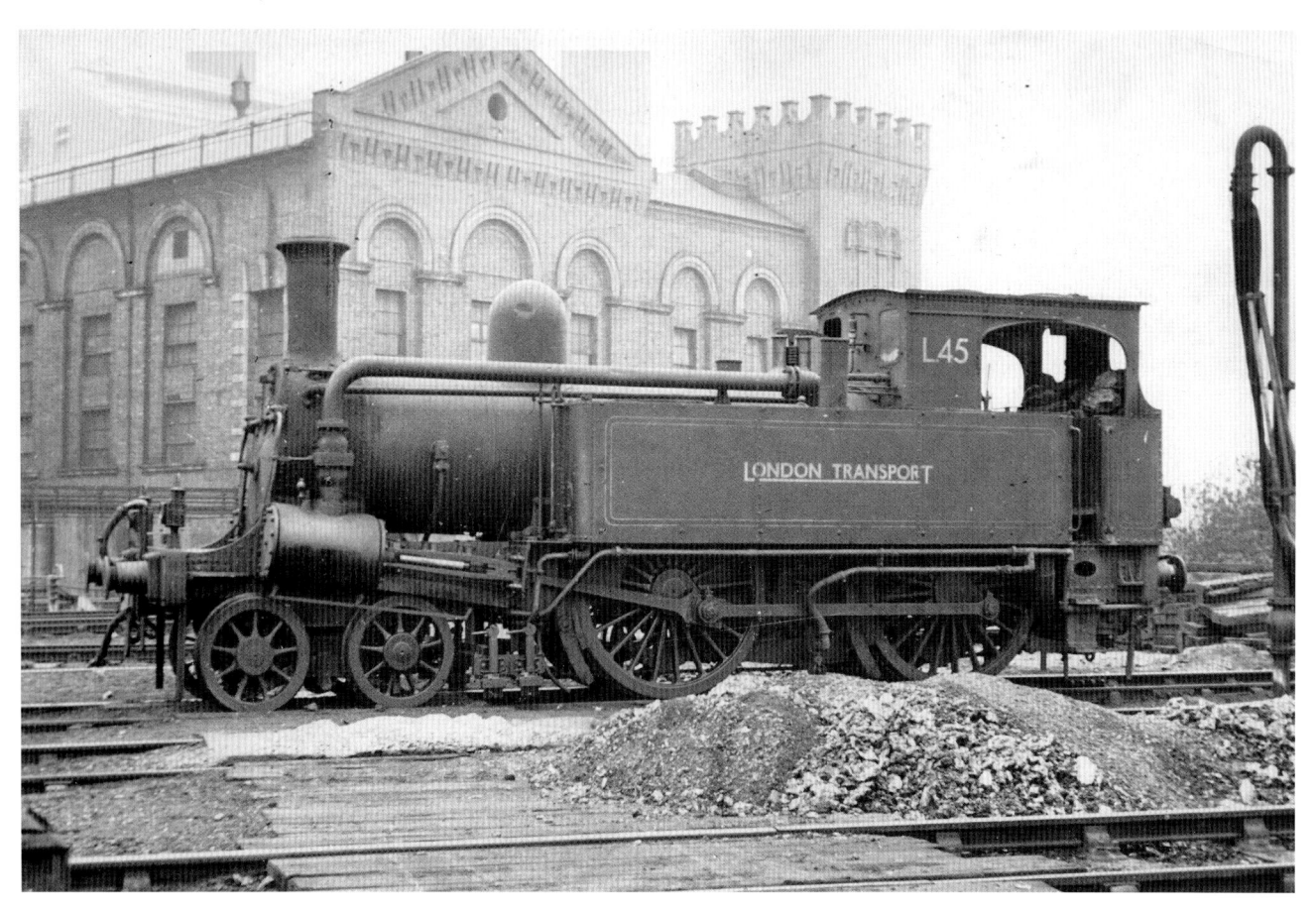

Above: Class A No 3 is seen on a Harrow train pre electrification. *Crecy Heritage Library*

Below: Electric No 1 on a Harrow train after electrification. *Crecy Heritage Library*

Neasden station with the power station in the background. *Ben Brooksbank*

consider seriously the idea of living outside London, but close to the railway that would take them to their place of work within a reasonable amount of time. So, if the steam trains had failed to turn the Metropolitan into a main-line railway, the electric trains succeeded in turning it into a busy suburban line.

The last of the steam rolling stock

Before studying the new electric stock, let us have a last glance at the steam stock. Fourteen years after the 'F' class engines, four 'G' class 0-6-4 tank locomotives were built by the Yorkshire Engine Company – No 94 *Lord Aberconway*, No 95 *Robert H. Selbie*, No 96 *Charles Jones* and No 97 *Brill*. They were also very much heavier than any other Metropolitan locomotive had been before; they started to run in 1915, and the company was very proud of them.

The next batch, which appeared in 1920-21, consisted of eight 'H' class 4-4-4 tank locomotives built by Kerr, Stuart & Company and designed by Charles Jones. They were numbered 103 to 110.

Finally, the last steam engines to be built for the Metropolitan Railway Company were the six powerful 2-6-4 'K' class tank locomotives built by Armstrong Whitworth in 1925, with unassembled parts that had been made by Woolwich Arsenal for the South Eastern & Chatham Railway at the Government's request just after the First World War to keep the staff employed.

The locomotives were mostly used north of Finchley Road for freight workings. Soon after, the Metropolitan Railway Company became part of the London Passenger Transport Board, and responsibility for steam working the timetabled passenger and goods trains passed to the London & North Eastern Railway. The 'G', 'H' and 'K' class locomotives also went to the LNER, which renumbered them, and became responsible for the steam haulage of passenger trains beyond Rickmansworth. The remainder, used for engineering works, remained with London Transport and were renumbered with the prefix 'L'.

To compete with the carriages of the Great Central in service over the line between Harrow-on-the-Hill and Verney Junction, the Metropolitan Railway brought out between 1912 and 1923 new stock nicknamed 'Dreadnought'. The vehicles were longer and higher off the ground than previous stock, and the roofs had a semi-elliptical shape. The compartment doors were rounded at the top, and of the swing type. They were fitted with

Class H 4-4-4T locomotive No 104.

Class G 0-6-4T locomotive No 94 *Lord Aberconway*.

Class K 2-6-4T locomotive No 114. *Stephenson Locomotive Society*

draught excluders and door locks with internal 'lift-to-open'-type handles. So as to spread the passenger load and reduce the stopping time at rush hours, the 3rd Class carriages were provided with groups of three compartments connected by a central corridor. These trains only had 1st and 3rd Class carriages, as 2nd Class was withdrawn from Metropolitan trains on 17 December 1906. There were seven compartments in the 1st Class carriages and nine in groups of three in the 3rd Class vehicles. The brake coaches had seven compartments. These were the first Metropolitan trains fitted with a passenger alarm system. The bogies were made of pressed steel with a wheelbase

A 1905 motor car. *London Transport Museum*

of 7 feet set at 35-foot centres, and 36-inch-diameter wheels.

The carriages were equipped with screw couplings and side buffers. The lighting was gas at first, but became electric in 1918. Most of these high-standard coaches remained in service over the non-electrified sections of the Metropolitan Railway until 1961 when, on 9 September, all steam passenger traffic came to an end.

New electric stock

Electrification brought an entirely new fleet of engines and carriages. The new electric carriages were of composite steel and timber construction and 52ft 6in long over the buffers, with bodies 8ft 9in wide. At first they were built with open end platforms and gates; these were enclosed later on. There were three types of carriages: 3rd Class motor coaches, 1st Class trailer coaches, and 3rd Class trailer coaches. Inside they were arranged with both transverse and longitudinal seats: 48 in the motor cars and 56 in the trailer cars. The 3rd Class seats were covered with buffalo hide and those in 1st Class cars with moquette. They were constructed by the Metropolitan Amalgamated Railway Carriage & Wagon Company, and the electrical equipment was made by the British Westinghouse Company (which later became the Metropolitan Vickers Electrical Company Limited). The motor cars had four axles each driven by a 150hp motor.

Each train was usually composed of six carriages: two 1st Class trailers in the middle, flanked on each side by a 3rd Class trailer, and a 3rd Class motor car at each end. The cars were coupled at first by a plain link and pin except for the outer ends of the motor cars, which were fitted with screw couplings; later all cars were fitted with automatic mechanical couplings of the 'buck-eye' type, and the end of each carriage was provided with sliding doors and patent swing gates (in 1906 the gate ends were converted to vestibule ends). All the carriages were brightly lit, nicely furnished, well heated and ventilated. The brakes were of the Westinghouse automatic quick-acting compressed-air type, with one brake block to each wheel; they could be operated by hand from the driver's compartment or from the platform at the end of the car. The brakes were inside hung so that there was hardly any cant to the truck when they were applied.

Then came another batch of 26 motor cars fitted with British Thomson-Houston equipment, 12 with

Camel-back electric locomotive No 1.

British Thomson-Houston electric locomotive number 11, part of the second batch of electric locomotives delivered to the Metropolitan Railway 1907-8.

150hp motors and 14 with 200hp motors. The Metropolitan also converted 22 old compartment stock coaches, and in 1913 bought a further 23 car sets fitted with British Westinghouse equipment; the equipment from 13 of them was fitted to new motor cars built by the Metropolitan Amalgamated Carriage, Wagon & Finance Company, the rest being used to replace the British Thomson-Houston equipment fitted to the previous batch.

As the Metropolitan Railway did not intend to electrify the whole of its network, it also needed powerful electric locomotives capable of hauling steam stock. The first ten, built in 1905-06 by British Westinghouse and the Amalgamated Railway Carriage Company, were known as 'camelbacks', since they had a central driving cab flanked by a bonnet at each end. Each engine had a length over buffers of 35ft 9in with bogie centres at 17ft 3in. The pressed steel bogies carried two Type 86M nose-suspended traction motors that drove the 36-inch-diameter wheels through a spur gearing having a ratio of 22:60.

These pairs of motors were controlled by 15 electro-pneumatic switches in the shape of a turret, which were set into motion by the low-voltage electricity supplied by a 14-volt battery, later on replaced by a motor generator set. The locomotives were also equipped with an electrically driven air compressor and two exhausters. As they had to haul trains with the Westinghouse brake system as well as trains with the vacuum brake, they were fitted with both.

The next batch of ten locomotives was built by British Thomson-Houston and delivered between 1907 and 1908. They were more box-like, having a flat-fronted driving cab at each end, and the equipment was fitted in the middle on each side of a central gangway. They were lighter and shorter than the previous ten. The 'deadman's handle' safety device was fitted on the master controllers. They were also equipped with buck-eye couplers and standard screw couplings, the latter being removable. At first these locomotives could only work as far as Willesden Green, but locomotive changing facilities were soon provided at Wembley Park on 1 November 1906, at Harrow-on-the-Hill on 19 July 1908, and on 5 January 1925 at Rickmansworth.

In 1919, the company needed more powerful engines, and decided to rebuild the 20 electric locomotives but, as the trials were unsuccessful, it was decided to have new ones built instead, and an order was placed with Vickers Ltd of Barrow in Furness. These new replacement electric locomotives went into service between 1922 and 1923. Each was 39ftb 6in long. They had four-wheel bogies which each carried 300hp nose-suspended motors, and four positive and two positive current collector shoes. There was a driving cab in each of the rounded ends and the mechanical equipment was fitted on each side of a centre gangway. They were also equipped with a dual brake system. Each locomotive weighed 60½ tons, their tractive effort was about 22,000lb, and within 25 seconds they could accelerate from a stand to 25mph. They could also reach a top speed of 65mph, or run at a shunting speed of 2mph. Their 29ft 6in wheelbase allowed them to deal easily with 3-chain-radius curves. Their livery was maroon with black and straw lining; the solebars, buffer beams and window frames were painted red. At first they were given only a number, but in 1926 it was decided to name them.

The 'MV' and 'MW' electric multiple-units were the last to be built for the Metropolitan Railway before it became part of the London Passenger Transport Board, which gave them the name 'T' stock in 1938 when they were made up into nine eight-coach and ten six-coach trains. In 1927 the Metropolitan ordered 12 compartment-type driving motor coaches from the Metropolitan Amalgamated Railway Carriage, Wagon & Finance Company; they resembled the 'Dreadnoughts', and each was fitted with four Metropolitan Vickers 275hp motors. They all had five passenger compartments, seating five-a-side, a luggage compartment and accommodation for the driver and guard. They were of two types so as to work with the existing trailer cars. Six of them formed the 'MW' stock ('W' standing for Westinghouse brake), were fitted with buck-eye couplings and no side buffers, and were designated to work with six 'Bogie' stock trailers. The other six were equipped with side buffers, screw couplings and vacuum brakes, and were used to work with five converted steam stock coaches. These formed the 'MV' stock ('V' standing for Vacuum brake). They were very successful, and in 1929 the Metropolitan ordered another batch of 30 motor coaches and 20 trailer coaches. The last batch was ordered in 1931, and consisted of 18 motor coaches, 14 1st Class trailer coaches and 14 control trailer coaches with 3rd Class accommodation, and 19 plain 3rd Class trailer coaches. They made up seven eight-coach trains. This multiple-unit compartment stock was mainly used on the line from the City or Baker Street to Rickmansworth and later on the Stanmore Branch until 1939, the date when the Bakerloo took over.

Metropolitan-Vickers locomotive No 7, named *Edmund Burke*. Stephenson Locomotive Society

The first Metropolitan Railway electric train was delivered in 1927.

A 'T' stock train, formerly 'M.W.' stock.

9

Amalgamation and nationalisation

Finally, we come to the end of an era for the Metropolitan Railway Company, with the formation in 1933 of the London Passenger Transport Board, which meant the death of the company's ambitions and pride.

The Metropolitan, which considered itself a main-line railway, since it carried goods and passengers and had connections with the four main-line railways, fought the project from the beginning, and when in the end the company was forced to comply with the Government's decision it is said that on the last day of its existence as an independent company, the people in charge, helped by some members of staff, made outside their headquarters at Baker Street a big bonfire from most of the company's old papers, thus putting an end to a dream that did not come true and to a chapter in the history of London's Underground.

However, even if the Metropolitan Railway Company did not approve of the project, something desperately needed to be done at that stage, since the whole of the London transport system was deteriorating rapidly, mainly because of a lack of coordination and increasing competition between the different independent passenger transport operators, which of course resulted in high fares and congestion. To deal with this problem, the Government started to take steps as early as

'K' class No 111 with a freight working passes Chorley Wood on 2 June 1934. *Crecy Heritage Library*

September 1919 when a Ministry of Transport was created, taking over the powers previously exercised by the Board of Trade. In a report published in 1920 the Ministry proposed the amalgamation of all railway lines into seven groups (which later were reduced to four groups), one of which was to be the amalgamation of all London's local lines. However, the project did not go far at first. The Underground group was prepared to negotiate some working arrangements with other transport operators as far as the organisation and management were concerned, but they did not want their interest or ownership to be involved. Though everyone knew what had to be done, no agreement could be reached.

In 1924, more or less as a result of the tram and bus strike, the newly elected Labour Government passed the Traffic Act of 1924, reducing the competition between buses and trams by controlling the number of buses on certain routes. It did this setting up a Licensing Authority that dealt with the setting of bus routes, the suitability of the vehicles used, the frequency of their services, and the number of buses allowed on certain routes. As a result the number of independent bus companies was reduced, but this was not sufficient, since many problems still remained to be solved.

Consequently, during 1925-26 some inquiries into the travelling facilities in London were carried out by the London & Home Counties Traffic Advisory Committee, which acknowledged the fact that a unified management between the companies was necessary if all wasteful competition was to stop. Frank Pick, who was then Joint Assistant Managing Director of the Underground group, suggested the formation of a common fund and a common management for all the passenger transport companies operating in London. The Minister of Transport asked the Committee to study the scheme and its report of October 1927 favoured the idea. Most of the passenger transport companies involved approved the scheme except for some independent bus companies and the Metropolitan Railway Company, which wanted to remain independent. The Labour Party also opposed the idea, considering the only solution to the problem to be public ownership; when it came to power again in May 1929, it rejected the proposed Bill for common fund and management. Herbert Morrison was then Minister of Transport, and on 2 December he made a public announcement of his proposals, which were based on his proposals. He wanted the unification to be under public control, the management to be a non-political body, the main line railways to participate without the transfer of ownerships and the system to be run commercially so as to be self-supporting and unsubsidised.

Settling the financial side of the scheme was the hardest task, if everyone was to be satisfied, and negotiations went on for many months until the final Bill was published on 13 March 1931. On 28 April it went before a Joint Select Committee of the Houses of Commons and Lords, which studied it during 35 sitting days. Finally, on 20 July, it was

Class A No 23 is seen at Brill on 17 March 1933, shortly before takeover by the LPTB. Two years later the branch was closed. *A. W. Croughton/Stephenson Locomotive Society Collection*

approved by five votes to four, and at that stage it looked as if the battle was at long last won. Unfortunately it was not, for in August 1931 a new 'National Government' came into power, and the Bill had to be considered by the new Parliament. However, the new Minister of Transport, P. J. Pybus, announced that the Bill would be carried out by the new Parliament from where it had been left in July, but the debate went on for some months before some agreements were reached. Finally, Royal Assent was given to the Bill on April 1933, and the London Passenger Transport Board came into existence on 1 July.

The seven members of the Board appointed by a body of Appointing Trustees on 18 May 1933 were Frank Pick, John Cliff, Patrick Ashley Cooper, Sir John William Gilbert, Sir John Edward Holland, Sir Henry Maybury and Lord Ashfield, who was appointed Chairman. The London Passenger Transport Board (LPTB), composed of five railway companies, seven tramway undertakings and more than 100 bus and coach companies, became the biggest urban passenger transport organisation in the world. It operated in an area of 1,986 square miles, served a population of about 9,400,000 people, and was given the big task of organising, improving and coordinating.

Though the Metropolitan Railway Company had been strongly opposed to the project, once it was carried out the company benefited quite a lot from it since a whole scheme of modernisation for the line was announced in November 1934. This included amongst other things:

• the disappearance of the bottleneck between Finchley Road and Baker Street by the provision of tube tunnels along that section of the line so as to enable Bakerloo trains to take over the running of the Stanmore branch
• the building of a 'fly-under' at Wembley Park
• the quadrupling of tracks between Harrow and Rickmansworth
• the electrification of the line as far as Amersham and Chesham
• the re-siting and rebuilding of Uxbridge, Aldgate East and King's Cross stations
• the reconstruction of Ruislip, Ruislip Manor, Eastcote and Rayners Lane stations and of Neasden Depot
• the provision at Cromwell Road, Kensington, of a fly-over junction to enable the trains of the Circle Line to come into direct cross-platform connections with those of the District Line
• the repeal of the 1879 Act forcing the companies to run a continuous service on the Circle Line
• the withdrawal of services on the Brill branch and between Verney Junction and Aylesbury after 30 November 1935 and 4 July 1936 respectively, because of the small number of passengers using these sections of the line
• the replacement of the diamond-shaped red backing plates used for the names of the stations by the standard Underground 'bull's-eyes'
• the change of livery for stock being renovated
• the introduction of new stock
• the taking over on 1 January 1937 of the steam-hauled Metropolitan trains between Aylesbury and Rickmansworth by the LNER

By 1939 much of the work had been carried out or was well under way. For example, the new Neasden Depot was finished in 1938, the Bakerloo link was opened on 20 November 1939 with intermediate stations at St John's Wood and Swiss Cottage, and new stations were opened at Rayners Lane on 8 August 1938, at Eastcote early in 1939, at Ruislip Manor on 26 June 1938, and at Uxbridge on 4 December 1938. Unfortunately, the outbreak of the Second World War in 1939 interrupted for a while all improvement work.

In 1945 the Labour Party came to power once more, bringing with it the plan of nationalising all the major industries. As far as transport was concerned, Labour intended to bring into one publicly owned and publicly controlled organisation all the overland transport facilities in Great Britain. A Transport Bill to that effect was introduced in November 1946, and it received Royal Assent in August 1947; on 1 January 1948 the London Passenger Transport Board became part of the British Transport Commission, but was worked as a distinct unit by the London Transport Executive. This change had little effect on the Metropolitan Line, since most of the improvement schemes put forward by the LPTB continued to be carried out. On 12 September 1960 electric trains started to run to Amersham and Chesham, but all services north of Amersham were handed over to British Railways on 9 September 1961. By June 1962 the modernisation of the Metropolitan Line was complete.

On 1 January 1963 the British Transport Commission was dissolved and London Transport reverted to its original status as an independent statutory undertaking and was given the name of the London Transport Board, which in its turn was dissolved by the Transport (London) Act of 1969 and became the London Transport Executive. This new body was only in charge of the management and the day-to-day operation of the services, as financial and policy control was given to the Greater London Council.

The GLC was disbanded in 1984 and responsibility for transport in London passed to London Regional Transport until the formation of Transport for London in 2000, the body now responsible for public transport in the capital.

Part Two: The Development of 'Metro-land'

If, unfortunately, the Metropolitan Railway did not survive in its pride and glory, it definitely left its imprint on the countryside it went through, since it brought thousands of people to a rural place which was subsequently named Metro-land.

John Betjeman who was fond of Metro-land gave a very good account of that chapter in the history of the Metropolitan Railway in a television film, called *Metro-Land*, first shown on BBC in 1973.

The next section of book will focus on the Metropolitan company's involvement in suburban development and the changes it made to Londoners' lives. And to understand how a railway company like the Metropolitan Railway Company became involved in suburban development it is necessary to first go back to the 19th century and the formation of the Surplus Lands Committee.

10

The Metropolitan Railway Surplus Lands Committee

In the 19th century the railways were granted the privilege of being able to purchase by compulsory procedure any property or land required for the building or extension of their lines, but most of the time they bought or had to buy more than they really needed. Unfortunately, the Land Clauses Act of 1845, which gave them the power to buy the land, also forced them to dispose of any surplus lands that they did not use within the ten years following the completion of the works; they were allowed to apply for an extension of the time period only if they could prove that they intended to require the land which they had not yet used. At the end of the ten years, before the surplus lands could be put up on the open market, they had to be offered back for sale to their previous owners or heirs, and if the latter refused or could not be found, to the people whose land adjoined the lands put up for sale by the railway companies.

During the period when the surplus lands were not used, the railway companies were allowed to let them or use them for anything they wanted, but they could not offer them for sale. Thus the railway companies could not draw any benefit from the rise in land value they had created. This applied to all the railway companies but one – the Metropolitan Railway Company – which was allowed by the Metropolitan Inner Circle Completion Act of 1874 to grant building leases and sell ground rents. One of the main reasons for this privilege was that, unlike the other companies, the Metropolitan line did not just terminate in London, but was built in London, and thus the land it had to acquire for the construction of the line was not empty rural land but valuable city land. Consequently, with the gradual extension of the line, the company acquired more and more surplus lands and properties and started to draw some revenues from them, as well as from the railway line itself. However, when the surplus lands' earnings began to increase, Sir Edward Watkin started to feel uneasy, for he thought that:

'Parliament might some day say that it was a dangerous thing for a small railway company to have a rent roll of £80,000 a year, with about 1,000 tenants, and they (the railway company) might be unwillingly compelled to sell the property.'[22]

This was something that of course the company did not want to see happen. The company was, indeed, not interested in selling the surplus properties and lands it owned. At a Board meeting of 24 March 1886, in answer to a question from Lord Redesdale, 'Why don't you sell?', Sir Edward Watkin answered:

'What are we to do with about two million of money? You cannot force men to take their capital back. You cannot buy up so large an amount … without probably raising prices, artificially, 50%.'[23]

It was therefore decided that the separation of the railway earnings from the land and property earnings would be a good idea, and in October 1885 instructions were given to arrange for the preparation of the plan and schedule required in connection with this separation. Watkin was very much in favour of the project as it would, he said,

'…improve the selling value and steadiness of the stock, and thus protect the investor from the speculator; avoid an attack upon the anomaly of such an immense proportion of surplus property; do no damage in any case to anybody; prevent exaggerated notions of the profits of underground lines, and therefore prevent competition based upon too high dividends; and facilitate future union, if desired, with other interests.'[24]

However, though it seemed a good idea, not everyone was at first in favour of it. Some, like Mr George Morphett, objected to the fact that the Committee would have too much power; others, like Mr Pochin, did not like the idea of the land being owned by a different organisation, fearing that in the future such an organisation, thinking only of their own interest, like the Metropolitan District Railway Company in the past, would turn hostile, which would create a lot of problems. He also thought that the setting up of this Committee would be a costly business and that in the end the market value of the two companies would be less than their market value was then as a whole.

On the other hand, some people, such as Mr Bradbourne, supported the project. In a letter to Watkin in March 1886 he wrote:

'It seems to me that a well matured plan of separation between what I may call the railway stocks and the land stocks of the Metropolitan Railway Company will be much more likely to secure both from legislature attacks than if they were to continue amalgamated. There is jealousy on the part of a portion of the public against the railway companies, as such being possessed of surplus property, and this separation, properly worked out, will, I think weaken the force of any attack which might be made upon us from this cause.'[25]

In the meantime, the preparation for the Plan and Schedule went ahead, and was approved by the Metropolitan Railway Act of 1885 and finally confirmed by the Metropolitan Railway Act of 1887. Thus the lands and properties not required for the purposes of the railway undertaking of the company, and the revenues drawn from them, were separated from the stations and works and the revenues drawn from the running of the line, and put under the control and management of the Metropolitan Railway Surplus Lands Committee, consisting of five persons (three appointed by the shareholders and two by the directors of the railway company). A stock known as the surplus lands stock was created to the amount of the capital determined at the sum of £2,640,915 and issued to the proprietors of ordinary stock registered on the books of the company on 30 June 1887 in the proportions of £1 of surplus lands stock to every £2 of ordinary stock of the company. However, the Surplus Lands Committee remained vested in the Metropolitan Railway Company, and any purchase or sale of property was to be done under the seal of the railway company, and all leases were granted in the same way. If the railway company required any of the properties for railway purposes, a fair price was paid to the Committee. The income arising from the surplus lands was applied in payment of a dividend on the surplus land

Advert for new houses on the Cecil Park Estate, Pinner, from the Metropolitan Railway's housing brochure *Near and Far*, May 1912.

stock each half year, and the proceeds of the sale of the properties were reinvested either in further leasehold or freehold properties or mortgages on real estate or investments authorised by the Trustee Act. Each half year the Committee also presented to its shareholders a report with a statement of account.

At first the Committee's interests were mainly focused on its properties in London, but just before the First World War it decided to take an interest in the land it owned in the suburbs, and the development of two residential estates was started on the north and south sides of Pinner station in Middlesex, becoming the Grange Estate and the Cecil Park Estate respectively. A direct entry and exit between Pinner railway station and the estate was also provided for the convenience of the residents during rush hours. The plots had frontages of 35 feet and upwards, and could be acquired from £5 to £6 per foot frontage. The purchase money could be paid by a deposit of £5 for a plot or £25 for a house, and the balance with interest extended over a period of years; the purchaser was free of surveyor's and legal charges with the exception of stamps, registration and out-of-pocket disbursements. The restrictions and reservations included that only one house would be built on a plot (a pair on two plots), and that no house would be erected of less value than £1,000. The houses could either be let at a rent varying between £40 and £75, or bought at a price varying between £1,300 and £1,600.

The Illustrated Guide to the Metropolitan Railway Extensions of 1905 advertised the Cecil Park Estate as follows:

'This estate is beautifully timbered, charmingly situated and is within a few minutes' walk of Pinner village and of the Metropolitan Railway station. The houses are unique and tasteful in design, thoroughly well built and have large gardens. They are planned and erected under the direct supervision of the Committee's architect. The sewers are connected with the main drainage system of the district, and great care is taken with the sanitary arrangement generally. Gas is laid on, and there is an excellent supply of water.'[26]

Pinner was chosen by the company since it was at the time a picturesque rural village whose population had started to grow by the end of the 19th century: in 1891 the population was 2,729, in 1901 it had increased to 3,366, in 1911 to 7,103, and in 1921 to 9,462. This is how Pinner is described in a Metropolitan Railway brochure of 1912:

'For long it has been a favourite resort for picnics and outings which fortunately have not had the too common result of vulgarising the neighbourhood. Indeed, the effect seems to have been to bring outsiders a knowledge of desirability of the village and its environs as a place of residence. Its situation on the northern slope of Harrow Vale gives it pure and invigorating air, while it is sheltered from north-easterly winds by the gentle slope above it. The main street, which forms the backbone of the village, is a happy combination of the old-fashioned and the modern, and the general effect is heightened by the fine old church that stands at the eastern side of the village… Pinner has become a popular place of residence, and the demand for up-to-date houses has led to considerable development lately. In the village itself a number of residences have been erected, and all round suitable land is available for further building. Until a short time ago the demand had been for detached houses, but lately a number of well-designed semi-detached houses have been built to supply the requirements of would-be householders. One property in particular, the Cecil Park Estate, which practically adjoins the station, has developed in this direction, and the well built, superior class, detached and semi-detached houses erected on it … can be highly recommended as desirable and comfortable residences. In all points

Advertisement for building plots on the Grange Estate in Pinner. The sites were sold by the Metropolitan Railway Surplus Lands Committee, advertised *Metro-land* in 1925, the guidebook for Metro-travelers.

Pinner, Middlesex.

Fast electric train service to and from Town.

The Metropolitan Railway Surplus Lands Committee have formed New Roads with main drainage, gas, electric light and water services on the Grange Estate situate on the North side of the Metropolitan Railway line, with access to the Pinner High Street.

THERE are many beautiful sites on this Estate, and the plots have frontages of 35 feet and upwards, and can be acquired from £5 per foot frontage.

The purchase money can be paid by a deposit of £5 and the balance with interest extended over a period of years.

The restrictions and reservations include that only one house shall be built on a plot (a pair on two plots) and no house to be erected of less value than £1,000.

The few remaining plots on the Cecil Park Estate can also be secured on similar terms.

Different types of Houses are for Sale, freehold, on advantageous terms of payment.

Further Particulars of H. GIBSON, General Offices, Metropolitan Railway, Baker Street Station N.W.1.

Telephone: Langham 1130.

"HOMES IN METRO-LAND," illustrating a number of Houses and Bungalows, for erection at inclusive prices, can be obtained on application to The Commercial Manager, Baker Street Station, N.W.1. Price 2s. 6d.

Pinner answers the description of a pleasing and convenient residential neighbourhood...'[27]

At the end of the 1920s there was talk that the Government intended to place all the capital's railways under one main body, the London Passenger Transport Board, and as we have already seen the Metropolitan Railway Company and the Surplus Lands Committee did not like the idea very much, especially the latter, which thought that since it had nothing to do with the railways it should not be included in the Bill. So it was decided that the Metropolitan Surplus Lands Committee should be vested into a new limited liability company called the Metropolitan Surplus Lands Company Limited, and that its shares would be distributed amongst the Surplus Lands stockholders. Thus, after the amalgamation of the railway company into the LPTB, the Metropolitan Surplus Lands Company Limited was formed and incorporated under the 1929 Companies Act on 29 June 1933. It was now completely independent but continued to maintain a close and good relationship with the parent company and to pursue its land development activities. In 1931, for instance, it had started the development of 8½ acres of freehold land to the north of Woodcock Dell Farm near Northwick Park Golf Course and within easy reach of Preston Road and Northwick Park stations. Some plots of land suitable for detached and semi-detached houses became available for sale from £150.

> **Woodcock Dell Estate, Northwick Park.**
>
> Only 8 miles from Baker Street, having the benefit of being within easy reach of 2 Stations on the Metropolitan Railway, Preston Road and Northwick Park, with an unexcelled service of fast electric trains to and from Baker Street and The City.
>
> THE Estate is actually the site of the old Woodcock Dell Farmhouse and nearby is Kenton and the old hamlet of Preston. There are many facilities for outdoor recreation, including Tennis Courts. The golf course at Northwick Park is immediately adjacent, and others are within easy reach, with the large Sports Ground of Messrs. Selfridge directly adjoining the Estate, adding much to preserve the attractive features of the open countryside.
>
> Schools, Churches and Shops are within easy distance.
>
> The Estate comprises some 8½ acres with about 2,800 ft. frontage of land ready for immediate building.
>
> Beautiful sites are now available from £150 suitable for the erection of Semi-detached or Detached Houses, and a single plot or large sections can be taken up on exceptional terms of purchase.
>
> For further particulars and a plan of the Estate apply:—
>
> **H. GIBSON,**
> **Metropolitan Railway Surplus Lands Committee,**
> General Offices: Baker Street Station, N.W.1.   Welbeck 6688.

1932 *Metro-land* advertisement for building plots in Woodcock Dell Estate, Northwick Park, available from the Metropolitan Railway's Surplus Lands Committee.

11
The Metropolitan Railway Country Estates Limited Company and Metro-land

The development along London's suburban railway lines really started after the First World War, but it was not at the time a new idea, and the process had in fact started before then.

Pearson, for instance, already had in mind the building of a suburban village of about 10,000 cottages, 6 or 7 miles from London, with easy access to the capital, so as to relieve overcrowding of poor people inside the City; however, the time was not ripe for such ideas, and the project did not materialise.

In the 1880s the Metropolitan Railway built some workmen's cottages at Neasden for its staff, and Sir Edward Watkin suggested in 1885 that railway companies in general might 'with very great good, be permitted to build little colonies in places contiguous to their railways'[28]. Yet, though he thought it was a good idea, he did not carry it out, for he was too busy extending his network in order to achieve his ultimate dream – to turn the Metropolitan into a main-line railway – and in order to do so successfully he could not start dealing with suburban development. This was another reason why the Metropolitan Railway Surplus Lands Committee was set up, so that land and property transactions would not interfere with the running of the railway. However, later on, before the First World War, as we have seen in the previous chapter, the Committee started to show an interest in the lands the company owned in the suburbs.

In 1911 the prospectus of the Ruislip Manor Limited Company contained the following statement:

'Since the electrification of the Metropolitan and District Railways and the opening of the Great Central Railway, the growth of London on the north has been rapid and continuous, and the whole of the land … is rapidly becoming ripe for immediate development.'[29]

And Ruislip is indeed a good example of how a small village along the Metropolitan Railway line started to develop before the First World War. The population in 1881 was 1,455, in 1891 it had risen to 1,836, in 1901 to 4,515, and in 1911 it reached 6,273. As early as 1903 King's College Cambridge, which owned some 1,300 acres of land lying between Ruislip and Northwood and between Ruislip and Northolt Junction, was interested in selling the estate for development, provided it would become a modern suburb for London, built on the most generous scale of town planning with every amenity that the new standard of housing required at the time; this new estate was to be called Ruislip Garden City. In 1907 a company registered under the name of Ruislip Building Company Limited (and in fact set up with the help of the college) took up the offer and bought a part of the King's College Estate, which it then started to develop. In 1910 an agreement with a private company called Garden Estates Limited, incorporated in August 1909, replaced the former arrangements and, under the new agreement, if 133 acres of the estate were acquired before 31 July 1911 the estate company would then be entitled (but not bound) during the next 21 years either to purchase or take up on Building Agreement or Lease additional lands at prices that averaged less than £167 an acre. Such an arrangement was advantageous, for the new estate company did not have to buy more land than it needed, thus avoiding the locking up of a big part of its capital and reducing the cost of repayments. With this arrangement the company was also free to stop developing, if at any time the demand ceased, without incurring great losses.

In 1911 a town planning competition was launched by the college and the local authorities. Some 60 plans for the layout of the Garden City were entered, but the winning plan was the one of Messrs A. & J. Soutar, who intended to divide the estate into four areas. Area 1, known as Copse Wood, was meant for the larger class of houses (three houses per acre, gross) and would comprise some parks and a golf course. Area 2, called Park Wood, was to be a mixture of good-class houses and fairly moderate-size houses (four and a half houses per acre, gross) and would include the reservoir that would be devoted to the purpose of swimming and aquatic sports and laid out as a pleasure resort. For Area 3, situated south of Park Wood and north of the Metropolitan Railway, the laying out of some playing fields, the transformation into ornamental waters of the River Pinn, and the building of some houses (eight houses per acre, gross), a shopping centre, public buildings such as a fire station, library, school, etc, was suggested. Finally, Area 4, situated south of the railway, was partly to cater for working class people (ten houses per acre, gross) and partly to be laid out for recreation grounds. It was intended to use up the land as follows:

Area devoted to building plots – 837 acres
Area devoted to open spaces – 255 acres
Area devoted to roads – 184 acres
Total area – about 1,276 acres

The total number of houses suggested was 7,642, which was to include 3,556 houses not exceeding £30 rental, 3,541 houses not exceeding £60 rental, 524 houses not exceeding £100 rental, and 21 houses exceeding £100 rental.[30]

In 1911 a new company called Ruislip Manor Ltd took over from Garden Estates Limited. In 1914 the plans for Ruislip Garden City were approved by the Local Government Board. Ruislip-Northwood Urban District Council was the first local authority to use the powers given by the Housing & Town Planning Act of 1909 and to produce a town plan.

At the request of Ruislip Manor Ltd, the building company, the Metropolitan Railway opened a halt at Ruislip Manor in 1912. By 1914 some 200 houses had been built, but the outbreak of war unfortunately put an end to such an ambitious project.

As to the Metropolitan Railway Company, it also started to show some serious interest in suburban development before the war, especially when Robert H. Selbie came on the scene (in 1903 he was appointed Secretary and in 1908 he became General Manager of the company).

The area between Wembley and Aylesbury was very attractive and suitable for residential development, and Selbie did not think that the company was making enough profit from the lands situated in the neighbourhood of its stations. He could see that some revenues could be drawn from the development of such areas where land could be secured at a comparatively low price. Indeed, if houses were built along the line, the people living in them would have to take the company's trains to travel to town, thus increasing the railway's revenues, all the more so since there was at the time a tendency for people to move away from the nearer suburbs to the more outlying districts. Since the company was widening the line between Wembley Park and Finchley Road, it would be able to offer them a good service to town and back.

So, at a Board Meeting on 3 December 1912, Robert H. Selbie 'called attention to the quantity of Surplus Lands in possession of the Company adjacent to the Railway which were not likely to be required for railway purposes and outlined a scheme for their development as building estates.'[31] And at the Board Meeting of 2 October 1913 he 'recommended that the scheme should take definite shape and that a few of the large shareholders of the Railway Company be approached with a view to the formation of a separate company to carry out the proposals.'[32] The lands adjoining the railway that were suggested as being suitable for development as building land were situated at Willesden Green, Neasden, Hendon, Wembley Park, Rayners Lane, Ruislip, Ickenham and Uxbridge. At the time, the report was approved only in principle. Then, unfortunately, came the war, and it was only in 1918 that the project was brought up again and finally carried out in 1919. By then there was a great demand for houses and also a great

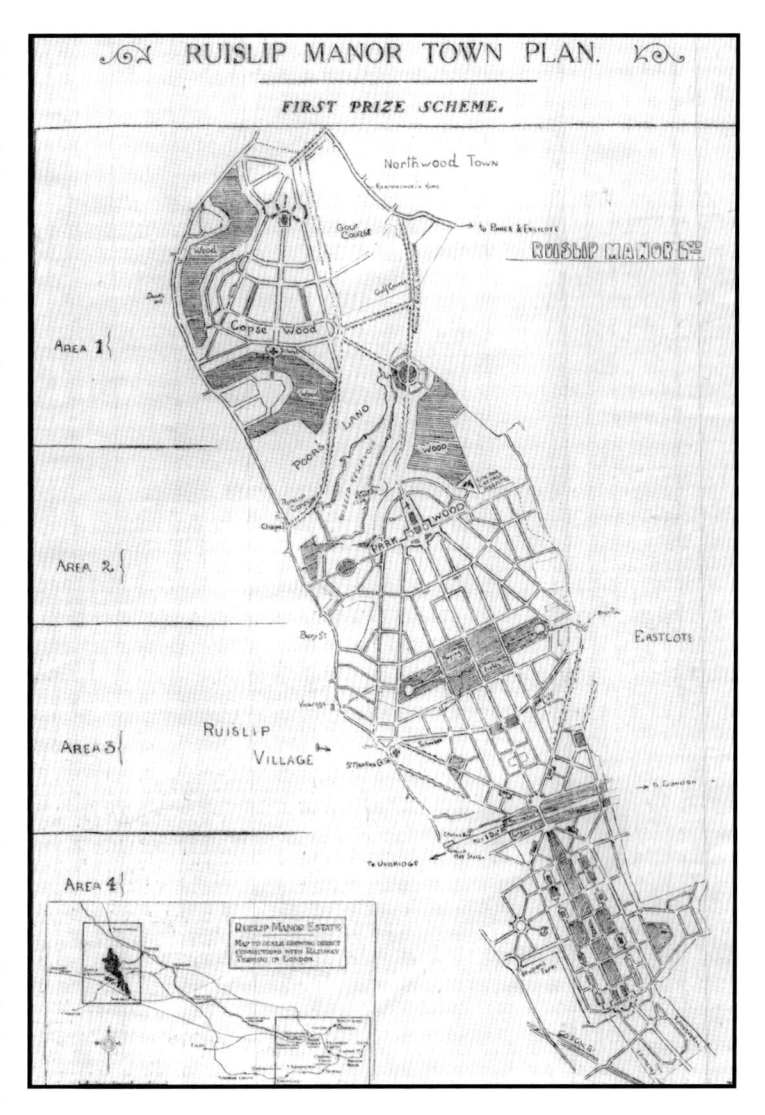

The prize-winning plan in 1911 for the development of Ruislip Garden City.

shortage of them, and with Lloyd George's policy 'to make Britain a fit country for heroes to live in'[33] Selbie did not find much opposition to his project. On 21 November 1918 he addressed the Board as follows:

'In view of the large demand there will be for houses as soon as peace is declared, and the forces demobilised and also in view of the advertisement the districts served by the Company's line have received during the war, I am of opinion that the scheme should be taken in hand forthwith.'[34]

In the minutes of 14 January 1919 it was reported that the subcommittee of the Board reconsidered the proposal and was of opinion that the arguments that had been advanced in its favour four years earlier were still sound and had been strengthened, first by the advertisement the districts served by their line had received in various ways during the period of war, and second by the fact that the cessation of building operations during the previous few years had caused a dearth of middle class residences, especially in the outer suburbs of London. In these circumstances the Committee recommended that the scheme should be proceeded with immediately, that the railway company should support it financially and otherwise, and in order to ensure that the operations of the company be confined to schemes that would benefit the railway, the virtual control of the undertaking be in the hands of the Metropolitan Railway Company.[35]

At a Board Meeting on 19 December 1918 it was suggested that...

'in order to obtain early possession of the properties'... '...a 'Syndicate' [should] be first formed for the purpose of providing the money required for the deposits under some such arrangements as the following: the Syndicate to have a capital of £10,000 to be divided into 10,000 £1 shares to be fully paid up in cash; the object of the Syndicate would be to enter into contracts and to promote and organise the main company.'[36]

It was also decided that the Syndicate should not make any profit on the transfer of the contracts to the main company.

Thus, in March 1919 a private company was registered under the Companies Acts of 1908 to 1917, with the name of North-Western Estates Syndicate Limited with a capital of £1,000 divided into 1,000 shares of £1 each. The Syndicate took powers to purchase lands and the memorandum was drawn so as to give the widest scope to the activities of the Syndicate in view of the fact that it was intended to keep it alive as possible machinery for future operations.

The first directors of the Syndicate, appointed as such by two signatories of the memorandum, were Mr Selbie and Mr Gibson. The Syndicate was to enter into contracts to purchase the estates and to transfer such contracts to the new company when incorporated. In order that the Syndicate might be put in funds to meet the deposits to be paid under the contracts for purchase and the preliminary and incidental expenses of the formation of the Syndicate, the Metropolitan Railway Company was to advance to the Syndicate the amount of the deposits plus a further sum to cover preliminary expenses. The Syndicate was to repay this advance together with interest, say at the rate of 5.5% per annum, out of the monies that it was to receive from the new company as consideration for transferring the contracts to the new company.[37]

However, at the last minute, after having sought the advice of the Hon Frank Russell KC, it was unfortunately revealed that it would not be a good idea for the railway company to take a financial interest in the new company as, should the latter's venture fail, 'the directors might be attacked on the grounds that they have not invested or prudently invested the funds of the Company but had employed them on a hazardous and speculative venture, and Mr Russell thought in the event of the new company failing, the court would be bound ex-hypothesi to hold that the venture was hazardous and speculative.' Moreover, although

'...from a legal and technical aspect the scheme does not involve the Metropolitan Railway Company holding land, nevertheless in effect it does enable a railway company to purchase and hold land without acquiring the necessary statutory authority. In other words, the scheme does not enable a railway company to evade the rule or anyhow the policy of the legislature that a railway company shall not acquire or hold land otherwise than by statutory sanction. He was therefore of opinion that if the scheme were in any way attacked the court might hold it to be invalid on the ground that it was against public policy.'[38]

So it appeared that the directors would be running some risks, at any rate of criticism, if they invested any part of the company's funds in the ordinary shares of the new company. In those circumstances, at a Board Meeting of 29 May 1919 the subcommittee decided to withdraw its recommendation that the railway should take a financial interest in the new concern, and proposed that in place of doing so the railway company should enter into an agreement with the estate company permitting it to use the name of the railway company in its title and undertaking, to give it all possible assistance in the development of the estates to be purchased by means of the railway organisation; the railway company was to have in exchange the nomination of the chairman and two directors of the new company for a period of ten years.[39]

On 7 June 1919 the Metropolitan Railway Country Estates Company was incorporated under the Companies Acts of 1908 to 1917, with a capital of £200,000 divided into 400,000 shares of 10 shillings each. In its prospectus issued at the end of June 1919, the company explained its object as follows:

'The company has been formed with the object ... of acquiring from the North Western Syndicate Limited and from the Metropolitan Railway Company, respectively ... freehold estates... These estates comprising some 627 acres are served by the Metropolitan Railway and the Metropolitan and Great Central Joint Line and are being acquired with a view to their being laid out in an attractive manner and resold in plots of varying sizes. For many years the development of land in the home county districts served by the Metropolitan Railway has been seriously hindered by reason of the difficulty experienced by the purchasers in acquiring sites on which to erect their houses; the available land for the most part being for sale in large parcels only, and quite outside the ordinary buyer's means or requirements. The company's scheme will thus throw open large areas for development, and the company are confident that there will be a ready sale of the plots especially in view of the excellent service of fast trains to the City (through Baker Street) and also to Marylebone, such services linking up with the 'Tubes' and the great railway termini of London. In their scheme of development, the company contemplate the erection of houses on portions of several estates to meet the requirements of all classes of residents, including the provision where necessary of shops in convenient positions, and it is intended to arrange a scheme whereby purchasers will be able to acquire land and properties on convenient terms by deferred instalments.[40]

As we have seen, this whole project was the idea of some of the directors of the Metropolitan Railway Company, who could see in the venture a way of bringing additional traffic to their line, but unfortunately their statutory powers did not allow them to invest any money in the company. However, the railway was able to grant the new company the part-time services of Henry Gibson (the surveyor and valuer to the railway company's Surplus Lands Committee), and some of his staff. The railway also put at the disposal of the estates company the assistance of its publicity department, offering premises at Baker Street station; also, as already mentioned, it gave the new company the right to use the railway company's name. Later the Metropolitan Railway also gave the estate company some financial help; on 25 July 1928 it advanced to the estate company the sum of £45,000 at an interest of 4% per annum, secured by a debenture that provided as security the estate company's lands at Rayners Lane. This debenture, which was due for redemption on 15 July 1933, was extended on 24 March 1932 to 1 January 1940, at an interest that would rise to 5% on 15 July 1933, but in fact the

Front cover of the *Metro-land* guidebook.

outstanding balance was redeemed on that date. The Metropolitan Surplus Lands Committee also advanced money to the estate company: £15,000 on 12 May 1920, and a further £2,500 on 15 August 1921 at an interest of 6% per annum in exchange for the handing over of £20,000 war stock as collateral security.

In return for the services rendered, the railway company had the right for a period of ten years to be represented on the Board of Directors of the new company, three of whom, including the Chairman, were to be members of the board of the railway company or nominees of that company, and the Metropolitan Railway Company and the Metropolitan Railway Surplus Committee stockholders were to be given preferential consideration as far as the application for shares in the new company was concerned.

From then on the new company embarked on the development of estates along the main line and its branches, thus launching a new era for the Metropolitan Railway, the era of 'Metro-land'. Metro-land was more a symbol than a place with defined boundaries. However, it is true that when one talks of Metro-land, one refers to the land along the suburban branches of the Metropolitan Railway lying in Middlesex, Hertfordshire and Buckinghamshire. But these places are still there, and no one ever talks of Metro-land any longer.

> # METRO-LAND.
>
> WITH a view to bringing the Londoner into closer acquaintance with the rural districts they serve, the Metropolitan Railway have prepared an artistic comprehensive Guide, entitled "Metro-land," containing numerous colour illustrations, maps, etc.
>
> It will take the reader into a score of romantic villages, and half a dozen little country towns. It will take him into parks like those of Latimer and Shardeloes; to places of historic interest and "haunts of ancient peace," to a multitude of out-of-the-way nooks and corners, where the life of the country goes on serene, unspoilt by the changes which have overwhelmed the countryside elsewhere.
>
> *This entertaining handbook may be readily obtained at any "Met." Station; Information Bureau, 20, The Arcade, Liverpool Street, E.C.; or direct from Commercial Manager, Baker Street Station, N.W. 1.*

Live in Metro-land from *The Railway Magazine*, February 1927.

Metro-land was in fact a slogan used for publicity from 1915 onwards and invented, it seems, by a popular journalist and versifier named George R. Sims, who wrote in 1915 the following poem:

'I know a land where the wild flowers grow,
Near, near at hand if by train you go,
"Metro-land", "Metro-land",
Meadows sweet have a golden glow,
Hills are green as the vales below

In "Metro-land", "Metro-land."
"Metro-land", "Metro-land",
Leafy dell and woodland fair,
Land of love and hope and peace,
Land where all your trouble cease,
"Metro-land", "Metro-land",
Waft, oh waft me there:
Hearts are lighter, eyes are brighter
In "Metro-land", "Metro-land" '.[41]

Thus, Metro-land became synonymous with visiting or living in countryside that was situated along the railway line and was quite appealing. At the beginning of the 20th century London gradually became a rather unpleasant place to live in since it was getting very crowded as well as increasingly expensive, and the countryside was of course much nicer but inconvenient to live in without adequate means of transport (it took, for instance, 12 hours to go by horse from Ruislip to London).

However, the railway was soon to remedy that situation, since it then became the necessary link between London and its surrounding countryside, thus making middle class people's dream come true; indeed, thanks to the good service provided by the railway, they could now live in the country and in the house of their dreams, while still going to work in the City. By encouraging people to go and live in the country, the Metropolitan Railway Company could reap some handsome profits, and to that end it did a lot of advertising. 'Live in Metro-land' became the slogan of the period between the two wars. It was found everywhere on posters, in brochures, in newspapers and even on the door handles of Metropolitan Railway carriages. The railway did not wait for the setting up of the Metropolitan Railway Country Estates Company to start advertising the glories and charms of the rural arcadia lying beyond Baker Street station, since it was already doing it before the First World War. In the 1900s, for instance, it used to publish a *Guide to the Metropolitan Railway Extensions* with a list of flats to let in the neighbourhood of the company's stations in Middlesex, Hertfordshire and Buckinghamshire. Then

> # METRO-LAND.
>
> WITH a view to bringing the Londoner into closer acquaintance with the rural districts they serve, the Metropolitan Railway have prepared an artistic comprehensive Guide, entitled "Metro-Land," containing numerous four-colour illustrations, maps, etc.
>
> It will take the reader into a score of romantic villages, and half a dozen little country towns. It will take him into parks like those of Latimer and Shardeloes; to places of historic interest and "haunts of ancient peace," to a multitude of out-of-the-way nooks and corners, where the life of the country goes on serene, unspoilt by the changes which have overwhelmed the countryside elsewhere.
>
> As an aid to those seeking a house amid congenial surroundings "Metro-land" will also prove useful, and the excellent Residential Estates that are being vigorously developed by the Metropolitan Railway Country Estates, Ltd., are fully dealt with.
>
> *Obtainable at any "Met." Station; Information Bureau, 20, The Arcade, Liverpool St., E.C., or direct from Commercial Manager, Baker St. Station, N.W.1.*

Advertisements for the *Metro-land* guidebook circa 1920.

came a brochure called *Country Homes*, replaced later by *Country Homes in Metro-land*. There was also *Country Walks* advertising walks and rambles in Middlesex, Hertfordshire and Buckinghamshire and accompanied by sketch maps of routes (incidentally the shape of the pamphlet was oblong so as to fit the coat pockets of the time). There was also a handbook called *Near and Far*, very similar to the famous *Metro-land* which was frequently published between 1919 and 1932 (published once or sometimes even twice a year if the demand called for it). All these brochures and many others, which were well illustrated, described the countryside at its best with the hope of stimulating people to become residents there, or at least frequent visitors.

An account of the history and a description of the towns and villages served by the railway, was also given. However, *Metro-land* was the best; it was a real vade mecum for Metro-travellers, comprising sections such as 'How to get about London', 'Historical notes on Metro-land', 'Country homes in Metro-land', descriptions of Metro-land's towns and villages, and information on golf courses, places of interest, educational facilities, fares, hotels, caterers, flats, housing development... In the 1912 edition of *Near and Far* may be found the following statement:

'To each of us at some period there comes the vital question 'Where shall I live?' and it is not easy to answer. The day when it was possible for the City merchant or professional man to reside over, or in proximity to his place of business is long past and gone, and the morning scenes at the London termini of railways serving the suburban and rural districts indicate how greatly are appreciated the facilities now provided for living outside the business area. The extension of the urban districts, combined with the development of the older and more immediate suburbs due to the ease of access thereto, has caused the latter to become a part of the Metropolis, separate from it in name only. Hence, these one-time attractive suburbs where development was first commenced have become busy townships and are no longer, perhaps, the most desirable places of residence for the class they were originally intended for. Those, therefore, who seek quiet, combined with a healthy and restorative atmosphere, must go farther afield and it is here that the Handiest of Handy Lines, the Metropolitan Railway, comes with suggestions.'[42]

Front cover of the *Metro-land* guidebook, 1924.

Advert from *The Railway Magazine*, April 1929, aimed at house-seekers in Metro-land.

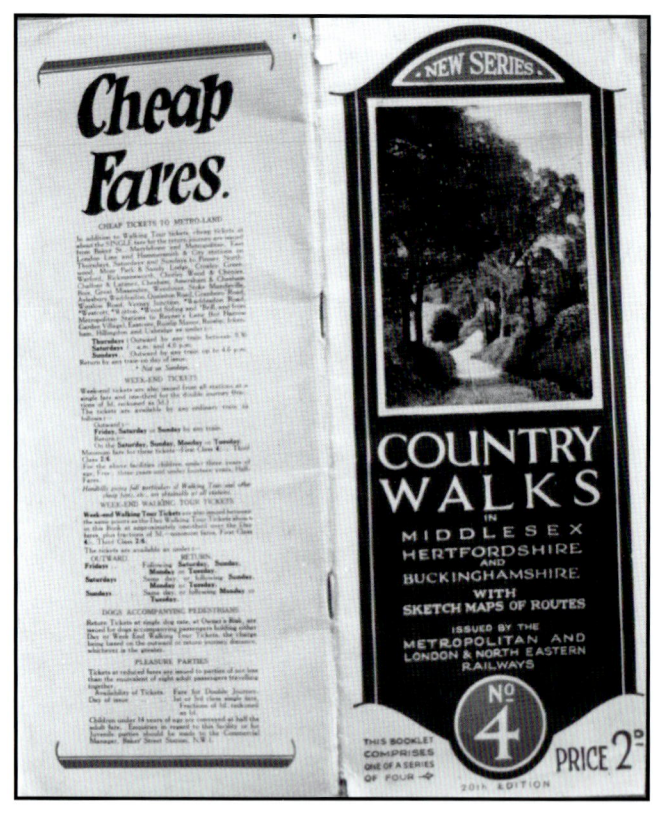

Rambles in Metro-land from *The Railway Magazine*, October 1928.

Advert from *The Railway Magazine*, September 1922.

In the 1923 edition of *Metro-land* G. R. Sims wrote the following poem:

My Metro-land

Realm of Romance that lies around my home
                    My Metro-land,
Sweet peaceful scenes that I with joy may roam,
                    My Metro-land,
Fir-countryside, green girdling toil and town,
The Verdant Vale, the gentle flower decked down,
With these you gem the sceptred City's crown,
                    My Metro-land.

Dear Realm of rest from London's weary ways,
                    My Metro-land,
Brightly you beam beyond the City's haze,
                    My Metro-land,
My town tried nerves, when work-a-day is o'er,
Where comes no echo of the City's Roar ,
You brace to health and calm content restore
                    My Metro-land.[43]

But the best description of Metro-land is to be found in a leaflet published in the early 1920s by the Metropolitan Railway to advertise its handbook *Metro-land*:

'A few years ago Londoners were offered a new word – Metro-land. They adopted it at once, and though the gazetteers may not recognise it, it is now part of the living speech of men. Metro-land is Middlesex in one part, Herts in another, and Bucks in a third. Those who dwell within its borders pay their rates and taxes in those particular counties, but their homes are in Metro-land.

The precise boundaries of Metro-land are a little elusive. No one quite knows where Metro-land really begins – how far beyond the long tunnel which forms the dark avenue of its approach from Baker Street. Does Metro-land begin at Willesden Green? I should rather guess Neasden or the pleasant slopes of Dollis Hill. But the crossroads by Blackbird Farm, and the old church at Kingsbury above the lake-like reservoir standing in the square camp which the Romans made, before London was, these certainly belong to Metro-land.

Then take a stretch of country five or six miles wide on either side of the shining rails and follow on past Harrow and Rickmansworth, and through the Chilterns, and out into the vale beyond, and all that lies to right and left beyond Aylesbury to Quainton Road and the Claydons and Verney Junction, where London is far out of sight and mind, all this is Metro-land.

It is a strip of the Home Counties, and for charm and beauty, its like is hard, its superior harder still, to find. What is the particular charm of Metro-land? It is not "violently lovely", as Byron said of one of his early loves, but, like her, it "steals upon the spirit like a May-day breaking". Its charms are

Metropolitan Railway's 'Where to Live' guidebook, advertised in the *Railway Magazine*, 1926.

Metro-land Homeseekers Guide from *The Railway Magazine* December 1927.

CHEAP :: :: RETURN TICKETS

Are issued to Parties taking not less than SIX First Class or TEN Third Class whole Tickets for Pleasure Excursions to

Eastcote, Ruislip, Ickenham, Uxbridge, Pinner, Chorley Wood, Great Missenden, Wendover, Aylesbury,

And other places from

ALL METROPOLITAN RAILWAY STATIONS

Applications should be made by letter, not less than three days before the proposed Excursion, stating:

The Date of the proposed Excursion,
The Station from and to which Tickets are required,
For which Trains,
Class of Carriage,
The probable number, and
That it is exclusively a Pleasure Party.

ILLUSTRATED BOOKLET giving full particulars post free on application to

"**TRAFFIC SUPERINTENDENT,**"
32, Westbourne Terrace, London, W.

To whom all communications respecting Pleasure Parties should be addressed.

SHOPPING TICKETS
(FIRST-CLASS) AT REDUCED RATES
are now issued by all trains between 10.30 a.m. and 4.0 p.m.

TO	St John's Wood Rd.	Marlboro' Rd.	Swiss Cottage.	Finchley Rd.	West Hampstead.	Kilburn.	Willesden Green.	Dollis Hill.	Neasden.	Wembley Park.	Preston Road.
	d.	d.	d.	d.	d.	d.	d.	s. d.	s. d.	s. d.	s. d.
Finchley Road	...	...	...	...	...	4	5½	6	8½	11
Kilburn	5	4	...	...	...	...	3	4	6	8½
South Kensington	7	7	7	7	7	7	9½	10½	10½ 1	1 1	1 3
Notting Hill Gate	6	...	...	...	...	...	8½	9½	9½ 1	0 1	2
Bayswater	5	6	6	6	6	6	7	8½	...	...	...
Edgware Road	...	4	5	...	...	...	...	...	...	...	...
Baker Street	...	...	4	5	5	5	...	...	8½	11	1 1
Portland Road	...	4	...	6	6	...	...	...	...	...	...
Euston Square	4	5	5	...	...	...	7	8½	...	...	...
Aldersgate Street	...	...	...	...	...	...	8½	9½	9½ 1	0 1	2
Liverpool Street	6	7	7	7	7	7	9½	11	11 1	1 1	3
BAKER ST. & WATERLOO RY. Via Baker Street.
Oxford Circus	4	...	6	7	7	7	9	10	10 1	1	...
Piccadilly Circus	5	5	7	8	8	8	10	11	11 1	2	...
Trafalgar Square	6	6	8	9	9	9	11	1 0	1 0 1	2	...
Gt. NORTHERN, PICCADILLY and BROMPTON RLY. Via Baker St.& Piccadilly Circus
Dover Street	...	...	7	9	9	9	11	1 0	1 0 1	2	...
Knightsbridge	...	...	8	9	9	9	11	1 0	1 0 1	3	...
Brompton Road	...	...	9	10	10	10	1 0	1 1	1 1 1	4	...
CENTRAL LONDON RLY. Via Baker St. & Oxford Circus
Bond Street	...	...	7	9	9	9	11	1 1	1 1 1	3	...
Marble Arch	...	...	7	9	9	9	11	1 1	1 1 1	3	...
Tottenham Court Road	...	...	7	9	9	9	11	1 1	1 1 1	3	...
British Museum	...	...	7	9	9	9	11	1 1	1 1 1	3	...
Chancery Lane	...	...	7	9	9	9	11	1 1	1 1 1	3	...

Tickets are issued to Children up to twelve years of age at half the Adult Fares.

Cheap Excursion Tickets

ARE NOW ISSUED

On SUNDAYS, *MONDAYS, THURSDAYS & SATURDAYS,

FROM AND TO

LONDON STATIONS

AND

Chorley Wood	Great Missenden
Chalfont Road	Wendover
Chesham	Stoke Mandeville
Amersham	Aylesbury

And other Stations,

BY CERTAIN TRAINS.

* No Excursion Tickets issued TO London on Mondays.

For Particulars see Excursion Programme.

Cheap Week-End Tickets

Are now issued by any Train on

FRIDAYS, SATURDAYS & SUNDAYS

available for return by any Train on Sundays, Mondays or Tuesdays

From LONDON

(BAKER ST. and certain other Metropolitan Railway Stations)

to the following Stations:

TO	RETURN FARES	
	1st Class s. d.	3rd Class s. d.
CHORLEY WOOD	4 0	2 0
CHALFONT ROAD	4 0	2 0
CHESHAM	4 6	2 4
AMERSHAM	4 3	2 4
GREAT MISSENDEN	5 6	2 10
WENDOVER	7 0	3 6
STOKE MANDEVILLE	7 6	3 9
AYLESBURY	8 0	4 0

Similar Cheap Tickets are issued to London from most of the above Stations.

For further particulars see handbills and programmes.

From *Near and Far,* 1912.

many and varied. Middlesex, where it still contrives to escape the fast spreading tide of London, wears a pleasant homely face. The elms grow tall in its field and pastures and in the broad plain stretches below Harrow's airy ridge towards Uxbridge.

Harrow-on-the-Hill, crowned by church and school, is the capital of this Riding of Metro-land; Ruislip and Northwood are its lake district; Eastcote and Ickenham, Harefield and Pinner are its rustic townships. London is at your very door, if your needs must keep in touch with London, but it is always pure country at the corner of the lane beyond your garden fence. The town has stained the country less here than in Essex, Kent or Surrey, at the same radius of ten or twenty miles from Charing Cross. But for many the best of Metro-land begins where the iron road starts to climb in among the Chilterns, which are the very heart of Metro-land – the flinty Chilterns with their tangled ridges, their stony yet fruitful fields, their noble beech woods and shy coppices, their alluring footpaths, their timbered cottages, scattered hamlets and pretty Georgian townships strung out along the high roads.

I know no more dainty group of little country towns than Rickmansworth, Amersham, Chesham, Missenden and Wendover leading on to the fine old market town of Aylesbury – English to the core – each with its ancient church, its old manor house, its picturesque inns, and its exquisite setting of hill and wood. I know few more charming villages than the twin Chalfonts, Latimer and Chenies, Little Missenden, Penn, windy Cholesbury, the Hampdens, Great and Little, the Kimbles and a score of others that might be named. Few streams run a brighter course than the Chess, and where will you find woods more delightful than those of Shardeloes and Penn, Hampden, Chequers and Halton?

Only a narrow tongue of 'homely, hearty, loving Hertfordshire' lies in Metro-land, but within its pale are Rickmansworth and its lovely parks, and here is the waters-meet of Chess, Gade and Colne. Rickmansworth is a delightful old-world town, and Chorley Wood Common flames into yellow gold when the gorse is in flower. Historical associations from the earliest times, camps and earthworks, old churches, old cottages, old inns, and a pleasant, simple country-folk to talk to, good roads, good paths and quick change of scene and view – Metro-land falls short in nothing which the heart of man can desire…

Metro-land the land which the Metropolitan Railway is proud to serve – is a strip of England at its fairest, a gracious district formed by nature for the homes of a healthy, happy race.'[44]

Front cover of *Metro-land* magazine from 1928.

However, advertising the place was not enough. The railway company had to offer more than pictures, words and dreams, if it wanted to attract more customers. And it did. At first, it offered the possibility of buying cheap tickets: for instance, the city gent could purchase a season ticket for a period of a week, a month or even longer; workmen's tickets for the working class people could be obtained at certain times of the day only; the housewife was not forgotten since she could buy a shopping ticket if she wanted to go and visit London's big department stores; as for children under 3, they did not pay, and for those aged between 3 and 14 there were half-price fares available; special school party fares could also be obtained, and a whole train could be booked in advance for a day trip in the country; cheap day return tickets at about the single fare for the double journey were issued on Thursdays, Saturdays and Sundays to any station in the country; walking tour tickets were available to members of rambling clubs in parties of not less than eight adults, who could travel out to one station and return from another at a fare approximately equivalent to the higher of the two single fares involved; as to the weekend walking tour tickets, they were issued between the same points as the day walking tour tickets at approximately one-third over the day walking tour fares; and finally, weekend tickets could be bought from all stations at a single and one-third for the double journey.

During the hunting season, the Metropolitan Railway provided special trains with boxes for horses. For the wealthier people, the company

LOCAL DATA OF RESIDENTIAL DISTRICTS IN "METRO-LAND."

Station.	Trains (each way) daily.	Journey time to or from Baker St.	Local Rates (in the £)	Gas. Per 1000 feet (a); per th'm (b).	Charge for Water.	Range of Rents.	Altitude (above sea level).	Subsoil.
Willesden Green	209	8 mts.	13/6	3/7(a)	7½% rate val.	£50-£150	180 ft.	Clay
Neasden & Kingsbury	184	11 ,,	13/6	3/7(a)	7½ ,, ,,	£50-£150	127 ft.	Gravel and clay
Wembley Park	179	11 ,,	10/2	10d.(b)	9 ,, ,, (apprx)	£55-£70	234 ft.	Clay
Preston Road	82	13 ,,	10/2	10d.(b)	9 ,, ,, ,,	from £45	162 ft.	,,
Northwick Pk. & Kenton	82	14½ ,,	9/11	11d.(b)	11½ ,, ,, ,,	from £50	175 ft.	,,
Harrow-on-the-Hill	131	15 ,,	10/-	4/1½(a)	11½ ,, ,, ,,	£40-£400	400 ft.	,,
Eastcote	44	22 ,,	11/-	1/1(b)	7-9 ,, ,, ,,	from £40	196 ft.	Loamy clay
Ruislip	45	25 ,,	11/-	1/1(b)	7-9 ,, ,, ,,	from £45	168 ft.	Gravel and clay
Ickenham	43	27 ,,	10/-	1/1(b)	7½ ,, ,,	from £40	207 ft.	,, ,,
Hillingdon	43	29 ,,	14/2	1/1(b)	7½ ,, ,,	from £45	117 ft.	,, ,,
Uxbridge	43	31 ,,	11/3	1/-(b)	2/- in £ ,,	£40-£120	200 ft.	Chiefly gravel
Pinner	45	19 ,,	8/-	1/1(b)	7-9% ,,	from £40	163-230 ft.	Clay
Northwood	46	21 ,,	11/2	1/1(b)	7-9 ,, ,, (apprx)	£45-£250	200-450 ft.	Gravel and clay
Moor Pk. & Sandy Lodge	29	26 ,,	12/-	1/1½(b)	7 ,, ,,	up to £350	380 ft.	Gravel and chalk
Rickmansworth	50	25 ,,	12/-	1/1½(b)	7 ,, ,,	£40-£120	150-270 ft.	,, ,,
Chorley Wood & Chenies	38	32 ,,	10/-	1/6 (b)	7½ ,, ,, (apprx)	£50-£120	368 ft.	,, ,,
Chalfont & Latimer	36	36 ,,	10/9	1/- (b)	7½ ,, ,,	from £35	410 ft.	Gravel
Chesham	26	48 ,,	13/2	4/9½(a)	5 ,, ,,	£40-£60	330-526 ft.	Gravel and chalk
Amersham & Chesh'Bois	28	39 ,,	11/-	1/- (b)	7½-10 ,, ,,	from £40	300-540 ft.	,, ,,
Great Missenden	27	47 ,,	10/-	1/1(b)	7 ,, ,, (apprx)	£45-£75	400-600 ft.	,, ,,
Wendover	26	55 ,,	11/7½	1/5(b)	7½ ,, gross val.	£35-£150	450-900 ft.	,, ,,
Aylesbury	25	67 ,,	14/10	1/3(b)	7½ ,, ,,	£30-£60	275 ft.	Clay & friable rock

From *Metro-land*, 1925.

SEASON TICKET RATES IN OPERATION TO AND FROM METRO-LAND.

FROM.	LIVERPOOL STREET.						BAKER STREET.					
	First Class.			Third Class.			First Class.			Third Class.		
	3 months	1 month	1 week	3 months	1 month	1 week	3 months	1 month	1 week	3 months	1 month	1 week
	£ s. d.	£ s. d.	s. d.	£ s. d.	£ s. d.	£ s. d.	£ s. d.	£ s. d.	£ s. d.	£ s. d.	£ s. d.	£ s. d.
Willesden Green	3 14 9	1 9 6	8 0	2 14 3	1 1 9	5 9	2 3 3	17 6	5 0	1 9 6	11 9	3 3
Neasden	4 7 3	1 15 3	9 9	2 19 6	1 3 3	6 3	2 13 3	1 1 3	6 0	1 15 6	14 3	4 0
Wembley Park	4 13 0	1 17 6	10 6	3 3 0	1 3 3	6 3	3 3 9	1 6 0	7 3	2 2 6	17 6	4 9
Preston Road	5 5 6	2 1 0	11 6	3 11 0	1 6 9	6 9	3 13 0	1 9 6	8 3	2 8 3	19 3	5 2
Northwick Park & Kenton	5 15 9	2 3 6	11 9	3 12 9	1 6 9	6 9	3 19 0	1 11 0	8 9	2 11 3	1 0 6	5 2
Harrow-on-the-Hill	5 16 0	2 5 0	12 0	3 17 3	1 8 9	7 3	4 2 9	1 12 6	9 0	2 13 0	1 1 3	6 0
West Harrow	6 1 6	2 5 9	12 9	3 19 0	1 10 3	8 3	4 8 3	1 15 0	9 9	2 16 9	1 3 0	6 6
Eastcote	6 16 0	2 12 9	14 9	4 11 6	1 15 0	9 9	5 1 9	2 0 0	11 0	3 8 9	1 6 6	7 6
Ruislip Manor	7 0 3	2 14 3	15 0	4 13 6	1 16 3	10 0	5 5 9	2 0 9	11 3	3 9 6	1 7 0	7 6
Ruislip	7 0 3	2 14 3	15 0	4 13 6	1 16 3	10 0	5 5 9	2 0 9	11 3	3 9 6	1 7 0	7 6
Ickenham	7 7 9	2 14 3	15 0	4 13 6	1 16 3	10 0	5 11 9	2 1 9	11 6	3 9 6	1 8 0	7 9
Hillingdon	7 16 9	2 17 6	16 0	5 2 0	1 18 6	10 0	6 0 6	2 6 6	13 0	3 18 9	1 10 0	8 3
Uxbridge	8 1 3	2 19 3	16 6	5 7 6	1 19 6	11 0	6 5 9	2 10 0	13 9	4 1 9	1 13 9	9 6
North Harrow	6 7 6	2 7 3	12 3	4 0 6	1 11 0	8 3	4 12 9	1 17 3	10 3	3 0 0	1 4 0	6 6
Pinner	6 14 0	2 9 6	12 5	4 3 6	1 13 9	8 6	5 7 0	2 1 0	11 0	3 5 6	1 6 6	6 8
Northwood	7 12 3	2 16 0	14 6	4 17 0	1 15 9	9 0	6 6 0	2 8 6	13 0	3 14 6	1 9 6	7 10
Moor Park & Sandy Lodge	7 16 9	2 17 6	14 9	4 17 6	1 16 3	9 2	6 18 9	2 11 0	13 3	4 3 6	1 11 6	8 0
Croxley Green (via Direct Route)	8 2 3	2 19 6	14 11	4 18 3	1 16 6	9 3	7 6 3	2 13 9	14 6	4 6 9	1 12 3	8 1
Watford (via Direct Route)	8 2 3	2 19 6	14 11	4 19 6	1 16 9	9 3	7 6 3	2 13 9	14 6	4 6 9	1 12 3	8 1
Croxley Gn. (via Rickmansworth)	8 5 9	3 1 0	16 0	5 10 6	2 0 9	10 9	7 7 7	2 14 3	14 6	4 13 6	1 16 3	9 6
Watford (via Rickmansworth)	8 5 9	3 1 0	16 0	5 10 6	2 0 9	10 9	7 7 7	2 14 3	14 6	4 13 6	1 16 3	9 6
Rickmansworth	8 5 9	3 1 0	16 0	5 10 6	2 0 9	10 9	7 7 7	2 14 3	14 6	4 13 6	1 16 3	9 6
Chorley Wood	8 14 9	3 4 3	17 9	5 16 6	2 2 9	12 0	7 16 9	2 17 6	16 0	4 17 6	1 18 6	10 9
Chalfont & Latimer	9 8 3	3 9 3	19 3	6 5 6	2 6 3	12 9	8 10 3	3 2 6	17 3	5 5 6	2 1 9	11 6
Chesham	10 1 9	3 14 0	1 0 6	6 14 6	2 9 6	15 0	9 9 3	3 7 6	18 9	5 13 9	2 5 0	12 6
Amersham	9 17 3	3 12 6	1 0 0	6 11 6	2 8 3	13 6	8 19 3	3 5 9	18 3	5 9 9	2 4 0	12 3
Chesham & Amersham	10 8 3	3 17 0	—	6 18 3	2 11 0	—	9 11 0	3 10 6	—	5 17 6	2 6 6	—
Great Missenden	10 19 6	4 0 6	1 2 3	7 6 3	2 13 9	15 0	10 0 6	3 14 0	1 0 6	5 17 6	2 7 3	13 0
Wendover	11 17 0	4 7 0	1 4 0	7 18 0	2 18 0	16 0	10 14 0	4 0 6	1 2 3	6 16 0	2 13 9	15 0
Stoke Mandeville	12 10 3	4 12 0	1 5 6	8 6 0	3 0 6	17 0	11 12 6	4 4 3	1 2 6	7 13 0	2 17 0	15 9
Aylesbury	12 17 9	4 14 9	1 6 3	8 11 9	3 3 0	17 6	12 1 6	4 8 9	1 4 6	8 1 0	2 19 3	16 6

Metro. Season Tickets can be obtained for any period of one month or over, including "broken periods," such as 1 month and 5 days, 4 months and 18 days, etc. Weekly Season Tickets can be obtained available between any pair of Stations on the Metropolitan, Met. & G.C. Jt., Met. and L. & N.E., and Hammersmith and City Lines, and also from all Stations Swiss Cottage to Watford and Rickmansworth inclusive through to Oxford Circus, Piccadilly Circus, Trafalgar Square, Charing Cross and Waterloo. Weekly Season Tickets are available from Sunday to the following Saturday. Particulars of Season Ticket Rates between all points readily supplied by the Commercial Manager, Baker Street Station, N.W.1.

Season ticket rates, 1928. *Metro-land*

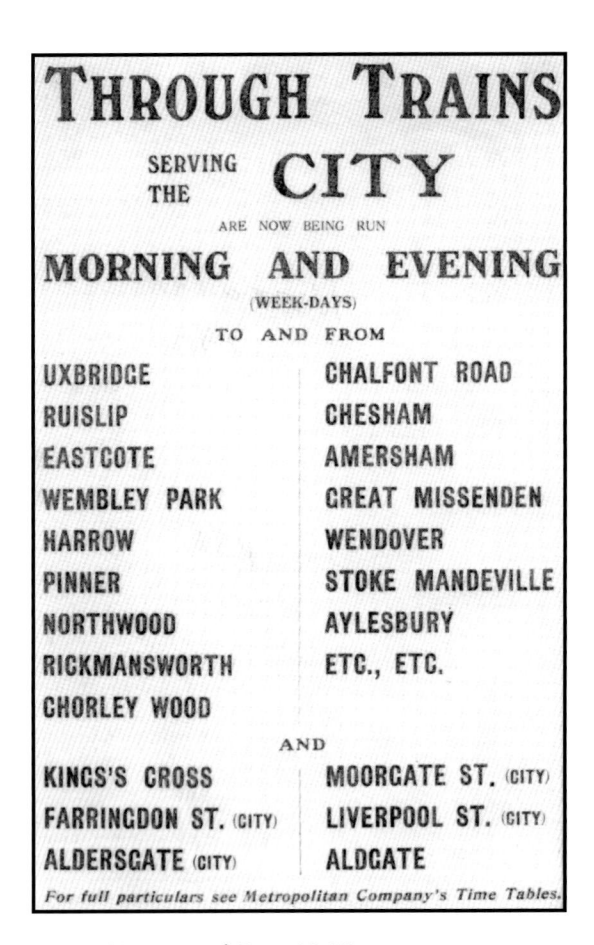

From *Near and Far*, 1912.

Advert from *Country Homes* in *Metro-land*, 1917.

From *Metro-land*, 1931.

From *Metro-land*, 1925.

1927/1928 adverts for travelling on the Metropolitan or buying a property in Metro-land.

put into service on 1 June 1910 two Pullman cars called *Mayflower* and *Galatea*, with the purpose of rendering the rich city gentleman's journey to and from the City more pleasant and comfortable. This service was available during rush hours, and late at night for theatre-goers. For an extra fare of 1 shilling (if you were beyond Rickmansworth) or 6d (for any distance between Aldgate and Rickmansworth – in 1915, for a time, the extra fare was 6d all the way), and in a luxurious interior of beautiful carpets and fittings while sitting in an upholstered armchair, one could in the morning enjoy a delicious breakfast and read one's newspaper in peace and quiet before going to work. In the early evening one could relax after a tiresome day and enjoy one's journey back home while sipping one's favourite drink available from the bar, and finally, late at night, one could be served a light supper after an enjoyable evening at the theatre. This Pullman service was the first to be electrically hauled in Europe, and the two carriages were rented from the Pullman Car Company but maintained (apart from the internal fittings) by the Metropolitan Railway Company. Unfortunately, they were withdrawn on 7 October 1939.

But the Metropolitan was not just a passenger line, since the trains also carried goods and parcels, which ranged from Chesham's watercress

Pullman car *Mayflower*. Stephenson Locomotive Society

and Uxbridge's flowers to the transportation of livestock, minerals or building material required for the construction of the new estates, and at certain stations the collection and delivery of goods by cars and vans was undertaken.

The goods could also be forwarded beyond Metropolitan stations, as the company had links with the railways of London and with most of the main lines, including the LNWR, Midland, GCR and GWR.

The company's second move to attract more customers was, as we have already mentioned earlier, to promote suburban development, and its first venture was that of the Metropolitan Surplus Lands Committee at Pinner. The Metropolitan also helped financially the Wembley Park Estate Company, which was building houses in that suburb. But its

Advert from *Near and Far*, 1912.

Pullman service advertised in *Country Homes* in *Metro-land*, 1917.

PULLMAN SERVICE
(WEEK-DAYS)

TO THE CITY.					FROM THE CITY.						
	a.m.	a.m.	p.m.	p.m.		a.m.	a.m.	p.m.	p.m.	p.m.	p.m.
				SE				SE	SO	SO	SE SE
Verney Junction	...	...	...	8 14	Liverpool Street	10 16	11 52	1 05	5 25	6 14	...
Aylesbury	8 24	...	4 14	8 46	Moorgate Street	10 17	11 53	1 15	5 26	6 15	...
Stoke Mandeville	8 30	...	4 20	8 52	King's Cross	10 23	11 59	1 75	5 32	6 21	...
Wendover	8 37	...	4 27	8 59	Baker Street	10 30	12 7	1 55	40 6	30 11	35
Great Missenden	8 46	9 26	4 36	10 8	Harrow	10 48	12 25	1 32 5	57 6	47 11	52
Amersham	8 55	9 35	4 45	10 17	North Harrow	10 54	12 31	1 38	...	6 54	11 59
Chesham	...	...	...	...	Pinner	10 57	12 34	1 41 6	4 6	57 12	2
Chalfont & Latimer	8 59	9 39	4 51	10 23	Northwood	11 3	12 40	1 47 6	10 7	3 12	8
Chorley Wood and Chenies	9 3	9 43	4 55	10 27	Sandy Lodge	11 7	12 43	1 50	...	...	...
Rickmansworth	9 8	9 48	5 1	10 34	Rickmansworth	11 10	12 47	1 546	17 7	9 12	14
Sandy Lodge	...	9 52	5 5	...	Chorley Wood and Chenies	11 18	12 54	2 06	23 7	16 12	21
Northwood	9 15	9 56	5 9	10 41	Chalfont & Latimer	11 23	12 59	2 6 6	29 7	21 12	27
Pinner	9 19	10 1	5 14	10 46	Chesham	...	...	...	...	...	...
North Harrow	...	10 3	5 16	10 48	Amersham	11 31	1 8	2 12 6	35 7	28 12	33
Harrow	...	10 10	5 24	10 55	Great Missenden	11 38	1 17	2 20 6	43 7	35 12	41
Baker Street	9 44	10 27	5 45	11 17	Wendover	11 47	1 26	2 28 6	51 7	44 12	49
King's Cross	9 50	10 32	5 53	...	Stoke Mandeville	11 52	1 31	2 33 6	56 7	49	*
Moorgate Street	9 56	10 38	5 59	...	Aylesbury	11 57	1 36	2 38 7	1 7	54 12	56
Liverpool Street	9 58	10 40	6 1	...	Verney Junction	...	...	...	...	8 23	...

S E—Saturdays excepted   S O—Saturdays only.

* Calls if required on Saturdays only to set down passengers, on notice being given to the Guard at the previous Station.

CHARGE FOR ANY DISTANCE . . . . . . **6^D**
POPULAR TARIFF OF REFRESHMENTS.

Metropolitan Railway

EXPRESS
PARCELS
SERVICE

A BOON TO ALL RESIDENTS
ON THE
METROPOLITAN RAILWAY.

PARCELS RECEIVED AT ALL
THE COMPANY'S STATIONS
FOR DELIVERY BY ALL
:: TRAINS TO ALL PARTS ::

The most Expeditious Delivery

CHARGES LOW.

FOR DETAILS SEE PROGRAMMES.

> **Kingsbury Garden Village Neasden.**
>
> Situated close to Neasden & Kingsbury (Metro.) Station, about 6 miles from Baker Street, with an unexcelled service of trains occupying 10-12 minutes' journey and additional through trains morning and evening to City. (Only one station from the British Empire Exhibition).
>
> THE attractions of Neasden—and they are many—lie up the hill towards the cross-roads and beyond. These roads branch off towards Dollis Hill on the one hand, and down towards the Brent on the other, while beyond the Brent are the rural lanes which lead to old Kingsbury Church, near the Reservoir and Forty-lane which carries one on towards Wembley Park. Peace and quiet prevail, and the stretches of country around afford plenty of opportunity for invigorating exercise to those who incline to walking and cycling.
>
> A Model Garden Village, at which a number of Semi-detached Residences have been erected, partially meeting the continuous demand for small houses, and all these properties have been acquired.
>
> Well-known firms of Builders are actively continuing operations on this Estate, and Houses can be secured from £950 Freehold, with 3 bedrooms, bathrooms, dining room, drawing room, kitchen, etc., and payment made on easy terms to suit a purchaser.
>
> The attention of Builders is specially drawn to the Freehold Sites which may be acquired on payment of a small deposit and balance over a term of years.
>
> These Sites are particularly suitable for Houses eligible for the Government Subsidy.
>
> Full particulars, and a plan of the Estate, may be obtained on application to—
>
> **H. GIBSON**, *Estate Agent*,
> The Metropolitan Railway Country Estates, Ltd.
> General Offices: Baker Street Station, N.W.1.   Langham 1130.
>
> "HOMES IN METRO-LAND," illustrating a number of Houses and Bungalows, for erection at inclusive prices, can be obtained on application to The Commercial Manager, Baker Street Station, N.W.1.   Price 2s. 6d.

Advert from *Metro-land*, 1925.

Advert from *Where to Live*, a brochure issued by the Metropolitan Railway.

> **FREEHOLD HOUSES AT VILLAGE WAY,**
> KINGSBURY GARDEN VILLAGE, NEASDEN.
>
> £725 for a Centre House.   £775 for an End House.
>
> secures £50 possession.
>
> Centre House stands on a Plot with 19 ft. frontage and a depth of about 120 ft., and each End House has an additional 9 ft. frontage, which can be utilized for the erection of a Garage, if required.
>
> An unequalled opportunity for those of moderate means.
>
> *For further details of repayment scheme see page 3.*

biggest venture in that field was of course reflected in the support it gave to the Metropolitan Country Estates Company, which it helped to set up in 1919. The latter's first undertaking was to buy from the Syndicate three estates known as the Neasden Estate, the Chalk Hill Estate and the Cedars Estate, and to develop them.

The Neasden Estate, also called the Kingsbury Garden Village Estate, was situated 6 miles from Baker Street and close to Neasden station. It covered an area of 40 acres and was bought by the company for £12,000 with the intention of building about 384 detached and semi-detached houses. The estate was planned on garden village lines with wayside greens and quadrangles. Most houses had a frontage of about 30 feet and a depth of 120 feet, and contained three bedrooms, a bathroom and toilet, two reception rooms, a combined kitchen-scullery, a bicycle or pram store and a porch entrance. The prices varied between £1,100 leasehold and £1,250 freehold, but in 1930 some houses were advertised for £675. Sites alone could also be purchased. At the beginning the estate was not very successful, and in 1921 there were complaints from the management that the houses were selling too slowly. It was therefore decided to try and popularise the estate more, by displaying more posters, by improving the estate office, and by fixing under Neasden station's nameboards a sign reading 'Alight here for Kingsbury Garden Village'.

The Chalk Hill Estate comprised 123 acres of undulating land extending from Wembley Park station to Neasden. The property was bought for £25,000 and planned in half-acre and acre plots for the erection of small houses of a country type with ample grounds for gardens and orchards. The plots were selling at about £600 per acre or £325 per half-acre, freehold. By 1930, 105 acres had been sold and most of the estate was covered with detached houses and bungalows. The remainder could then be acquired as freehold building sites of a quarter of an acre for £175 or pro rata for a larger area. Plots for shops were also available from £10 per foot frontage.

The Cedars Estate was the company's biggest. It was bought for £50,000 and originally covered 454 acres of elevated ground near the Metropolitan Railway and Great Central Railway joint station at Rickmansworth. It extended on both sides of the railway line, towards Chorley Wood station on one side and Chorley Wood Common on the other. This estate was divided into several sections: there was a main parcel of 207 acres with a 4,700-foot frontage to Chorley Wood Lane, offering fine views over the River Chess on the north side; a parcel of 50 acres falling towards the north from Chorley Wood Lane to the Chess Valley, with frontages of 1,500 feet to Chorley Wood Lane and 1,050 feet to Solesbridge Lane; another parcel of 73 acres situated about half a mile from Chorley Wood and overlooking the Common to the north, with a frontage of 700

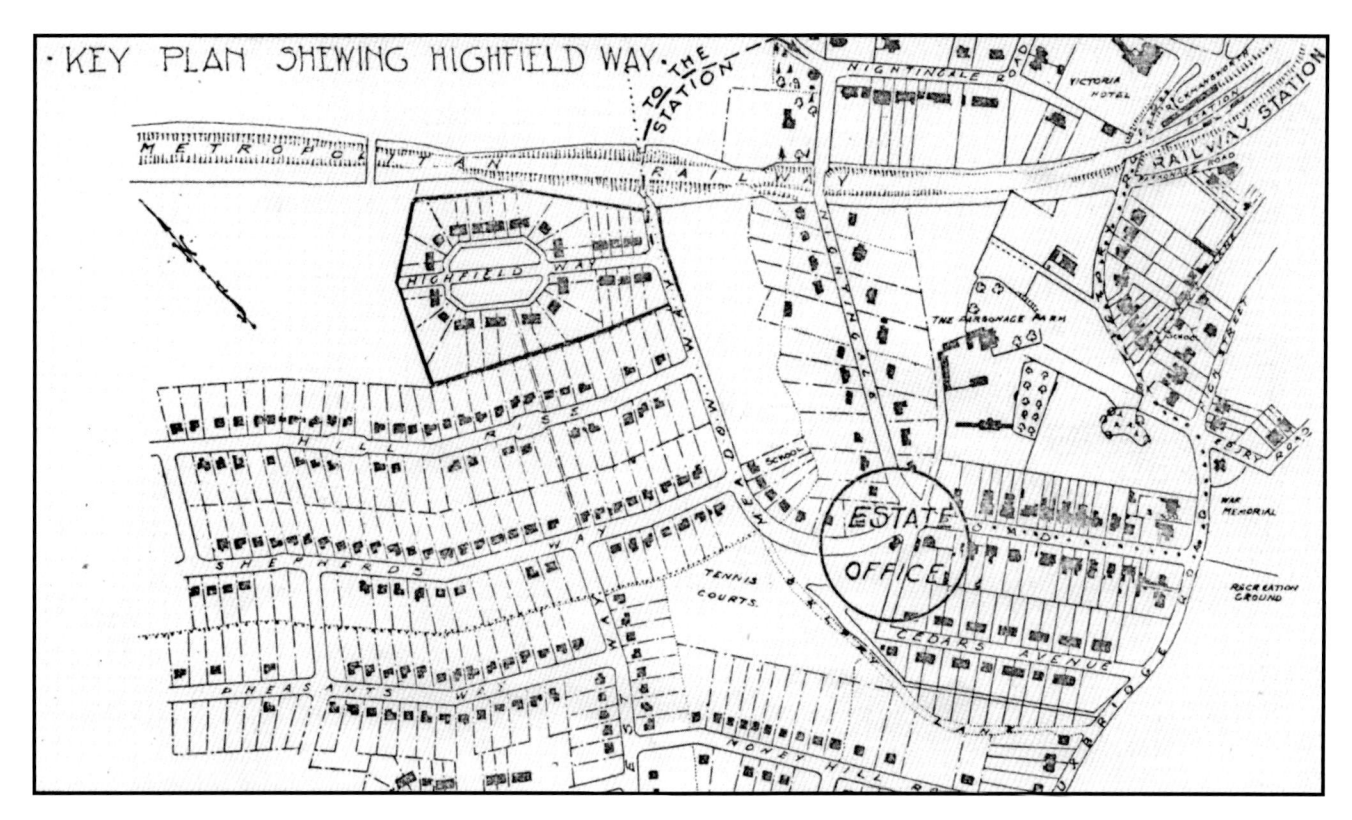

From a leaflet advertising the Cedars Estate, published by the Metropolitan Railway Country Estates Company.

Adverts from a brochure on the Cedars Estate, published by the Metropolitan Railway Country Estates Company.

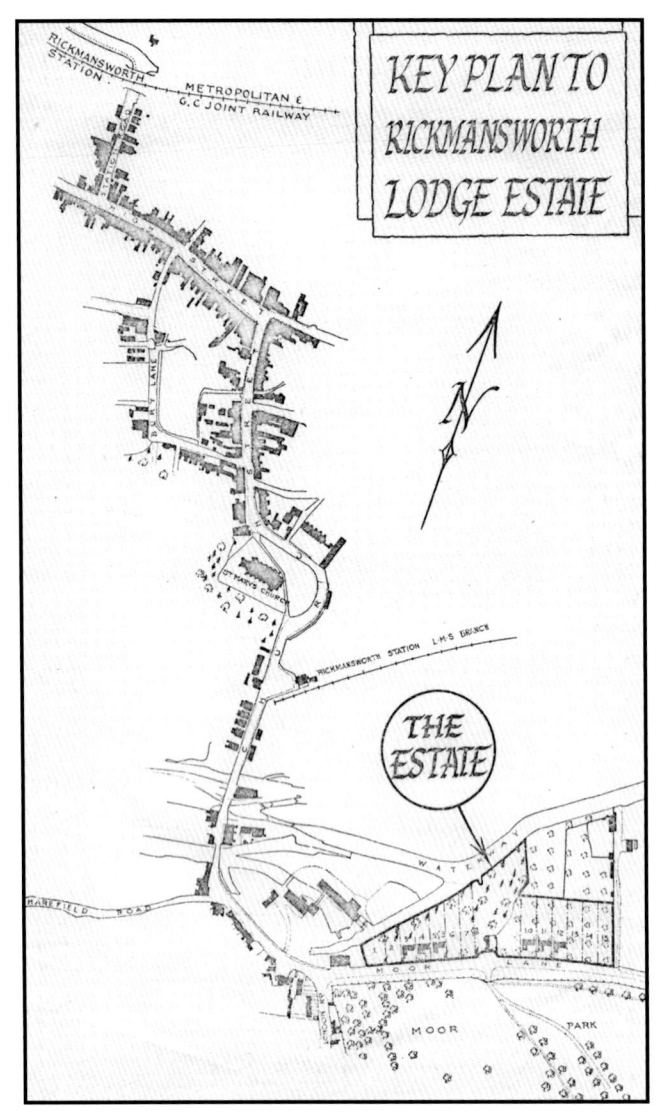

line and on the unattached portion of the estate, adjoining Chorley Wood Common. There, houses started at £725 freehold. Plots of land were also available from half an acre upwards at £650 per acre, or at £800 per acre in some select positions. Near Chorley Wood Common sites of a third, half and three-quarters of an acre were for sale at £600 per acre, and smaller plots 50 feet by 150 feet could be acquired on the south side of the railway line from £200 per plot.

As the years went by and the demand for new housing grew, the company bought and developed other estates along the line, such as the Manor Farm Estate situated in an undulating and well-wooded area, within 5 minutes' walking distance of Ruislip Manor and Ruislip stations and on the north side of the main Eastcote-Ruislip road. Soon after the purchase of the land, freehold building sites with a minimum frontage of 30 feet and a depth from 180 to 250 feet became available on the Manor Farm Estate at a price starting from £5 per foot frontage. Then bungalows, detached and semi-detached houses were offered for sale at prices that ranged between £770 and £1,100 freehold, but a large section was also reserved for a future recreation

From a leaflet published by the Metropolitan Railway Country Estates Company, advertising the Rickmansworth Lodge Estate.

feet to Catlip Lane; and finally a long strip of 124 acres alongside the southern bank of the railway with frontages of 1,500 feet to Berry Lane and 1,200 feet to Nightingale Road. Later on, more land was purchased, such as the Money Hill Park Estate, some land at Shepherd's Lane, and 78¾ acres of land fronting the Uxbridge Road, thus extending the estate to an area of about 600 acres.

When the company bought the estate it decided to preserve its open and rural character, to take advantage of its woodland, and to build good-class residences, mainly detached, of exclusive design, varied in character and accommodation, and surrounded by a good area of land. The estate was divided into sections so that the higher-priced residences were not affected by the cheaper type. The most expensive properties, found mainly on the north side of the railway line, stood in grounds from an acre upwards, and their prices ranged from £1,900 to £3,250 leasehold or £2,500 to £4,000 freehold. Smaller houses and semi-detached ones could be found on the south side of the railway

Advert from a brochure on the Highlands Estate, published by the Metropolitan Railway Country Estates Company.

ground and some tennis courts. By 1930 all the plots fronting the main Eastcote-Ruislip road were sold and the company started the development of some 50 acres at the rear of the estate.

Then, in the rural neighbourhood of Eastcote station, the company purchased in 1927 10¾ acres of land known as the Eastcote Hill Estate, for £3525, and soon afterwards some attractive semi-detached residences at a price starting from £975 freehold, as well as some sites from £5 per foot frontage and some shop plots on the main country road from £10 per foot frontage became available. There, too, some land was kept for tennis courts.

In 1930 the company started the development of the Elm Grove Estate situated next to Ruislip station, on the south side of the Metropolitan Railway. There, plots with a 50-foot frontage and varying depth, suitable for the erection of bungalows and small detached and semi-detached houses, became available at prices starting at about £4 per foot frontage.

The Hillingdon Mount Estate, a 7½-acre site adjoining Hillingdon station, was bought by the Metropolitan Railway Company in September 1922 at an auction sale of the Swakeleys Estate with the intention of building a goods yard. But later the railway was given by the Metropolitan Railway

Manor Farm Estate, Ruislip

REAL Houses of Value are now available on this charming residential Estate adjoining large Public Recreation Park and hundreds of acres of permanently preserved woods. Prices from £875 Freehold. Each with 3 or 4 Bedrooms, brick built-in Garage, Verandah, Tiled Kitchenette and Bathroom, 2 large Reception Rooms, 2 W.C.'s. Bungalows from £675. No Extras. No Stamp Duties. Properties erected on selected site to order. Further particulars from—

MARKS & GULLETT

SALCOMBE, EASTCOTE ROAD,
MANOR FARM ESTATE, RUISLIP

Advert from *Where to Live*, published by the Metropolitan Railway.

Houses and bungalows which could be found on the Manor Farm Estate and advertised in a brochure of the Metropolitan Railway.

MANOR FARM ESTATE, RUISLIP

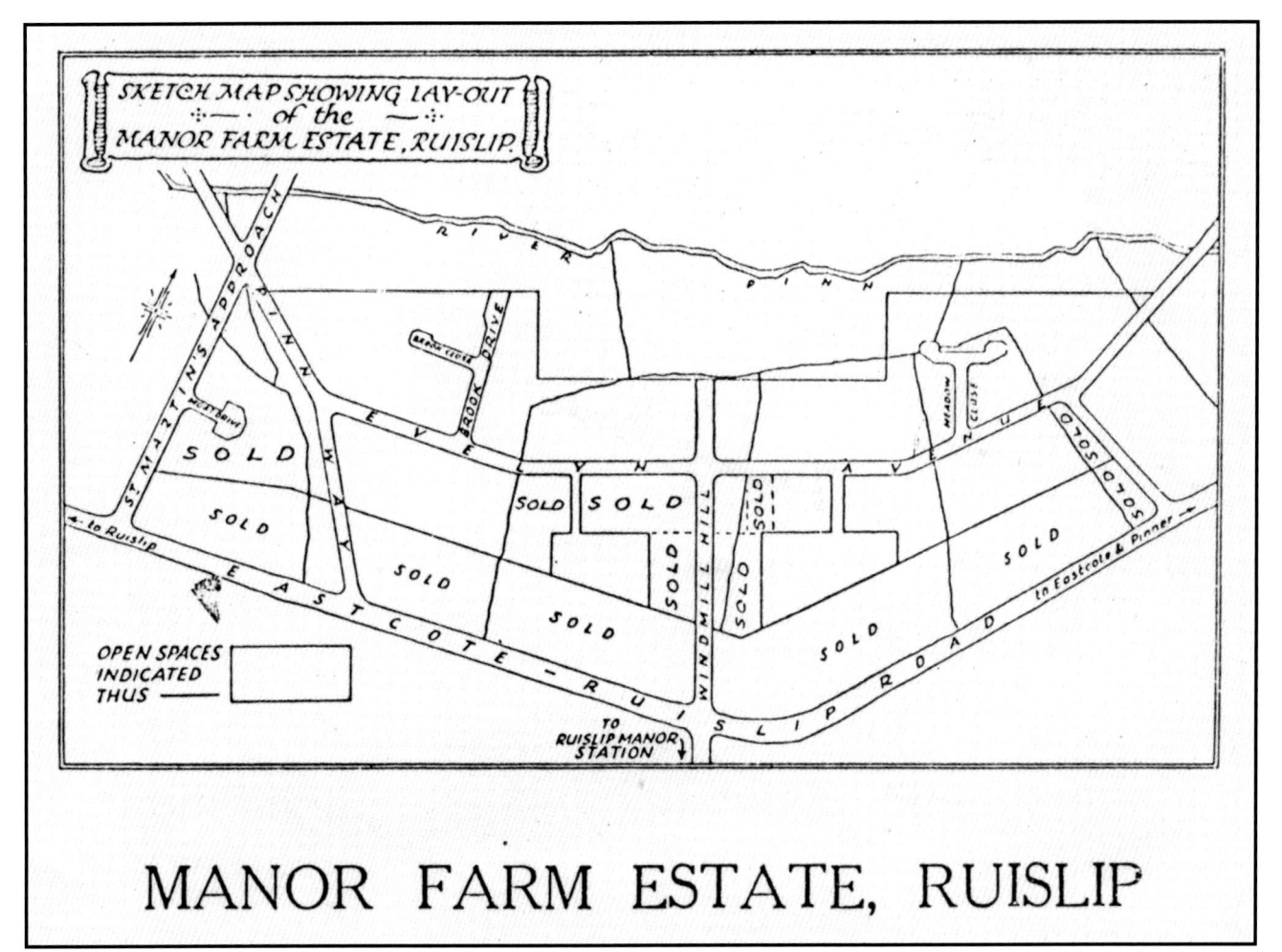

Hillingdon Mount Estate, Hillingdon.

Only 15 miles from London in a delightful rural district, and possessing many attractions for a Resident. This Estate adjoins Hillingdon Station on the Metropolitan Railway, and is within easy reach of the quaint old Market Town of Uxbridge—the time of journey to Baker Street being only 29 minutes, by an unexcelled electric train service—and travelling facilities are also available to Ealing, Earls Court etc., by a direct route via South Harrow.

THE development of this Estate has been carried out on unusual lines, affording amenities to Residents not generally met with, and a large area has been reserved for Tennis Courts with Car Park.

Sites with good frontages and large depths are available on the main County Road, at the nominal price of £4 10s. per foot frontage, and all services such as main drainage, gas, water and electric light are available.

Full particulars, and a plan of the Estate, may be obtained on application to—

H. GIBSON, *Estate Agent*,

The Metropolitan Railway Country Estates, Ltd.,

General Offices: Baker St. Station, N.W.1. Langham 1130.

"WHERE TO LIVE," illustrating a number of Houses for erection at inclusive prices, can be obtained on application, post free, to The Commercial Manager, Baker Street Station, N.W.1.

Eastcote Hill Estate, Eastcote.

This Estate has the distinct advantage of being immediately adjacent to Eastcote Station on the Metropolitan Railway, with its electric train service to all parts of London, the time of journey to Baker Street occupying only 22 minutes, and there is also a direct route from Eastcote to Ealing, Earls Court, etc., via South Harrow.

VERY fine BUILDING PLOTS are available from £5 per foot frontage, suitable for the erection of Detached or Semi-detached Houses or Bungalows.

Easy terms of payment are obtainable, and the Land forms a very attractive Investment, even if an owner does not wish to build at once.

High Class Residences are being erected for sale at £975 Freehold, and possession may be secured on payment of a nominal deposit of £25.

Full particulars, and a plan of the Estate, may be obtained on application to—

H. GIBSON,

The Metropolitan Railway Country Estates, Ltd.

General Offices: Baker St. Station, N.W.1.   Welbeck 6688.

Adverts from *Metro-land*.

Country Estates Company another piece of land on the opposite side, which was better suited for that purpose, and the original piece of land was subsequently let for grazing at £12 per year until June 1926, when the Metropolitan Railway Country Estates Company showed an interest in it and bought it for residential development for £1,170. In October 1926 another strip was added, worth £10. All the residences had garages and were sold from £800 freehold. Sites on the main road were also available from £4 per foot frontage, and at the rear a large area was specially reserved for tennis courts.

Then came the development of the Harrow Garden Village Estate, which the company bought in 1928, and which covered an area of about 213 acres between Rayners Lane station and Pinner. The following article appeared in a local newspaper of the time:

'London's latest Garden Suburb Amazing changes in a year.

Rayners Lane a short year ago was the loneliest station on the Metropolitan Railway. To-day it is the centre of a 'brand new' residential district complete with shops and schools and inhabited by hundreds of City workers. How this wonderful transformation has come about is a tribute to modern methods, mechanical science and hard work. For a year an army of workers aided by huge mechanical diggers and other up-to-date devices, have been building roads by the mile, laying a network of sewers and erecting houses, and what was virgin soil, since, save for the station and the remote farmstead no building obtained, has every promise of becoming one of the most popular residential districts around London.

No 'Gridiron' development

There are many things novel about the scheme and the 'gridiron' form of development that unfortunately characterises so much of post-war Suburbia has been definitely barred. Instead there are wide avenues, generous circles and closes, all well-timbered, recreation grounds, and upwards of 16 acres of open spaces. Grass rides take the place of the conventional curbs; green fields abound on all sides, and whilst all amenities of town have been duly provided, the rural nature of the locality has been carefully preserved. The Garden Estate, which is named Harrow Garden Village, lies off the slopes

Eastcote Halt in rural surroundings. *Stephenson Locomotive Society*

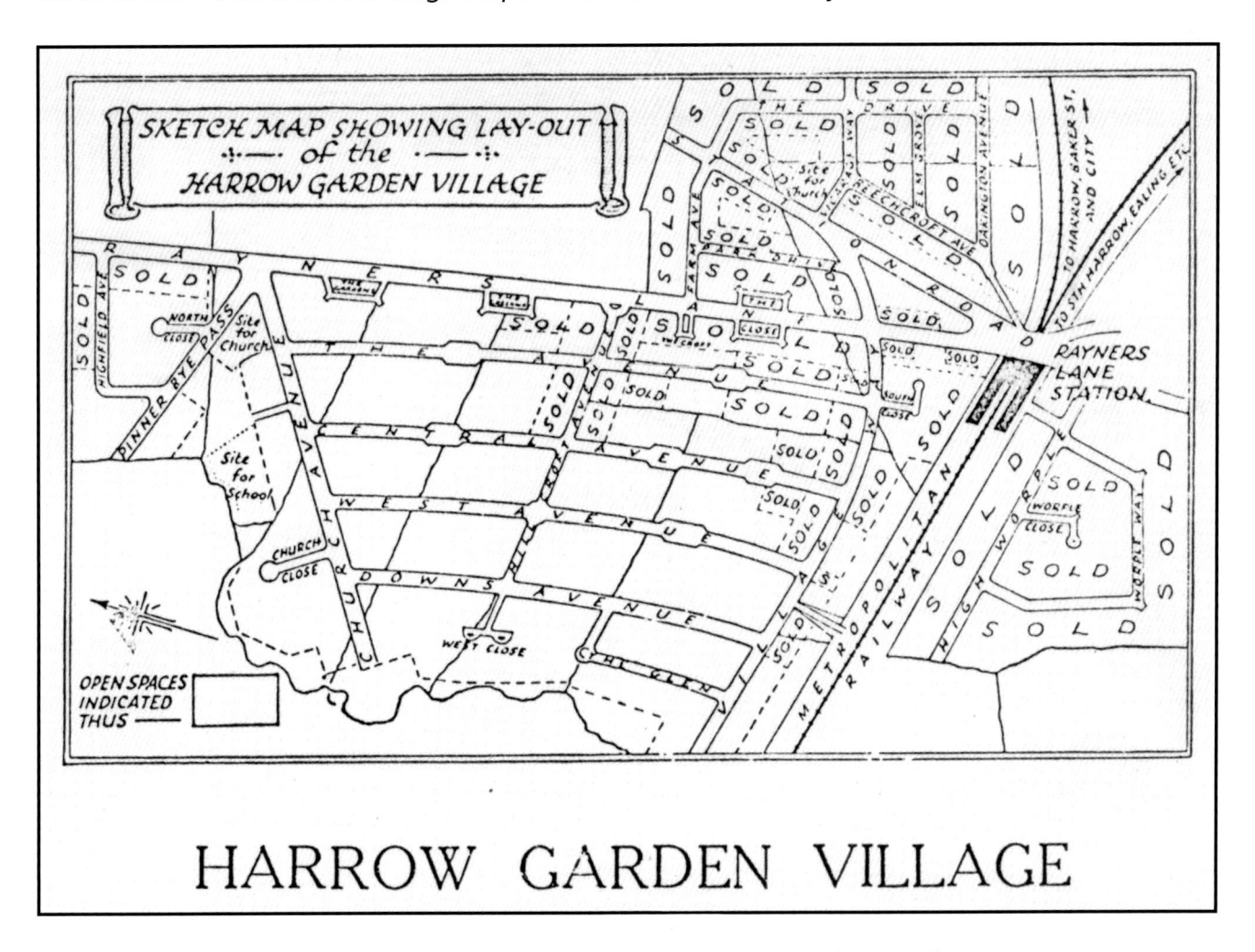

HARROW GARDEN VILLAGE

Advert from *Where to Live,* a brochure published by the Metropolitan Railway.

Rayner's Lane station, 1933. *London Transport Museum*

of Harrow's hill and is within twenty minutes of Town. It is being developed under the auspices of the Metropolitan Railway, and at the moment 214 acres are being dealt with, and provision made for some 1,600 houses. Its success is already definitely assured, and as evidence of the interest evinced in the scheme it may be mentioned that over 19,500 feet of frontage has been disposed of, and that sites for a cinema, hotel, churches and additional schools have already been earmarked.'[45]

A great variety of well-planned houses (to avoid the monotony of mass-produced houses) both large and small were available at prices ranging from £680 to £1,500 freehold, and were therefore accessible to the lower middle class. Some 25 builders were involved in the building of the estate, but the most important one was E. S. Reid, who had been a Deputy Surveyor to the Hendon Rural Council and who started working on the estate on 5 July 1929. In July 1930 a local newspaper made the following report:

'Mr Reid has made great progress in a year of much activity and he is to be congratulated on what he has achieved. Several houses were sold before even a turf had been cut. The first house was occupied three months later. To-day one road is completed and made up.'[46]

The reporter also points out that Mr Reid had succeeded admirably in making his estate as varied as possible, and he continues by adding that 'a wonderful feature of Mr Reid's particular estate is its uniformity. He has taken sufficient land so that no other builder can interfere with his own development.'[47]

Among the many builders of the Harrow Garden Village Estate were B. D. Bird & Sons, W. M. Atkinson, W. C. Dickinson, A. Robinson, R. Anderson & Son, J. G. Dowden & Son, F. Iredale, R. H. Sugar, Healey & Squire, Haigh Brothers, Jenkins, A. J. Bedford, and A. V. Evans. This shows that the Metropolitan Railway Country Estates Company was dealing essentially with land development rather than house-building, since most of the time the houses it was selling through its Baker Street office were built by contractors.

Rayners Lane's wooden halt, when it was first opened on 25 May 1906, stood in the middle of open fields, and was thus given the nickname of 'Pneumonia Junction' by those who used it. The houses in the area were scarce then, but when the Metropolitan Railway Country Estates Company started to develop Harrow Garden Village, Rayners Lane was soon transformed and the fields quickly disappeared under bricks and mortar, and while at the end of the 1920s about 22,000 people used the wooden halt every year, by the end of the 1930s there were about 4 million who used the brand-new station which opened on 30 August 1938. There they could take 'early' trains, 'late' trains, 'non-stop' trains or 'cheap' trains.

The last estate to be built before the Metropolitan Railway Company became part of the London Passenger Transport Board was the Weller Estate, which was bought by the company in April 1930 for the sum of £18,000 with the intention of erecting some 535 houses and 51 shops at prices ranging between £875 and £1,225 freehold. The land covered 78.722 acres and was situated on both sides of the Metropolitan line in the vicinity of Amersham station. After development, some freehold sites with a minimum frontage of 30 feet from £4 per foot frontage and some shop plots from £15 per foot frontage also became available. The southern part of the estate included Batchelor's Wood and some sites fronting Station Road and overlooking the old town of Amersham, as well as some beautiful stretches of countryside. In the northern part one could find Hoodside Farm, an historical building associated with Cromwell and William Penn and the Quakers. After having bought the estate, the Metropolitan Railway Country Estates Company asked the railway company for some financial assistance towards its development (a subsidy varying between £10 and £15 per house or shop erected), but the Metropolitan refused to grant it on the grounds that it did not have the power to do such things.

Finally, before closing this chapter on the Metropolitan Railway Country Estates, we must mention the Chenies Estate. In 1935 the company bought parts of the Chenies Estate from the Duke of Bedford and developed 30 acres of it near Chalfont & Latimer station and a further 163 acres close to Chorley Wood station. As we can see, the suburban development gradually crept up the railway line as time went by, and though Chorley Wood station was situated 22 miles from Baker Street, the rail journey only took about 40 minutes. The Estate was advertised as being on high and undulating ground with a subsoil of gravel and sand on chalk, enjoying wide uninterrupted views over the delightful countryside, and being surrounded by glorious woods, hills and valleys.

Houses varied between £700 and £1,400. After the nationalisation of the railway company, the Metropolitan Railway Country Estates Company went its own way and developed land all over England.

Advert from *Metro-land*, 1932.

Advert from *Metro-land*, 1932.

SEIZE THIS OFFER

WE set ourselves the seemingly impossible task of producing an £850 house for £750—a clear saving of a hundred pounds to the purchaser—and by cutting profits, mass purchase of materials, keen methods and painstaking care we have succeeded, and no matter where else you go you will not find anything to approach them for value, excellence of construction or elegance of design.

The houses are situated on the Harrow Garden Village Estate immediately adjoining Rayners Lane Station.

The Estate is one of the most accessible and attractive around London and there already exists a thriving residential centre complete with shops, schools and limitless recreative facilities. The accommodation of the houses comprise: three excellent bedrooms; two attractive reception rooms; tiled kitchen; tiled bathroom with panelled bath; spacious hall, together with a host of labour-saving features. Again, the frontal elevations are varied, and there are two distinct types from which you can choose.

The freehold price of £750 is definitely inclusive, and there are no road charges, no legal costs, no stamp duties, no survey fee, in fact no extras of any kind. A particularly reasonable deposit secures immediate possession, whilst the purchase repayments are only 22/9 weekly.

The houses can be inspected any day, including Sundays, and our representatives, who are always available, will readily answer any question or explain any point without obligating you in the slightest degree.

A. ROBINSON
HARROW GARDEN VILLAGE

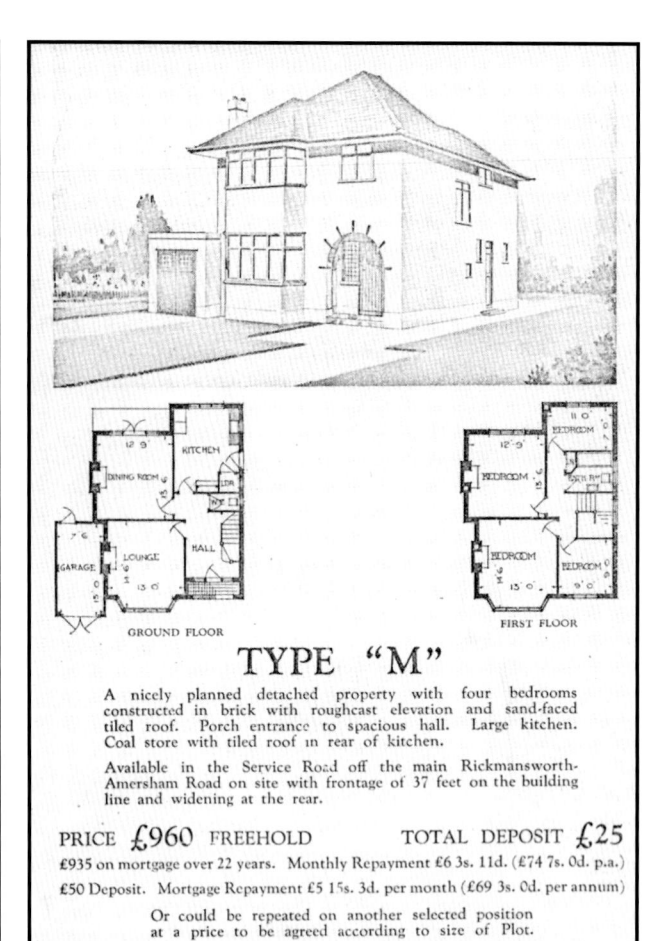

TYPE "M"

A nicely planned detached property with four bedrooms constructed in brick with roughcast elevation and sand-faced tiled roof. Porch entrance to spacious hall. Large kitchen. Coal store with tiled roof in rear of kitchen.

Available in the Service Road off the main Rickmansworth-Amersham Road on site with frontage of 37 feet on the building line and widening at the rear.

PRICE £960 FREEHOLD   TOTAL DEPOSIT £25

£935 on mortgage over 22 years. Monthly Repayment £6 3s. 11d. (£74 7s. 0d. p.a.)
£50 Deposit. Mortgage Repayment £5 15s. 3d. per month (£69 3s. 0d. per annum)

Or could be repeated on another selected position at a price to be agreed according to size of Plot.

Approximate Rateable Assessment £36.

Left: One of the houses which could be found on the Chenies Estate and which was advertised by the Metropolitan Railway Country Estates Company

Far left: Advert from *Homes in Metro-land, House Seeker's Guide*, October-December 1933.

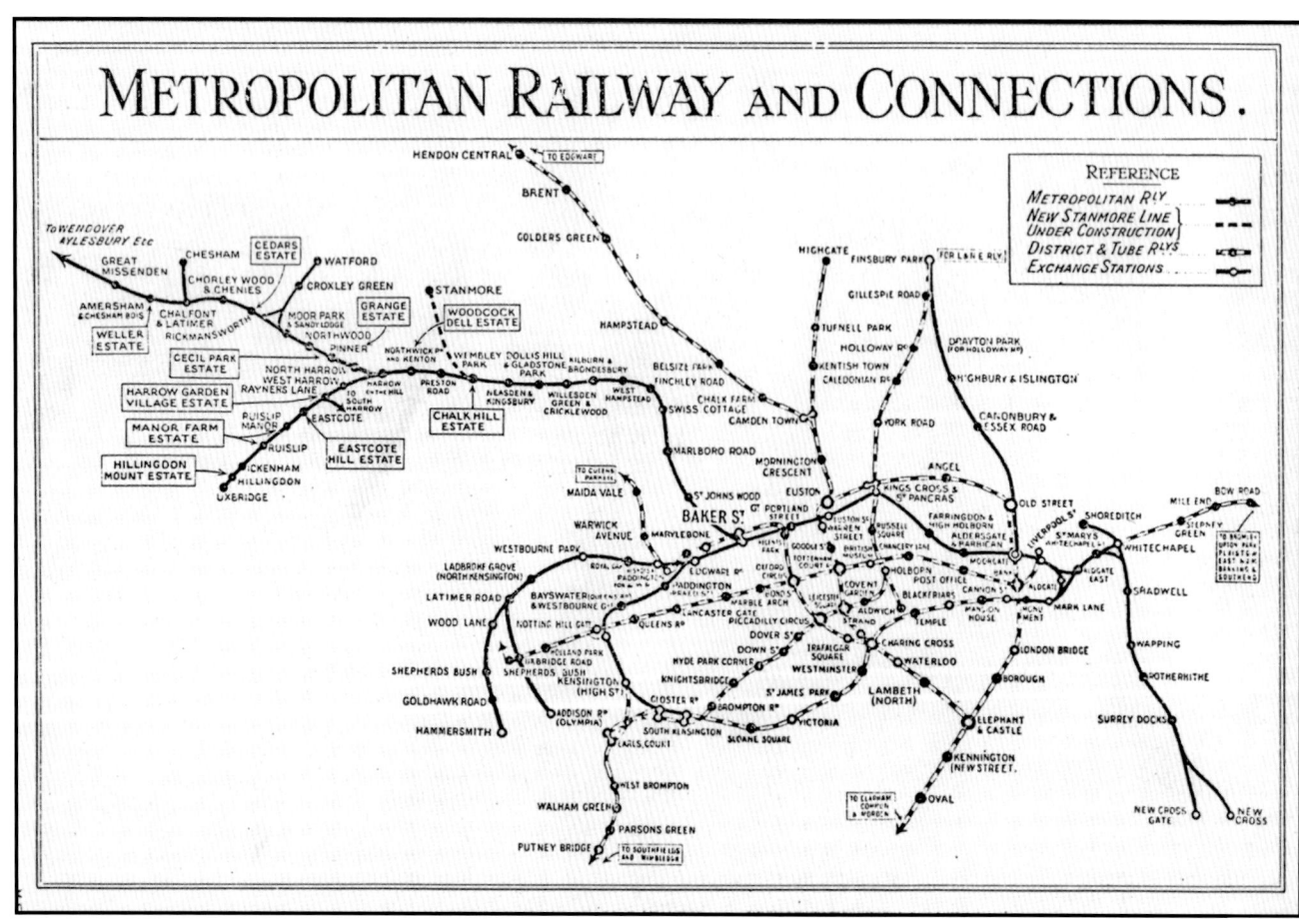

Map of the London Underground railways in the early 1930s showing the Metropolitan Railway Country Estates Company's housing estates.

12
The suburban development - Why? How? Who?

It is undeniable that the improvement of transport played a crucial role in the rise of suburbia between the two wars since it provided a cheap, fast and convenient means of commuting; especially after the electrification of trams and railways, the motorisation of omnibuses and the availability of cheap fares for workers. The latter were introduced in 1864 by the Metropolitan Railway Company and made compulsory by an Act of Parliament in 1883, which increased the population's mobility and hence helped to ease the problem of overcrowding in the central areas of the city. However, it would not be true to say that improved communication was the sole causative factor that contributed to the housing boom of the inter-war period, as other agents were indeed at work. First of all, let us consider the development of the building trade.

From the turn of the century onwards the construction industry went through quite a few ups and downs. At first, until about 1905, it boomed, but then the price of capital became high and people preferred to invest abroad. Lloyd George's People's Budget on Land Taxes and the Town Planning Act of 1909 caused some uncertainty; and the builders, who were then building mainly for renting, became discouraged by the fact that the rents, which were controlled, remained steady. Consequently, the building trade entered a phase of depression. Then came the war, much of the labour force was called up and materials became very scarce, causing building activity to come to a standstill. After the war, building a house became a costly business (costing about four times more than it had in 1914), mainly because there was not enough labour available, not only bricklayers but especially skilled workers in the necessary different trades such as glaziers, plumbers, tilers and carpenters. Most young people at the time preferred different careers, such as engineering and clerical work, rather than entering the building trade. This forced the Government to negotiate with the trade unions regarding apprenticeship conditions, so that the training age could be extended to 26, in order to allow demobilised men to undertake that profession if they so wished. The efficiency of the labour force had also deteriorated; workers, not being as skilled as before the war, took of course more hours to complete their work. The higher standards that were now required and the high interest rates also contributed to the desertion of the housing market by most investors, for such costly houses could not be rented at a profit. They could have built for a speculative sale, but it was risky and buyers were not numerous. Thus buyers and builders wisely waited for a fall in price.

However, despite the caution of buyers and builders, the demand for houses, especially small ones, grew. This preference for smaller and more easily manageable houses fitted with labour-saving equipment – bathroom, inside toilet, gas, electricity – developed mainly from the increase of family units and a reduction in household size (due mainly to an improved expectation of life, an increase in the marriage rate, and a fall in the birth rate), and also because of the growing scarcity and cost of domestic help. The only thing that was not a problem was land, since a lot of agricultural land, once used to feed London's horses and people, became available at low prices.

The agricultural depression of the 1920s, together with high taxation and death duties that landowners had to pay as well as the availability of more favourable alternative investment opportunities, pushed owners, especially those who were financially stretched, to sell their land and reinvest their capital in areas offering better prospects. They rarely developed their land themselves for fear of failing and thus reaping no benefits. They usually liked to sell their estate as a whole, so as to avoid being left with small areas less favourably situated that would not sell easily. However, they often had to divide their estate into lots, either because they could not obtain the price they wanted or the land developer considered it to be too big to be developed successfully. Most of the land was sold freehold.

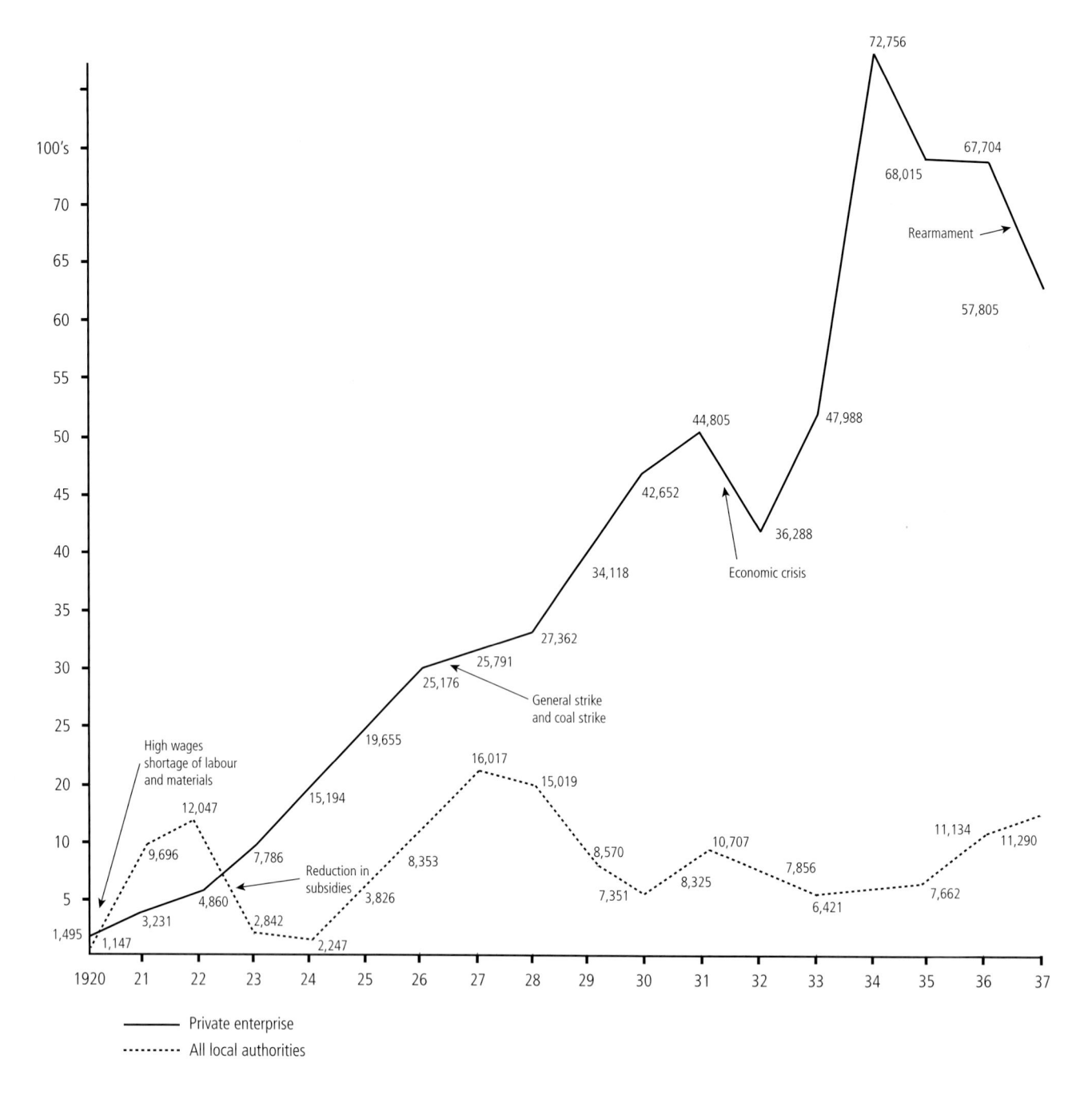

Houses built in Greater London, 1920-37.

But the fact of plenty of land and many people wanting a house was not enough to solve the problem, which became so serious that the Government had to intervene in order to provide the necessary housing. That task was first entrusted to local authorities, which, under the Housing & Town Planning Act of 1919 (introduced by the first Minister of Health, Dr Christopher Addison), were given the task of providing for low-rent accommodation, in exchange for which they were guaranteed that the Government would pay for any loss above a penny-rate. The rents of such places were to be calculated according to the tenant's income and not exceed the control rent level. In the same year, a second Act granted private builders a subsidy varying with the dimensions of the house being built (the maximum of £160 granted in 1919 was increased to £260 in 1920), regardless of whether the house was for sale or for rent. Unfortunately, with the sharp increase of building costs during the period of inflation, those subsidies became costly and ceased in 1922. In 1923, the Bonar Law government introduced a new Housing Act, known as the Chamberlain Act, favouring private building so as to reduce rent control. This time the local authorities were not granted any subsidy unless they could prove that private building was inadequate in their area. The money was paid out to builders – £6 a year for 25 years or a lump sum of £75, per house built – by the local authorities, which in their turn received the money from the Treasury on condition that what they built was either a two-storey house with a floor area varying between 620 and 950 feet or a self-contained flat or a bungalow with a floor area varying between 550 and 880 feet, all of which had to be fitted with a bath and to be finished by 1 October 1925.

In 1923 a Labour Government came into power, and a new Act known as the Wheatley Act was introduced, extending the latter subsidies to houses completed by October 1939 and giving back to the local authorities the power to build houses, and granting them a subsidy of £9 a year for 40 years for each urban house they built and let out at restricted rents.

In 1924 the Conservatives returned and decided not to grant the 1923 and 1924 Act subsidies to houses completed after 20 September 1927, to cut down even more the 1924 Act subsidy, and to cancel the 1923 Act subsidy for houses completed after 30 September 1929. Then a Labour Government returned in 1929 and abolished the subsidy reduction in the 1924 Act. Finally, the Conservatives' Housing (Financial Provisions) Act of 1933 cancelled all subsidies for houses completed after 30 June 1934.

So at first, as we have seen, building remained costly, but from 1926 onwards (with the exception of 1929) building costs gradually started to decrease to reach their lowest level in 1934, and the introduction of a cheap money policy after 1932 caused the interest rates to decrease, which gave private investors fewer opportunities to find good investments and made them turn towards building. Moreover, labour was available, wages remained stable and there was fierce competition between builders, all of which contributed to a boom in the building trade in the 1930s. And as can be seen on the accompanying graph (Page 108), the peak period for private enterprise was in 1934, with 72,756 houses built in the Greater London area.

However, it is also necessary to point out that building societies played an important part in housing development. The first building society appeared in 1781, but it was only in 1874 and 1894 that they were given a statutory basis. After that, as their assets increased their influence started to grow, especially in the period of general economic uncertainty between the two wars, as they presented an attractive investment.

'In 1913 total building society advances on new mortgages totalled £13 million, and in 1923 approximately £32 million. By 1929 the value of total new advances had increased by well over 1½ times to £74.7 million, with the amounts advanced in 1933 and 1936 standing at £103.2 million and £140.3 million respectively. The rise in the number of borrowers was similarly rapid, increasing from 553,900 in 1928 to 948,500 in 1933 and 1,295,200 in 1936, while the number of shareholders increased by approximately 3.7 times between 1922 and 1938.'[48]

Building societies had become less reluctant to lend money and finance house purchase, because they

Private building companies such as Haymills introduced a modernist - or 'Moderne' - style to their house building programme in the 1930s.

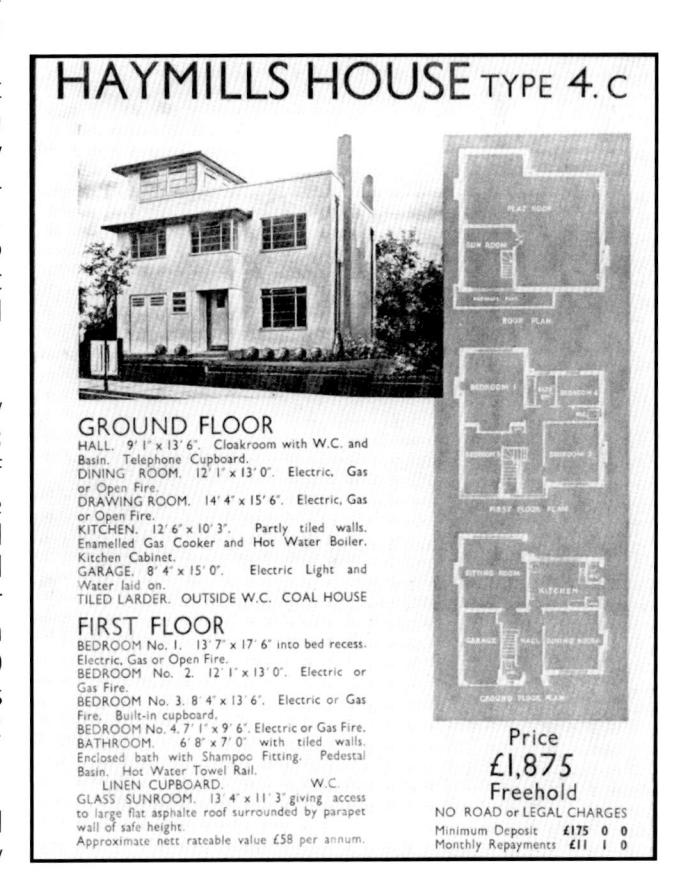

were now given more guarantees than before that they would be paid back, since the 1923 Act gave local authorities the power to guarantee payments by house purchasers to building societies; also some insurance companies started to guarantee building societies by offering single premium policies to house-buyers. They then became able to advance a maximum sum of 90 per cent of their surveyor's valuation instead of the usual 75 per cent, and to extend the repayment period from the normal 15 or 16 years to 25 or even 30, thus reducing the monthly instalments by nearly a third. The interest rates, which varied between 5 and 6½ per cent between 1924 and 1932, went down to 5 per cent in 1933, and to 4½ per cent in 1935; the competition between the different societies also helped to keep them at that level for the rest of the 1930s. The initial cash deposit, which used to be 20 or 25 per cent, also went down in the 1930s to 10 per cent and even 5 per cent. Thus to buy, for instance, a £600 house, there was no longer a need to save an initial deposit of £150 or £125 but just £30.

In some cases the building companies, which usually arranged the mortgages for their customers, also managed to have that deposit reduced. They might have an arrangement with a building society, such as the Builder's Pool, whereby the builder would deposit a certain amount of money with the building society as collateral security, in exchange for which the building society would grant to the house buyer a 95 per cent mortgage or allow the payment of the deposit by instalments over a certain period of time, hence providing a kind of second mortgage to cover the cost of the deposit. The societies could thus win a clientele who could not otherwise afford a purchase, such as the lower middle class. And very often building companies' advertisements announced that £5 was sufficient to secure the purchase of a house; most of them would also advertise no road charges, no legal costs, no stamp duty, and no survey fees.

A good publicity campaign was also essential, as purchasers had to be convinced that they were doing the right thing. Most companies stressed the fact that the instalments only slightly exceeded what would be payable in rent; that borrowers were getting the satisfaction of knowing that they had some ownership in what they were paying for, and that after the final payment the property would be theirs; that the purchase of a house by that system represented a good investment, as every payment the borrowers made reduced their liability, so that they were really saving money and building up a fund eventually towards their houses, instead of spending it, as in the case of renting a house; and that the purchasers were not deprived of their freedom of mobility, for they were entitled to sell their interest in the properties if they wished to, without losing any money. So, if at first people were hesitant as regards this new method of buying a house, they soon became aware of its advantages, and more and more people started to use it to buy their first house.

More examples of Haymills' 1930s 'Moderne' style of housing.

Buying a house became even more popular when the prices started to go down: the price of a parlour-type house, which cost £944 in 1920-21, was £513 in 1922 and £487 in 1936, and the price of a non-parlour-type house, which cost £863 in 1920, was £436 in 1922, £296 in 1934 and £363 in 1937. This drastic fall in house prices was not only due to a drop in the cost of materials and labour, but also due to the fact that most people who could afford to buy a house were now provided for and that speculative builders had to find a way of selling their houses, in order to attract the less wealthy part of the population, which they did by reducing costs and prices (sometimes, unfortunately, at the expense of quality). They also advertised all the new technical devices that had been absent in pre-war houses, such as electricity, labour-saving devices, nicely fitted bathrooms, inside toilets, modern kitchens, etc. Thus the period between the two wars saw an increase in the building trade and the appearance of many private building companies; some were good and became successful, like Taylor Woodrow, Costain, Nash, Haymills, Wimpey, etc, while others, more adventurous, after having built a few houses became bankrupt.

To return to the Metropolitan Railway Country Estates Company, which was one of the most important land developers in Metro-land (as we have seen, they developed about ten estates in the area during that period), it was not only converting bare land into plots and having houses built upon them, but also used to sell the houses and even arrange the financing if necessary. Here is an example of how it used to advertise it houses:

Advert from *Metro-land*, 1931.

'However beautiful and healthy a countryside may be, it is unfitted for the erection of dwelling-houses until a certain amount of preparatory work has been accomplished on the land. An approved scheme, for instance, has to be laid down; roads must be made, a drainage system planned and constructed, water, gas and electric light laid on, etc.

These preliminaries, which occupy far more thought, time and labour than appear on the surface, form part of what is termed 'the development of an Estate', and have a considerable influence on its character. It is fortunate then for their prospective purchasers that the large, new residential estates at Chorley Wood, Rickmansworth, Pinner, Wembley Park, Neasden, etc, are controlled by such an organisation as the Metropolitan Railway Country Estates Ltd, whose Board consists of several of the Directors and the General Manager of the Metropolitan Railway Company, with their experts...

The prospective householder who desires to fix his residence in one of the most beautiful countrysides to be found in all England, situated at the same time within easy reach of his business in the City, has four courses open before him:

(1) He can acquire a site (or plot of land) amid lovely surroundings (if he chooses, on the instalment plan), either to sell over again, for the value of the plot will be constantly increasing as the locality develops, or to hold it in reserve to suit his own convenience. In buying a plot in 'Metro-land', he virtually banks his money at a high (and safe) rate of interest.

(2) When he has acquired a site, he can, if he pleases, build on it. In that case, cash advances will, if he desires, be made to him towards the cost of building.

(3) He can buy a freehold house ready for immediate occupation, which, at his option, he can pay for on instalment plan. Viewing these instalments as rent, he eventually acquires a freehold house and the land, which becomes his absolute property.

(4) Arrangements can be made for residences and bungalows to be erected on a selected site on any of the following estates, for a fixed sum, to include the plot of land. Building and all fees, and if desired the amount agreed can be paid by a deposit of not less than £200, and the balance over a period of years (not exceeding fifteen years) in quarterly sums, with interest at the nominal rate of six per cent per annum. By this means a purchaser can have his house built to his own requirements, and secure possession on payment of a small deposit, and pay the balance as rent.'[49]

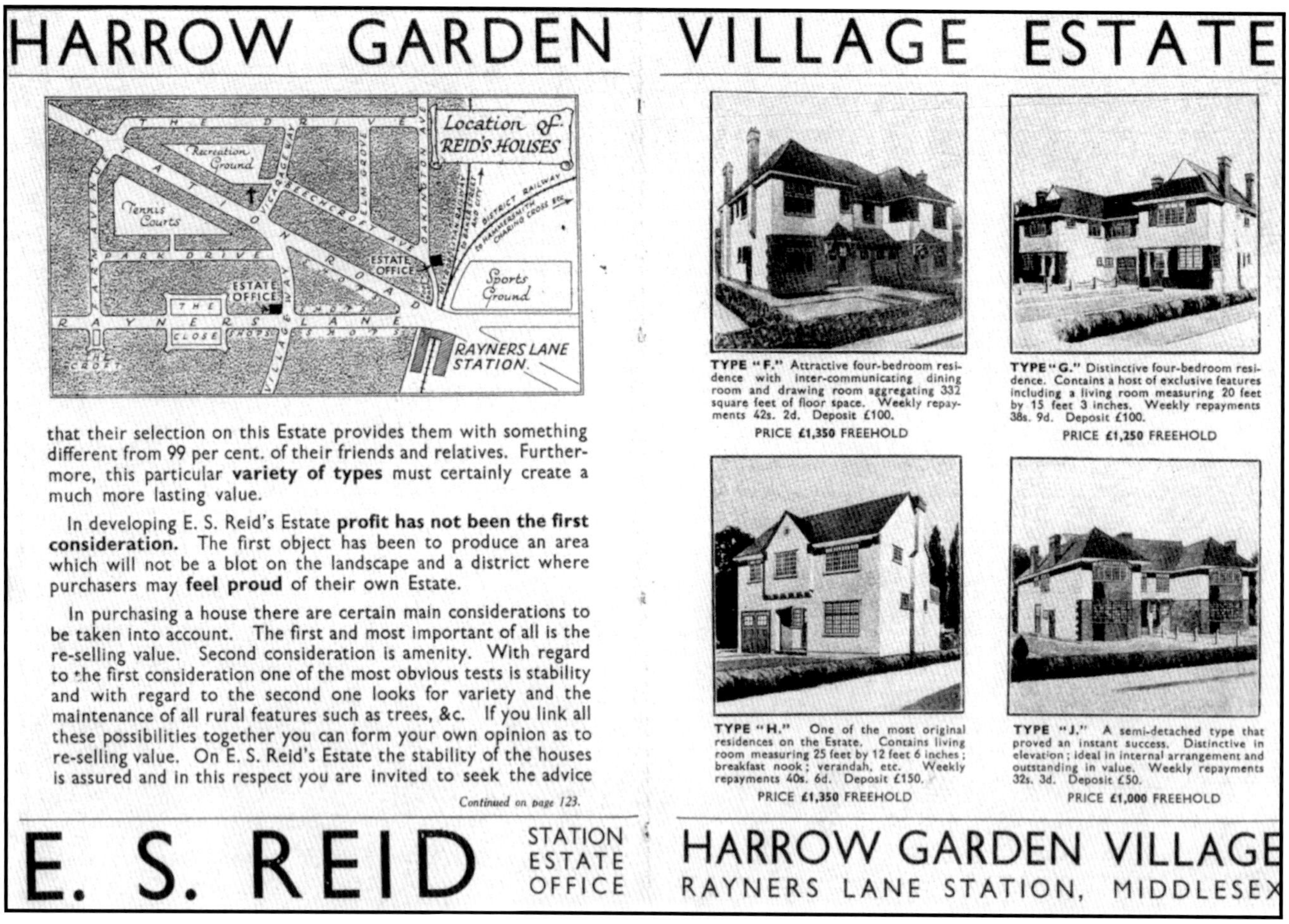

HARROW GARDEN VILLAGE ESTATE

that their selection on this Estate provides them with something different from 99 per cent. of their friends and relatives. Furthermore, this particular **variety of types** must certainly create a much more lasting value.

In developing E. S. Reid's Estate **profit has not been the first consideration.** The first object has been to produce an area which will not be a blot on the landscape and a district where purchasers may **feel proud** of their own Estate.

In purchasing a house there are certain main considerations to be taken into account. The first and most important of all is the re-selling value. Second consideration is amenity. With regard to the first consideration one of the most obvious tests is stability and with regard to the second one looks for variety and the maintenance of all rural features such as trees, &c. If you link all these possibilities together you can form your own opinion as to re-selling value. On E. S. Reid's Estate the stability of the houses is assured and in this respect you are invited to seek the advice

Continued on page 123.

TYPE "F." Attractive four-bedroom residence with inter-communicating dining room and drawing room aggregating 332 square feet of floor space. Weekly repayments 42s. 2d. Deposit £100.
PRICE £1,350 FREEHOLD

TYPE "G." Distinctive four-bedroom residence. Contains a host of exclusive features including a living room measuring 20 feet by 15 feet 3 inches. Weekly repayments 38s. 9d. Deposit £100.
PRICE £1,250 FREEHOLD

TYPE "H." One of the most original residences on the Estate. Contains living room measuring 25 feet by 12 feet 6 inches; breakfast nook; verandah, etc. Weekly repayments 40s. 6d. Deposit £150.
PRICE £1,350 FREEHOLD

TYPE "J." A semi-detached type that proved an instant success. Distinctive in elevation; ideal in internal arrangement and outstanding in value. Weekly repayments 32s. 3d. Deposit £50.
PRICE £1,000 FREEHOLD

E. S. REID STATION ESTATE OFFICE

HARROW GARDEN VILLAGE RAYNERS LANE STATION, MIDDLESEX

Adverts from Metro-land 1932.

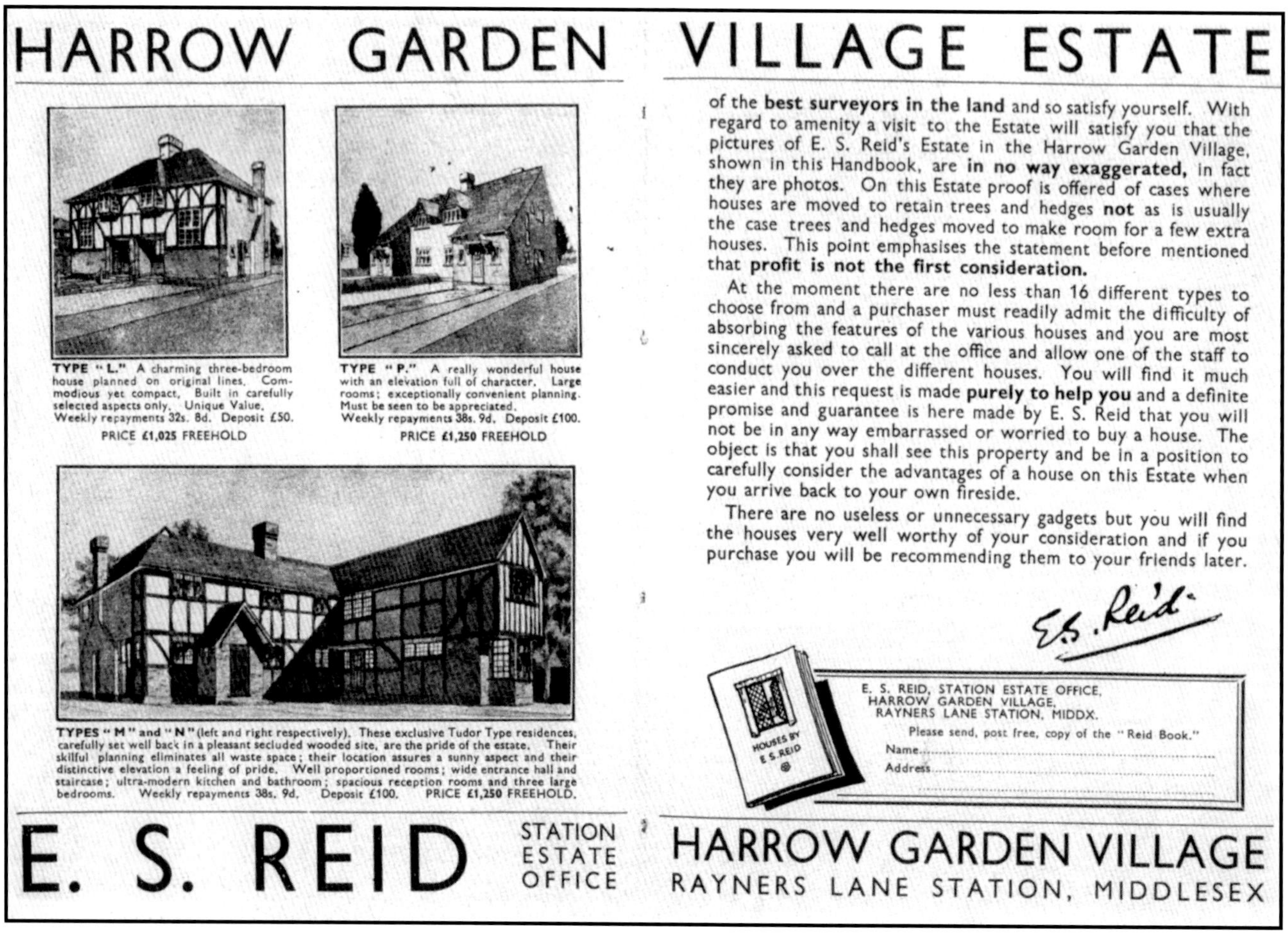

HARROW GARDEN VILLAGE ESTATE

TYPE "L." A charming three-bedroom house planned on original lines. Commodious yet compact. Built in carefully selected aspects only. Unique Value. Weekly repayments 32s. 8d. Deposit £50.
PRICE £1,025 FREEHOLD

TYPE "P." A really wonderful house with an elevation full of character. Large rooms; exceptionally convenient planning. Must be seen to be appreciated. Weekly repayments 38s. 9d. Deposit £100.
PRICE £1,250 FREEHOLD

TYPES "M" and "N" (left and right respectively). These exclusive Tudor Type residences, carefully set well back in a pleasant secluded wooded site, are the pride of the estate. Their skilful planning eliminates all waste space; their location assures a sunny aspect and their distinctive elevation a feeling of pride. Well proportioned rooms; wide entrance hall and staircase; ultra-modern kitchen and bathroom; spacious reception rooms and three large bedrooms. Weekly repayments 38s. 9d. Deposit £100. PRICE £1,250 FREEHOLD.

of the **best surveyors in the land** and so satisfy yourself. With regard to amenity a visit to the Estate will satisfy you that the pictures of E. S. Reid's Estate in the Harrow Garden Village, shown in this Handbook, are **in no way exaggerated**, in fact they are photos. On this Estate proof is offered of cases where houses are moved to retain trees and hedges **not** as is usually the case trees and hedges moved to make room for a few extra houses. This point emphasises the statement before mentioned that **profit is not the first consideration.**

At the moment there are no less than 16 different types to choose from and a purchaser must readily admit the difficulty of absorbing the features of the various houses and you are most sincerely asked to call at the office and allow one of the staff to conduct you over the different houses. You will find it much easier and this request is made **purely to help you** and a definite promise and guarantee is here made by E. S. Reid that you will not be in any way embarrassed or worried to buy a house. The object is that you shall see this property and be in a position to carefully consider the advantages of a house on this Estate when you arrive back to your own fireside.

There are no useless or unnecessary gadgets but you will find the houses very well worthy of your consideration and if you purchase you will be recommending them to your friends later.

E. S. Reid

E. S. REID, STATION ESTATE OFFICE,
HARROW GARDEN VILLAGE,
RAYNERS LANE STATION, MIDDX.
Please send, post free, copy of the "Reid Book."
Name...
Address..

E. S. REID STATION ESTATE OFFICE

HARROW GARDEN VILLAGE RAYNERS LANE STATION, MIDDLESEX

The deposit usually varied with the value of the house. It started at £25 for a house valued between £650 and £1,000 and could reach £200 for a house valued at more than £2,000. The repayment period could be 10, 15, 20 or 22 years. The table below gives as an example a house costing £695 with a rateable value of £35.

But the purchasers could also adopt an alternative method. For instance, if they bought a freehold house for £695 and put down a deposit of £25, it would leave them with the sum of £670, which they could choose to pay over a period of 22 years by monthly instalments of not less than £2 10s 9d, plus interest, which meant that their first instalment would be of £5 12s 2d (£2 10s 9d plus one month's interest on £670, £3 1s 5d), his second £5 11s 11d (£2 10s 9d plus one month's interest on the sum of £667 9s 3d, £3 1s 2d), and so on. In this way, as the principal was being paid off, the interest was going down.

Naturally, the Metropolitan Railway Country Estates Company was not the only land developing or building company in Metro-land – there were many others. However, all the houses were more or less of the same type, though each company was claiming that its own were the best, and that no better could be found… The most popular houses were the three-bedroomed semi-detached ones with bay windows at the front, a small front garden and a larger back garden. During the building boom the companies were competing fiercely, trying anything to attract customers. They all published lavish brochures and most of them had show houses and arranged free transport for their visitors to come

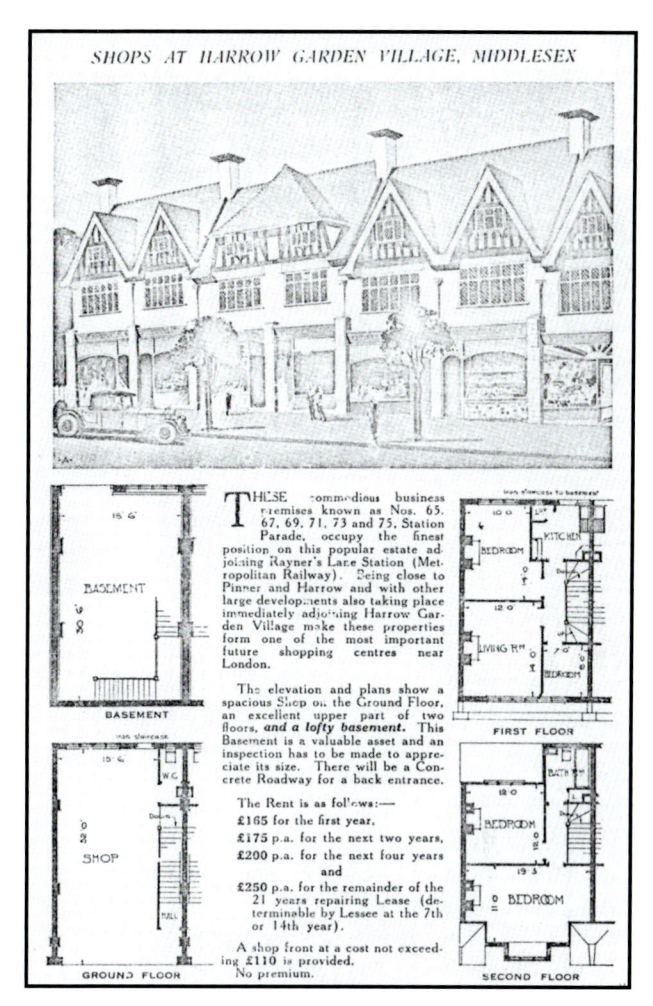

Advert from *Where to Live*, a brochure published by the Metropolitan Railway.

Deposit and repayments on a house costing £650

Purchase price (£)	Total deposit (£)	Amount of advance (£)	No of years	Monthly payments (12 per annum) (£ s d)	Annual payments (£ s d)
695	25	670	22	4 8 9	53 5 0
			20	4 13 10	56 6 0
			15	5 11 8	67 0 0
			10	7 8 6	89 2 0
	50	645	22	4 5 6	51 6 0
			20	4 10 4	54 4 0
			15	5 7 6	64 10 0
			10	7 3 0	85 16 0
	100	595	22	3 18 10	47 6 0
			20	4 3 4	50 0 0
			15	4 19 2	59 10 0
			10	6 11 11	79 3 0

and visit the property. Some offered extra features, such as some free furniture, or labour-saving devices such as a refrigerator, a cooker, a washing machine or some free electric fires, or a free radio, or a free season ticket to town for one year. Some even went so far as to organise big bonfires or firework displays, as for instance George Ball (Ruislip) Limited, which advertised its new estate at Ruislip Manor as follows: 'Free, tonight! Bring your friends to see the great fireworks and searchlight display at Ruislip Manor.'[50]

The suburban development was not specific to the interwar period. Suburbs were already in existence a few centuries earlier, but they were populated essentially by rich people who could afford to own a carriage. But with the improvement and development of the various means of communication throughout the 18th and 19th centuries, the suburbs gradually became available to more people, and this trend became strongly noticeable from 1880 onwards when one could commute cheaply over long distances either on the railway, by omnibus or by tram. The population of London's outer ring increased by about 50 per cent in each of the intercensal periods between 1861 and 1891, and by about 45 per cent during the period between 1891 and 1901.

The Victorian and inter-war suburbs both housed middle class people, but the main difference between the two was that the former were situated close to the city, whereas the latter developed further afield and in fact replaced the former where the working class, pushing out from the centre, started to move in. Thus the first factor that determined the suburban development was of course a demographic one. Gradually London was getting more and more populated, not just from natural causes but also because of the thousands of immigrants from the countryside or overseas pouring into it each year, thus increasing the built-up area until there was nowhere to build, causing overcrowding and consequently squalor and insalubrity. So, for most people life in the city became repulsive and unhealthy, which encouraged all those who could afford it to move out into the suburbs where they could breathe purer air, drink cleaner water, and feel less cramped and more independent. However, bad housing conditions and the badly polluted air, both a hazard to health, were not the only reasons that drove people out of the city into the rural areas around it.

As the cost of rented accommodation began to rise, people who had money started to realise that the purchase of a house through a building society was an investment and that, after a few years, it would give them something to show for their money, whereas rented accommodation produced no return. But such places could not be found in the city, where there was no available space to build. Thus the only areas left for such dwellings were the outskirts and, with an improved transport system, people became less reluctant to leave their abode near their place of work and did not mind lengthening their journeys to and from work. This is why they usually chose to go and live in a suburb served by a route (usually a railway line) that would take them directly to their place of work. They were also strongly influenced by the growing popularity of the single family dwelling.

Front cover of Metro-land, 1921, with an idealised suburban squire's half-timbered residence.

Moreover, a house in the suburbs offered much more than an investment, privacy or better health – it also meant security in a period of uncertainty and depression when people were trying either to forget bad wartime memories or ignore threats of future hostilities (low housing density was indeed one of the factors that saved the suburbs from destruction during the war). It also offered respectability: the possession of a house, in the inter-war period especially, became a symbol of social status. It meant that one had gone a step upwards on the social ladder and it created of course snobbery, especially among the new members of the middle class who enjoyed showing their friends and relatives round their new residence, demonstrating that they no longer belonged to the poverty in which they had been brought up. And usually, after moving in, the new residents, frightened of losing this newly acquired status, would try hard to keep up appearances; they would, for instance, improve their accents, stop swearing, try to send their children to private schools, employ some sort

The Coliseum: one of the cinemas in Harrow in 1921.

of domestic help, and keep the house inside and outside spotlessly clean, trim and well-groomed at all times.

Moreover, suburbia gave its inhabitants the opportunity to express themselves. Some people might think that the suburbs are made of nothing but strings of houses that look exactly the same, but in the case of Metro-land it was not true. There may have been some similarities in the architectural design, such as the presence of bays, of back and front gardens, of gables, of porches, of similar layouts, etc, but in fact each house was different from the others in the street, since the occupiers could choose the paint they wanted, fix the door knocker of their choice on the front door, lay out their gardens as they pleased, give their house a name, and so on. Still, it was inside that the differences were the most striking: people decorated the interior to their own taste, following the latest fashion and trying to acquire some showpieces like expensive furniture or a wireless or the latest domestic appliance, of which they would be very proud. They were then able, amidst the anonymity that suburbia engenders, to create a world of their own where they could give way to their idealistic and creative instincts so as not to lose their identity.

Like many other suburbs of the inter-war period, Metro-land represented an escape – an escape from the daily brutalities, from the tightly packed and socially mixed community of the city, and from the stress of everyday work, while offering at the same time all the charms of rural life. Hence the suburban man could enjoy the best of both worlds: a job in the city, which was bringing him a good income, and a home in the country, where he could enjoy his leisure time and his family life, in the same way as Mr Wemmick in Dickens's *Great Expectations* some 50 years earlier. In the novel, Pip says: 'Wemmick's house was a little wooden cottage in the midst of plots of garden', but he also points out that for him it was his 'castle', which he even made to look like one by cutting and painting the top 'like a battery mounted with guns', by adding 'gothic windows … and a gothic door', a 'bridge' which he took pride in hoisting up and down, by building 'an ornamental lake' in one part of his garden with 'a fountain in it' and growing vegetables in another part of it.[51] All this, of course, he did by himself, and very proudly he explains to Pip: 'I am my own engineer, and my own carpenter, and my own plumber, and my own gardener, and my own Jack of all Trades.'[52] Which is exactly what the suburban man was during his spare time, and he also felt like Wemmick when the latter says to Pip that '…the office is one thing, and private life another. When I go into the office, I leave the Castle behind me, and when I come into the Castle, I leave the office behind me.'[53]

Hence it is true to say that for each suburban dweller, his semi-detached house or bungalow or, if he was wealthier, his detached house was his 'castle', and not just a castle in the air, but a real castle on the ground where he could be his own master and thus create a world of his own. In other words, where he could be or play the country gentleman.

There was a lot of romanticism and nostalgia for the past attached to these dwellings. For instance, the oak beams, the red roofs and chimneys, the pebble-dashed walls, the lattice windows, the stained glass, the well-tended gardens, the tradesmen's entrances at the side of the houses, the brick fireplaces – all were reminiscent of manorial England. The names given to houses (Hill House, Caenwood, Riversdale, Glendale, Meadowside…), to the streets (Shepherds Way, Pheasant Way, Elm Way, Valley Road, the Clump…), or to the estates (Northwick Park Estate, Harrow Garden Village, Barn Hill Estate…) all had a romantic and pastoral touch that corresponded with the suburban man's wish to put down roots.

But who were all these new suburban squires, and how did they live?

The improved education facilities gave most children the opportunity to reach a standard that enabled them later to undertake a white-collar career in a world where clerks of all sorts were starting to be in great demand due to the expansion of public services and transport, the growth of the armed forces, the creation of numerous new laws, etc, requiring a greater number of civil servants. It was due also to such things as the booming of commercial and building activities, the development of banks, insurance companies, new consumer industries (such as the motor car), new domestic appliances, and joint-stock limited liability companies. All these prosperous activities gave birth to a multitude of clerks, senior officials, managers and directors of all kinds and of all trades. Thus, all these middlemen involved in distribution activities became the members of the new middle class who created the new suburbs.

Most of these people earned a good salary, which allowed them to put down a deposit for a house and maintain regular payments. Usually they could also afford some domestic help, a holiday at the seaside once a year and sending their children to private schools. In the 1930s the price of houses went down due mainly to lower building costs which fell by about 7% between 1926 and 1930, and by about 10% between 1930 and 1933. The interest rates and the amount required for a deposit went down too. In addition, there was also a gradual increase in real incomes which went up by about 10% between 1925 and 1930 and by about 7% between 1930 and 1933. All these changes enabled sections of the lower classes to fulfil their dream, which was to become house-owners in their turn.

Some firms offered special privileges to civil servants or those working for a public body, such as railway or bus workers or officials (who had travelling concessions and did not have to worry about travelling costs), or to bank and insurance employees because they were considered to have very secure jobs.

Having explained who the Metro-land people were and why they had come to Metro-land, let us now see what sort of life they lived.

Suburban men, being the breadwinners, were those who were spending the least time in the houses they had bought, as they had to leave it six times a week at regular hours to face the strain of daily work. Their journey to and from might have been strenuous too, but they had the possibility of making it either pleasant by chatting or playing cards with friends, or less tiresome by reading a book, a magazine or a paper, or doing a crossword, or even making it profitable by writing or settling business matters. Thus the station, the platform and the train became for them a centre of social life, a place where information could be exchanged and new acquaintances made – in other words a sort of link between the 'castle' and the office.

Once at home, their precious leisure time was divided between gardening, pottering about, playing with the children and hobbies such as sport, fishing, hiking or collecting stamps.

On the other hand, the housewives led a more isolated and lonely life, especially when the children were at school and the husbands at work. Not many went to work in those days, as their task was to be a home-maker, which meant looking after their house and family, thus having fewer opportunities to make new acquaintances, which could end up being rather depressing for some. Their weekly routine consisted of doing the washing on Monday, the ironing on Tuesday, the shopping on Wednesday or Thursday and the housework on Thursday or Friday. And Sunday was of course spent preparing Sunday

Advert from *Near and Far*, 1912.

THE PAVILION, Eastcote

J. HEYWOOD
Proprietor

By Royal Warrant to
H. M. THE KING

A. E. BAYLY
Manager
Phone 7555 Mayfair

The Ideal Spot
For School and Other Parties

SPECIALLY DESIGNED AND ARRANGED FOR LARGE PARTIES.

WITHIN FIVE MINUTES' WALK OF STATION

EXTENSIVE ACCOMMODATION.   PERMANENT BUILDINGS.
EXCELLENT CATERING AT MODERATE PRICES.   UP-TO-DATE
LAVATORIES.   LARGE PLAYING FIELDS.   EASY OF ACCESS.
ELECTRIC TRAIN SERVICE.   COLNE VALLEY CO. WATER
LAID ON.   AMUSEMENTS.

Illustrated Booklet with full particulars from

A. E. BAYLY, The Pavilion, Eastcote

Adverts from an early *Metro-land* book.

lunch and tea. However, not all housewives were lonely; they had the possibility, if they wanted to, to join associations, mainly charitable ones, organised usually by the church, or they could meet with others at a friend's house for tea or coffee or go shopping up in Town. If they were not too shy, they could also make new acquaintances when taking the children to school or to the park to play, or in the small local shops, or by chatting to the next-door neighbour over the garden fence.

The most popular form of entertainment offered in the evenings or Saturday afternoons was the cinema, especially in the 1930s when the sound film became available and when picture houses started to open all over the suburbs. In the county of Middlesex, for instance, there were about 82 picture houses in 1920, and by the end of the 1930s one could count about 138. They could seat up to 1,000 people, sometimes more, and could take as little as five months to erect at a cost that might vary between £50,000 and £100,000. Inside they were provided with an organ and a stage and luxurious décor; they also offered large and cosy vestibules or halls where patrons could wait comfortably before going into the auditorium, and one could also obtain refreshments in the tea lounge or coffee lounge built over the foyer. Another feature, which was popular with ladies, was the luxuriously fitted powder- and wash-room. However, what attracted people to the cinemas was mostly the relief it provided from the daily drudgeries and worries of life by taking them on a low-price trip to the world of dream, fantasy and beauty. The cinema architecture was usually grand and reminiscent of some sort of temple, while their names were evocative of opulence, eminence, splendour or exoticism: Embassy, Mayfair, Majestic, Coliseum, Capitol, Paramount, Dominion, Granada, Rio. It is also interesting to note that sometimes they were built even before churches.

The second most popular leisure activity was sport. Tennis was one of the favourites, and there were many clubs in the suburbs where one could go and enjoy a relaxing game during the day and a pleasant social reunion or dance in the evening. In Metro-land, many builders provided tennis courts or at least the space for them on their estates. But Metro-land was most famous for its golf links. As one early *Metro-land* brochure put it:

'To the City Man, the "Met" is a short cut to the nearest golf course. From his office, he can step in at any of the "Met" stations close by, and be taken in a few minutes by electric train to the links without a change.'

Adverts from an early *Metro-land* book.

THE PADDOCKS
SOUTH HARROW

Proprietor   -   -   -   A. B. CHAMPNISS
Telephone:—HARROW 173

ASSEMBLING FOR TEA, PADDOCKS, SOUTH HARROW.

The FAVOURITE RESORT for School Treats,
Summer Outings, etc., in West Middlesex.

Excellent Catering
Accommodation for 2,500 at one sitting.

Very large permanent shelters in grounds in case of rain.
Extensive grounds, 30 acres. Swings, See-Saws, Donkeys,
Roundabouts, Wonderful Miniature Railway.
TOYS, SWEETS, MINERALS AT POPULAR PRICES.
Liberal water supply from Colne Valley Water Co.'s Mains.
Up-to-date Sanitary arrangements.
Brakes and Wagonettes for Drives at moderate charges.
Frequent Service of ELECTRIC TRAINS from all Parts of London.
Close to South Harrow Met. and District Railway Stations.

ILLUSTRATED BOOKLET FREE from the Proprietor.

On nice summer days the suburban dwellers could join the crowds of city excursionists in one of the pleasure grounds along the 'Met' line, as for instance the Pavilion at Eastcote, covering an area of 32 acres and equipped with numerous items of amusement, entertainment and sports; games and dances were often organized, and swings, roundabouts, helter-skelters, a cycle circus, coconut shies, donkeys, a putting green, a miniature golf course and a bowling green could be found, amongst many other things. Refreshments and food were also provided at the outside stalls or inside the buildings that were capable of seating 4,000 people at a time. Adequate shelters were also provided in case of inclement weather. There were many more recreation parks like this, for example at Wembley Park, where one could go boating on a spacious ornamental lake, or The Paddocks between South Harrow and Northolt.

Tea rooms such as the Ye Cocoa Tree in Pinner, The Ship in Eastcote or The Orchard in Ruislip were quite popular too, but the most famous was The Poplars in Ruislip, where the waitresses used to be called after flowers and wear an imitation flower of that name. The place even had its own 'pop' song, The Poplars Waltz, the score of which most visitors bought and brought home as a souvenir. Here is the song.

Adverts from an early *Metro-land* book.

Adverts from an early *Metro-land* book.

They also listed in that brochure 14 golf courses, all situated along the 'Met' Line in the immediate vicinity of a 'Met' station between Neasden and Chesham. Through trains were run regularly, and special facilities were offered by the 'Met' to regular golf travellers. One station on the line was even built and opened as the result of a request made by a golf club. Sandy Lodge Halt opened in 1910 for the use of the golfers of Sandy Lodge Golf Club, 'on the guarantee that the receipts from golfers travelling to and from the Halt [would] not be less than £350 per annum and also that the club [would] construct and maintain free of cost to the Committee a footpath approach from the east side of the links to the station entrance.'[54] The station was renamed Moor Park & Sandy Lodge in 1923, and Moor Park in 1950.

Hiking in the beautiful surrounding countryside was also a popular Sunday activity, for which one could get a special train ticket. And if one did not know where to go, one could purchase for twopence one of the booklets published by the Metropolitan Railway Company called *Country Walks in Middlesex and Buckinghamshire*, which offered a great variety of pleasant itineraries illustrated with sketch maps. The book's rectangular shape was designed to fit the raincoat pockets of the time.

The Poplars tea rooms at Ruislip.

'Neath the Shade of the Ruislip "Poplars"

1 – Neath the shade of Ruislip Poplars;
We go by cycle for a country trip,
Every Man in London will tell you all about the merry Poplars at Ruislip,
It's there each one spends a good time
Walking past the tall trees and flowers,
To admire the marvellous scenery, just among the sweet Poplars bowers
And they…

Chorus:
Spend the Day with Rose you see,
At the Poplars where sweet Bluebell serves the Tea,
And Lily's white hands, bring Cake and Jam,
And don't we enjoy Miss Pansy's cold Lamb!
The Jellies and Custards by Poppy and May,
And the Cream brought by Daisy is as sweet as Hay;
It's a very short distance by Rail on the "Met"
And at the gate you'll find waiting, sweet Violet.

2 – Neath the shade of Ruislip Poplars;
That cool and leafy pleasant snug retreat
Every weekend very large Parties make arrangement, for their new-made friends to meet,
There Sisters meet Brothers' new chums,
And delight in the shady walks,
And a little spooning perhaps is done by the tone of highflown talks.

Then they…

Chorus

3 – Neath the shade of the Ruislip Poplars;
You'll notice soon a very lively batch,
Probably find their way to the sporting fields to play at Tennis or a Cricket match,
And coconut shies, quoits, or swings,
Delight customers by the score,
After all the games, and the fun is done, you will feel you can eat some more,
So they…

Chorus' [55]

Social activities were not lacking in Metro-land, and the suburban dweller could join one of the many societies or clubs and enjoy the expression of some concealed talents. There were dramatic societies such as 'The Vagabonds' in Pinner; operatic societies such as the Gilbert & Sullivan companies, the Pinner and Hatch End Society or the Wembley Choir Society; music societies such as The Pinner Players or The Pinner Orchestra; horticultural societies such as those in Harrow, Pinner or Wembley; political societies such as the Harrow Liberal Club or the Pinner Conservative Club; literary societies such as the Young Men's Literary Institute in Wembley or the Harrow Literary Institute; and so on. Most of these associations would also organise dances, shows, matches, etc. For those who would rather remain at home, other activities were available: they could invite relatives or friends to tea and take the opportunity to boast about their new status by showing their guests round their 'castle' then retire to the sitting room for a chat, more drinks and most certainly to listen to some music. If they wanted to enjoy a comfortable and peaceful evening at home, they could do so by listening to the wireless, of which they were very proud and which offered them a great variety of educative, informative and entertaining programmes, including the regular daily broadcasts of news, which started in 1922. Or they could read a book that they might have borrowed from their nearest library (there were not many public libraries, but there were many shop libraries, also known as 'Twopenny Libraries', because they lent all sorts of novels for twopence a week per book).

Metro-land did not only provide homes and entertainment, but also schools for the children, churches for the devout, shops for the housewives, and even work for some of the inhabitants. Educational facilities were never overlooked by the suburban dwellers, as they were hoping that their children would be able to rise a few more steps on the

Advert from *Metro-land* 1925.

GOLF COURSES IN METRO-LAND.

HARROW GOLF CLUB.—Adjoining Preston Road Station. 18 Holes.
NORTHWICK PARK GOLF CLUB.—Adjoining Northwick Park & Kenton Station. 18 Holes and a 9-hole course for Ladies.
RUISLIP GOLF CLUB.—King's End, 5 minutes from Station. 18 Holes.
HILLINGDON GOLF CLUB.—About 1 mile from Hillingdon and Uxbridge Stations. 9 Holes.
WOODLANDS PARK GOLF CLUB.—1 mile from Uxbridge Station. 18 Holes.
DENHAM GOLF CLUB.—About 1½ miles from Uxbridge Station. 18 Holes.
GRIMM'S DYKE GOLF CLUB.—About 2 miles from Pinner Station. 18 Holes.
PINNER HILL GOLF CLUB.—About 2 miles from Pinner Station. 18 Holes.
NORTHWOOD GOLF CLUB.—About ten minutes' walk from Station. 18 Holes.
SANDY LODGE GOLF CLUB.—Adjoining Moor Park & Sandy Lodge Station. 18 Holes and a 12-hole relief course.
MOOR PARK GOLF CLUB.—Adjoining Moor Park & Sandy Lodge Station. Three 18-hole courses.
WEST HERTS GOLF CLUB.—About half a mile from Croxley Green and Watford Stations. 18 Holes.
CHORLEY WOOD GOLF CLUB.—Two minutes' walk from Station. 9 Holes.
HAREWOOD DOWNS GOLF CLUB.—Nearest Station Chalfont & Latimer. 18 Holes.
CHESHAM & LEYHILL GOLF CLUB.—Nearest Station Chesham. 9 Holes.

For further particulars apply to Secretaries.

EDUCATIONAL FACILITIES.

WILLESDEN GREEN.—Askes Haberdashers School; Willesden High School; Sunbury House Preparatory School; St. Agnes' R.C. School, Cricklewood; Vernon House School; St. Mary's (C. of E.) School; Private and Council Schools.
WEMBLEY PARK.—The Gables Preparatory Boys' School; Wembley Boys' College; "Ravenscroft," Kindergarten, Wembley Park Drive; Girls' Grammar School; Chalk Hill House, Kindergarten; "Mount Rich." Kindergarten and Preparatory School; Wembley College of Commerce; St. Christopher's Preparatory School and Kindergarten.
NORTHWICK PARK.—Northwick Park School, Northwick Park Road; Chester College, Sheepcote Road. Boys and Girls also attend Harrow Schools.
HARROW-ON-THE-HILL. — The Lower School (Lyon Foundation); Orley Farm School; Byron Hill School; Victoria Hall School; St. Margaret's Girls' School; South'ands Girs' School; High School College Rd.; Harrow Technical School; Girls' County School; Boys' County School; etc.
RAYNERS LANE.—Atholl House Preparatory School for Boys; St. Teilo, Beechcroft Avenue (Kindergarten), and Secondary and other Schools within easy reach.
RUISLIP.—Kelvin High School for Girls and Boys; Preparatory School for Girls and Boys, The Studio, Ickenham Road; Ickenham High School for Girls and Boys; Private Schools and Council Schools.
UXBRIDGE.—Middlesex County Council Secondary (higher) Schools, Hillingdon; Uxbridge High School; St. Helen's College, Hillingdon; Uxbridge Business College; St. Michael's Preparatory School; Private and Council Schools.
PINNER.—Royal Commercial Travellers' School; Woodridings School for Girls and Boys; Pinner High School; Barrow Point House School; Meriston House School; Private Schools and Council Schools.
NORTHWOOD.—Mr. Terry's School for Boys; Northwood College; St. Helen's Girls' School; Temple School, Chester Road (Kindergarten); St. Martin's School for Boys; Private and Council Schools.
WATFORD.—Watford Grammar School for both Boys and Girls; Shirley House School; High School for Girls; numerous Private Schools; Council Schools.
RICKMANSWORTH.—Joan of Arc Convent School, Kindergarten and Boys' Preparatory School; Council Schools, Boys and Girls also attend either Harrow, Northwood, Watford or Amersham Schools
CHORLEY WOOD AND CHENIES.—Preparatory, Private, Kindergarten and Council Schools. Amersham and Watford Grammar Schools within easy reach by railway.
CHALFONT AND LATIMER.—Chalfont Road Holne Preparatory School; Little Chalfont Preparatory School and Capt. Hogg's Preparatory School for Boys, Chalfont St. Giles.
CHESHAM.—Private Schools, Chesham Preparatory School, and Council Schools. Amersham Grammar School 1½ miles distant.
AMERSHAM AND CHESHAM BOIS.—Amersham Grammar School, Private and Council Schools. Amersham College; Turret House, Collegiate School; St. Hilda's Girls' School; Chesham Bois High School
GREAT MISSENDEN.—Private and Council Schools; Boys also attend Amersham and Aylesbury Grammer Schools.
AYLESBURY. — Aylesbury Grammar School; Temple School; Private and Council Schools.

From *Metro-land*, 1932.

social ladder. Estate builders were well aware of the fact, and educational facilities were often advertised in their brochures – in the *Metro-land* books a whole page was devoted to them. Most parents, whenever they could afford it, preferred to send their children to private schools, for reasons of snobbery perhaps but also because the state schools could not cope with the rapid growth of suburbia and tended to be overcrowded. The most famous private school in Metro-land was of course that at Harrow-on-the-Hill. There was also Merchant Taylors', which it is interesting to note moved out of the city to Moor Park in 1933.

Churches of all denominations appeared too. Their appeal was no longer as strong as it had been earlier in Victorian times (especially with the developing fashion of weekend rambling; indeed, many people would rather go for a picnic in the country than to church – in other words they would rather visit the temple of Mother Nature than that of God the Father), but their congregations, mainly women, were still quite substantial, since they continued to play the role of a social centre where people, especially newcomers, could meet and feel they were part of a community. However, though there was usually a site allocated for a church in the

---

Park Lane Estate, Wembley Park

HOUSES ON PARK LANE ESTATE.

WHY NOT live in the bracing air and rural delights of this beautiful and healthy suburb. This charming Residential Estate—nearly 200 feet above sea level—gives extensive views of a well-wooded and gently undulating countryside and adjoins Wembley's beautiful Public Park.

The Park Lane Estate is planned and developed on the best Garden Suburb lines, with semi-detached Houses to suit all tastes and requirements.

3 Bedroom Houses from £750 to £1,000
4   "   "   " £1,100 " £1,250

FREEHOLD or LEASEHOLD. Semi-detached with facilities for Garage.

Special Points: Sound Construction, Perfect Sanitation, Pleasing Design, Artistic Decoration.

Over 1,200 of these Houses built and sold by us at Wembley. Close to Golf Links and Tennis Courts. Low Rates, 10/3 per ann. Mortgages arranged if required. Five minutes from Wembley Park Station (Metro. Rly.). Cheap Season Tickets.

COMBEN & WAKELING, Ltd.

Telephone: 1656-7 WEMBLEY.   **52 Park Lane, Wembley Hill.**

large developments, it often took up to 15 years to find the money to build a permanent church and in the meantime people had to be content with a wooden hut or a small brick hall.

For their daily or weekly shopping, housewives did not have to go to London each time, since on most estates, big or small, a site was allocated for shops, usually along the main new or existing roads or in the vicinity of the railway station and not within the estate, so as not to spoil its respectability. In those small shops personal and friendly attention was given, and one could get one's bread, meat, vegetables, fruit, groceries, dairy products, newspapers, sweets – in other words, most of the essential things. Whether the shops had been opened or not by the time people moved into the houses was a different matter, but the housewife was never stuck as she could always call on the services of the many traders who were only too glad to deliver at home whatever she required. As a way of advertising themselves, it was customary for most of them to leave on the doorstep of a newly moved-in family a free welcoming parcel containing samples of the goods they were selling.

Many people living in Metro-land commuted every day to the city, but not all of them. As more estates appeared, more work could be found locally,

1927/1928 adverts for travelling on the Metropolitan or buying a property in Metro-land.

Advert for houses built on the St John Estate by Comben and Wakeling.

with traders, who often needed assistants, the Post Offices, the schools, the building and decorating trades, and so on – all offered a fair amount of jobs to local people. Factories, mainly light industry, also started to develop, attracted by the low rates and the abundance of space.

Thus, living in Metro-land did not mean living in an ugly dormitory suburb like many of those seen nowadays outside big cities. Metro-land was beautiful and alive. Many estate builders, especially the Metropolitan Railway Country Estates Company, tried to make their estates look attractive and pleasant to live in by following the pattern of Ebenezer Howard's Garden Cities. But although we may get the impression that life in Metro-land was nice and easy, or at least better than it is now, for the majority of those who had a mortgage to pay it was not always easy, as climbing up the social ladder sometimes meant sacrifices and frugality – but to all Metro-land people it was worth it.

13
Wembley: an example of suburban development

Wembley, a rural hamlet in the 19th century, is a typical example of the suburban development brought on by the development of railways at the beginning of the 20th. It had been for many years a small village of farms, cottages and green fields situated on the narrow winding Harrow Road, in the Parish of Harrow, but the development of modern means of transport, especially the railway, was to transform this little hamlet into one of the most densely populated industrial suburbs of London.

The first railway line to penetrate Wembley was the London & Birmingham Railway in 1837, with a station at Harrow (now Harrow & Wealdstone). At the point where the Harrow Road crossed the line in Wembley, a halt was first provided in 1842, followed by a station in 1844, named at first 'Sudbury (for Wembley)', then 'Sudbury & Wembley' in 1882, 'Wembley for Sudbury' in 1910, and finally 'Wembley Central' in 1948. (These consecutive changes of names are in fact quite significant in the growing importance of Wembley.) Though the line

Haymaking in Wembley in 1910. *Grange Museum/Brent Archives*

Wembley Park – the entrance in 1905. *Grange Museum/Brent Archives*

brought at first excitement to the people for whom a steam train was a novelty, it did not have much effect on the growth of Wembley as it had essentially been built to convey traffic between the two big cities, and the company was not then interested in local traffic.

The second railway to approach Wembley was the Metropolitan Railway, which extended its line to Harrow in 1880, and plans to build a station at Wembley Park, put forward in February 1890, were approved in the summer of that year, and the station was opened on 2 May 1894. It was the Metropolitan that was to have the most influence on the development of Wembley. It began with the purchase of the grounds of the Wembley Park Estate by Sir Edward Watkin, then Chairman of the Metropolitan Railway Company, who wanted to turn it into London's greatest pleasure ground.

The Wembley Park Estate had been owned by the Page family for 260 years when, in the early 1800s, it came into the hands of John Gray, who continued the improvement of the house and grounds started by Richard Page in 1793. In 1880 his son sold 47 acres of the estate to the Metropolitan Railway Company for its extension to Harrow. In 1890, a few years after his death, the rest of the estate was sold to the Metropolitan, in all 280 acres for £32,929 18s 7d.

Sir Edward Watkin intended to attract more passengers on his line by turning the estate into a sports ground and pleasure park. Amenities for football, cricket, cycling, tennis, running and athletics were provided. Advantage was taken of the waters of the Wealdstone Brook, also known as Lidding Brook, a tributary of the River Brent, which was winding its way through the park, to build an ornamental lake covering an area of 8 acres, crossed by ornamental bridges and provided with a boathouse and an artificial waterfall. The lake was very popular in the summer for boating, and in the winter when, if the weather was cold enough, it was used for skating. The park itself was nicely laid out with winding paths bordered with lovely and sometimes rare flowers, shrubs and trees, creating a delight for botanists. The buildings consisted of grandstands, tea pagodas, a restaurant, a shelter for wet days, bandstands and pavilions. Concerts were given on fine days, and all sorts of children's amusements were available too.

The park was officially opened on 12 May 1894, at the same time as the Metropolitan Railway station. The park was very popular at first, and many Londoners and school parties flocked there on nice spring and summer days. However, the park's main attraction was what is now remembered as 'Watkin's Folly'. When Sir Edward Watkin went to the Paris Exhibition of 1889 he fell in love with Eiffel's successful Tower, not just because of its beauty but mainly because of the handsome profits it brought (the company was indeed making £1,800

Wembley Park – the boathouse in 1900. *Grange Museum/Brent Archives*

Wembley Park – the lake in 1900. *Grange Museum/Brent Archives*

The refreshment pavilion in Wembley Park in 1900. *Grange Museum/Brent Archives*

a day and within seven months the cost of the Tower, £280,000, had been covered). He decided to have a similar but bigger one built in London. Various sites were suggested, but Watkin, who did not want to share the profits such a feature might bring with another company, decided that Wembley Park would be the best site for it. In October 1889 a new company, backed by the Metropolitan Railway Company and Sir Edward Watkin himself, was registered under the name of the Tower Company Limited. It leased from the Metropolitan Railway 124 acres of grounds in Wembley Park between the railway line and Wembley Hill for 999 years at a rental of £2,000 per annum plus a quarter of the annual profits after the lessees had received a dividend of 15 per cent.

A competition was launched in November 1889 to find a design for the Tower. Prizes of 500 guineas and 250 guineas were to be offered to the two best entries. By the end of February 1890, the closing date of the competition, 68 entries had been received, and all were exhibited in May in the Hall of the Drapers' Company. Later in the year a brochure with details and illustrations of all the entries was published by the company. Not many designs were suitable, since a lot of them were either ugly or extravagant, as for instance the two that resembled huge screws, or another that was supposed to be reminiscent of the monoliths of ancient Egypt, or

Wembley Tower – the winning design. *London Transport Museum*

A publicity handbill issued by the Metropolitan Railway in the 1890s showing the proposed tower in the pleasure grounds at Wembley Park.

the one that looked like a multi-tiered wedding cake, or even the round granite tower 2,296 feet high. All sorts of attractions were to be included, as for example hotels, temples, museums, shops and laboratories.

Finally, the first prize was awarded to Messrs Stewart, Maclaren & Dunn for their 1,200-foot-high steel structure. Mr Eiffel was asked to be engineer but declined the offer, and the appointment went to Sir Benjamin Baker (designer of the Forth Bridge) and Mr Allan Stewart. For the construction of the Tower a subsidiary company, called the International Tower Construction Company, was formed in August 1891; it had a capital of £200,000 and Watkin as Chairman and in October 1891 its name was changed to the Metropolitan Tower Construction Company. In December 1891 the new company leased the Tower Company's land for a period of 999 years at an annual rent of £2,000 starting from December 1892. The contract for the construction of the Tower was let to Messrs Heenan & Froude of Manchester, who had built the Blackpool Tower, and the steel was supplied by the Newton Heath Iron Works of Manchester.

The Tower was not built according to the original design, as it would have been too costly; four legs were to support the structure instead of eight, and the height was reduced from 1,200 feet to 1,150, but still 165 feet taller than the Eiffel Tower. The materials were brought down by means of a railway branch line built for the purpose. Originally it was to have three stages, with a Post Office and a telephone call office on the third stage and an observatory and a powerful electric light at the very top, but eventually, to lower the cost, it was reduced to two stages: one at 150 feet and the other at about 550 feet above ground level, and just a small area at the top. Each of the platforms was to be provided with dancing rooms, restaurants, theatres, Turkish baths, exhibition rooms and shops. The intention was to make of it the prettiest site in the area. Unfortunately, fate was to decide otherwise. When the recreation grounds were opened for a third season the public was finally given access to the first platform of the Tower. At first people came in great numbers to see the novelty, but soon their enthusiasm died.

During the 1896 season 100,000 people came to the park and 18,500 went up the Tower, but at the end of the season in October only 864 visitors ascended the partially built metal structure. Sadly, the second platform was never built because on one hand the company ran out of money and found it very difficult to raise more, and on the other the London clay could not cope with the weight of the Tower, and subsidence started to appear, causing the foundations to move. People soon came to look upon it as an eyesore. However, it remained open to the public until about 1902, then through lack of maintenance it started to deteriorate and became unsafe to use. In 1904 it was proposed to dismantle the Tower, but nothing happened until March 1906, when the derelict branch line was put into use again to remove the materials.

When the platform and the lifts were removed, it was the turn of the legs, which were blown up with a special explosive called roburite; the last leg was removed on 9 September 1907. The branch line was removed in 1909, and the concrete foundations in 1922, to allow the building of Wembley's famous Stadium (as part of the 1924/25 British Empire Exhibition), which turned out to be more successful than the Tower, since it brought international fame to Wembley, at least as far as the world of sport is concerned.

In the meantime, the Metropolitan Tower Construction Company went into voluntary liquidation in 1899 and its lease was returned to the Tower Company, which changed its name to the Wembley Park Estate in 1906, since beside maintaining the park it was now more interested in estate development – an interest that the Tower Company already had when a few years earlier it advertised plots for sale in Wembley Park Drive. However, the electrification of the Metropolitan Railway line in 1905 gave a boost to the idea of housing development, and the Wembley Park Estate Company, with the financial help of the Metropolitan Railway Company, started to develop the land it owned and, through contractors, to build houses in Oakington Avenue, Wembley Park Drive, The Avenue (later renamed Raglan Gardens and now known as Empire Way), Magpie Avenue (later renamed Beechcroft Gardens), Station Road, Wembley Hill Road and Forty Lane. Although the company did not build the houses that went for sale on its estate, it always made sure that they were of good class, as the following report shows:

'In order to ensure the erection of good class properties on the estate, the company have decided to insist on houses being erected at a minimum of £50 per annum rent, whilst the cost of building of a single house must not be less than £600, exclusive of any out-buildings, stables, etc, and in the case of semi-detached residences the lowest limit is fixed at £1,100 for the pair, so that investors can with confidence assume that nothing will be allowed on the ground at all likely to disfigure it or to interfere with the select nature of the existing houses. Further, the company very wisely require the designs and plans of all houses to be submitted to them for approval before building is commenced. Neat lawns and spacious gardens are features of the houses already erected, and it is intended that this should be so throughout the estate.'[56]

And according to the same paper the estate was to become 'one of the most sought after residential sites anywhere west of the City' and contribute to make of Wembley Park 'one of the most pleasant and important garden suburbs to be found anywhere round Town.' In spite of its popularity, all was not going well for the company, since all the profit it was making was spent on paying off the interest on its mortgage, preventing it from paying any dividends to its shareholders. The only company that was making any profit from the whole business was of course the Metropolitan Railway Company, which was not only cashing in on the interest on the capital it had lent the estate company, but was also drawing some nice profit

Wembley Tower as it stood before being demolished in 1906-7. *Grange Museum/Brent Archives*

	Ordinary bookings	Season tickets	Goods and parcels	Totals
1906	£2,930	£258	£619	£3,807
1914	£4,106	£924	£1,120	£6,150
Increase	£1,176	£666	£501	£2,343

from an increase of traffic in the area, as the above figures show [57]:

Since it was then in the interest of the railway company to encourage estate development, in 1915 it was decided amongst other things 'for a period of seven years to make it an allowance each year equal to 25 per cent on the increase in the receipts from traffic to and from Wembley Park station over and above the receipts for the year 1906 up to a maximum of £700 a year.'[58]

However, when the Metropolitan Railway Country Estates Ltd started to become involved in estate development in the same area from 1919 onwards, the railway company became less keen on renewing its arrangements with the Wembley Park Estate Company. All it agreed to grant the latter at the end of 1919 was a maximum allowance of £700 per annum for a further period of five years. The estate company also had problems with the park itself, the popularity of which gradually declined since fewer entertainers were willing to go so far out of London to give a performance. The old Variety Hall inside the park was leased to the Walturdraw Company as a film studio, but unfortunately it was badly damaged by a fire in 1911. In 1912 the park was let to a golf course company at a rental of £600 per annum, and an 18-hole course was opened. The original grandstands and the bandstand were pulled down, while the main pavilion was kept as a clubhouse and the refreshment rooms as a teahouse; but what the estate company really wanted was to sell the park. Though it claimed to have had many viewers and offers, the sale did not materialise because, according to the company, of last-minute disagreements. And it was only in 1922, when the site was chosen for the British Empire Exhibition, that the company was finally able to sell the park. However, things did not improve for the company, and on 24 December 1930 it was decided that it would be wound up voluntarily.

The liquidation was announced in the London Gazette of 1 May 1931, and the last meeting took place on 2 June. As Wembley Park was changing, so were Wembley and all the neighbouring hamlets (Alperton, Preston, Uxendon, Sudbury and Tokyngton), which gradually started to expand at the end of the 19th century, as the table below shows.

As can be seen, the increase between 1871 and 1896 was 3,196, and that between 1896 and 1921 12,551. To illustrate this new expansion, we can name the development of the Copland Estate, then named the Harrowdene Estate, by the Conservative Land Company, which started after the death of General Copland-Crawford in 1895. Then, between 1899 and 1901, the development of the Wembley Hill Estate (situated between Park Lane, Wembley Hill Road and the High Road) also commenced. In his 1902 report, the Wembley Medical Officer made the following observation: 'I have thought that the land between Wembley, Stanmore, Kingsbury and Willesden, including the Kenton District and all Wembley Park, would be a suitable and typical area for 'a garden city'. Even now it would not be too late to consider the matter, if only the landowners had not an exaggerated notion of the value of their property.' And in his 1903 report, after quoting an estimated population of 5,000, he added that 'in the near future we may certainly expect a large increase to this number with the continued building operations, the rapid development of the railway communication with the Metropolis and especially in view of the fact that so much of our district is still undeveloped.' Of

Expansion of Wembley and neighbouring hamlets [59]

Year	Population	Increase	Acreage	Density	No of in-habited houses	No of persons per house	Increase in houses
1871	444						
1896	3,640	3,196	4,282	0.85			
1901	4,519	879	4,282	1.05	833	5.43	
1906	6,000	1,481	4,564	1.31	1,418	4.23	585
1911	10,696	4,696	4,564	2.34	2,434	4.39	1,016
1916	14,611	3,915	4,564	3.20	3,486	4.19	1,052
1921	16,191	1,580	4,564	3.52	3,800	4.26	314

Wembley Hill station, opened by the Great Central Railway in 1906. *Grange Museum/Brent Archives*

course he was right, and if we refer back to the figures quoted earlier we can see that the biggest increase comes around 1905, which corresponds to a period of great railway improvements.

On 28 June 1903 the Metropolitan District Railway extended its electric line to South Harrow with intermediate stations at Alperton (then called Perivale-Alperton), Sudbury Town and Sudbury Hill. In January 1905 the Metropolitan Railway electrified its line between Baker Street and Uxbridge, and in 1906 the Great Central Railway opened its line between Marylebone and South Harrow to passenger traffic, with intermediate stations at Wembley Hill and Sudbury & Harrow Road. From 1908 onwards an electric tramway service became available along Wembley Hill Road, and in August 1910 it was extended along the Harrow Road and the Mall to Sudbury. There was also a bus service, which allowed Londoners to discover the beautiful countryside.

1906 also saw the development of the southern part of the High Street and the development of a 'garden city' in Sudbury. In 1909 it was the turn of the Wembley House Estate (facing the Wembley Hill Estate), and in 1910 that of the Wembley Dairy Farm Estate. During the period 1896-1910 many houses were also built around Sudbury & Wembley station, the future Wembley Central (as for instance in Thurlow Gardens, Turton Road, Copland Road, Station Grove, Chaplin Road, St Anne's Road, Ranelagh Road, Montrose Crescent, the Hampfields Estate, the Curtis Estate, Lancelot Road, etc), and after 1910 it continued in Chatsworth Avenue, Waverley Avenue, Flamsted Avenue. Etc. Part of the Wembley Park Estate, as we have already seen, was also developed by the Wembley Park Estate Company.

In 1913 Sir Audley Dallas Neeld, the owner of the Tokyngton Estate, started to develop his 220 acres of land on garden city lines; the estate was then named Wembley Hill Garden Estate and, when it was formally opened on 20 June 1914, 20 houses were already under construction. In 1920 the Metropolitan Railway Country Estates Company started to develop the Chalk Hill Estate, which has already been mentioned in an earlier chapter. Shops started to appear in the High Street near Sudbury & Wembley station in 1882, and on the Harrow Road

Adverts for houses built by Musgrove in Flamsted Avenue in 1911.

FLAMSTED AVENUE,
Harrow Road, Wembley.

WELL-FINISHED SEMI-DETACHED VILLAS.

Containing on Ground Floor :

Lounge Hall with stove, tiled floor and ornamental screen to Staircase.
Dining Room with large bay window, polished oak mantel and overmantel, good modern stove, panelled ceiling, picture and chair rails.
Drawing Room : ornamental mantel and overmantel, good modern stove with hearth and tiles of dainty design, and casement doors leading to tiled floor and glass covered verandah.
Kitchen fitted with good **gas and coal kitchener**, tiled hearth and jambs, glass enclosed dresser with good drawers.
Scullery with good white glazed butler's sink, tiled walls and floor, plate rack and draining board, good cupboards & shelves.

Upstairs :
Three or Four Good Bedrooms,

Bathroom with tiled walls, white glazed bath and lavatory basin, with hot and cold supplies, and hot linen cupboard, 2 w.c's.

Good Garden, back and front, well laid out.

Lease 99 years
Ground Rent £7.

Prices from
£425 to £510

INTERIOR OF HALL OF HOUSES FROM £425

Adverts for houses built by Musgrove in Flamsted Avenue in 1911.

at Wembley Green in 1911. In his 1910 report, the Wembley Medical Officer of Health pointed out that 'the greater number of the inhabitants' worked 'in London' and that 'the labouring class' formed 'a smaller proportion of the population in Wembley'. His 1912 report contained the following statement: 'The unusual railway facilities for reaching the Metropolis – embracing ten stations on four separate lines – the tramways, together with the knowledge of the undoubted salubrity of the place, make it evident to all that Wembley may very easily become a large residential suburb for the middle class in a few years.' Indeed, by 1920 the area between the Grand Union Canal at Alperton and Wembley Hill via Ealing Road and Wembley High Road and between Wembley for Sudbury station and Wembley Hill station had become a continuous built-up area. But the biggest expansion of all was yet to come, and it could be said that it was triggered by the creation of two brand-new attractions that were to make Wembley famous: the building of Wembley Stadium and the opening at Wembley of the British Empire Exhibition.

Work on Wembley Stadium started in 1922, on the hill where half a tower had once stood, and 250,000 tons of clay were excavated to make room for the bowl of the arena. Then 1,500 tons of steel, 25,000 tons of concrete and half a million rivets were used to build the stands, designed to accommodate 125,000 spectators. The work was completed in the record time of 300 working days, and gave work to many unemployed people. When completed, the stadium measured 900 feet by 650 feet, and the twin towers at the front were 126 feet high. The rounded oblong grass centre measured 492 feet by 260 feet and was surrounded by a cinder running track. Other amenities were also provided: accommodation for 1,000 competitors, a boardroom, a box office, a gymnasium, a recreation room, a banqueting hall with seating capacity for several thousand people, buffets, cloakrooms, office accommodation, a press gallery, an observation gallery, two running tracks, a quarter-mile round track and a 220-yard straight running track (the only one in Europe at the time), while 3½ acres at the centre were laid out for football. The stadium's strength was tested first by a battalion of soldiers marching in the stands for an hour, then by the incredible number of spectators who turned up for the first football Cup Final in 1923.

However, the greatest attraction of all, since it brought a lot of people to Wembley, was of course the British Empire Exhibition of 1924/25, held in the grounds of Wembley Park. The idea for the exhibition was not new; already in the 1890s and 1900s some politicians thought that it would be to Great Britain's advantage to trade more with the countries of the Empire by importing more goods from the colonies and by exporting to them British-manufactured goods. Great Britain could thus compete more efficiently with countries like the United States and Germany. Thus, in 1902, the idea of an Empire Exhibition, which would encourage such a policy and at the same time commemorate the Prince of Wales's recent tour in the colonies, was put forward by the British Empire League. Unfortunately, an outbreak of war in the Far East and the victory at the elections of 1906 by the Labour and Liberal candidates, who were opposed to that policy, put a stop to the project. However, it was revived in 1910 by Sir Pieter Stuart Barn and Lord Strathcona, and by 1913 the project had again many supporters. Unfortunately, it was once more frustrated, this time by the outbreak of the First World War. It was only after the Armistice that the suggestion was renewed at a luncheon of the British Empire Club on 20 May 1919, and two organisations, the British Dominion Exhibition Limited and the London Great Exhibition, started to show some interest in the project. Finally, they amalgamated on 3 June 1920 to form a registered company that, after several amendments, was finally called The British Empire Exhibition (1924) Incorporated, and was promised Government support.

Wembley was chosen because it offered a lot of open space and natural beauty, and though it might have seemed remote from the heart of London to those who were opposed to the choice, it was not really any less accessible than any other exhibition site in or near the capital, since the transport facilities were so good. Wembley could indeed be reached from about 126 stations in central London in an average time varying from between 10 and 20 minutes. From Baker Street to Wembley Park on the Metropolitan Railway, or from Marylebone to Wembley Hill on the LNER, successor to the Great Central Railway, the journey lasted 10 minutes. Wembley was also served by the LMS, successor to the London & North Western Railway, and the Bakerloo tube, with stations at Wembley and Stonebridge Park, and by the Metropolitan District Railway with stations at Alperton and Sudbury Town. Wembley was also in tramway communication with Finchley and Hampstead in the north, and Paddington and Willesden, Hammersmith, Putney, Acton and Ealing in the west. The trams ran past the south entrance of the Exhibition. New bus routes were also opened, and some roads were widened, such as Forty Lane, which was converted from a 12-foot carriageway to a 60-foot thoroughfare. New roads were laid out, such as the North Circular, to accommodate motor traffic.

Construction began in January 1922, giving work to some 2,000 men, and the Exhibition was opened officially on 23 April 1924 by His Majesty King George V. The first season was a great success, attracting people from all over the world. Within the grounds of this huge city of concrete, one could in a single day make a cheap journey round the world, enjoy oneself and at the same time learn more about the geography and the conditions of life of the various countries visited than one ever could in one solid year of study, for indeed pleasure, education and business could all be found there. And all those who went to the Exhibition probably remember the song 'Let's Go To Wembley'!

'Can't you hear old London calling,
Telling you today,
Of the finest place on earth
Beats ev'ry thing they say.
Listen to this good advice
When clouds seem very dark,
Just pack your troubles in a bag and come to Wembley Park.

Let's go to the Exhibition,
Exhibition 1924;
That's the place to be,
Oh! It's better than the sea.
So all take a holiday and go to Wembley;
Let's go to the Exhibition
For ev'ry one should know
That's the finest place to go,
Is the Exhibition 1924
Let's go.

You can go by Tram or Motor,
Or by Bus or Train,
But don't forget when you get there,
You must come home again;
There are wondrous sights to see,
My! Ev'rything so grand
Makes you think you've left this earth, and gone to Fairyland.'[60]

The British Empire Exhibition, Wembley, 1924-5.

Ariel View of GREAT LAKE AUSTRALIA & STADIUM

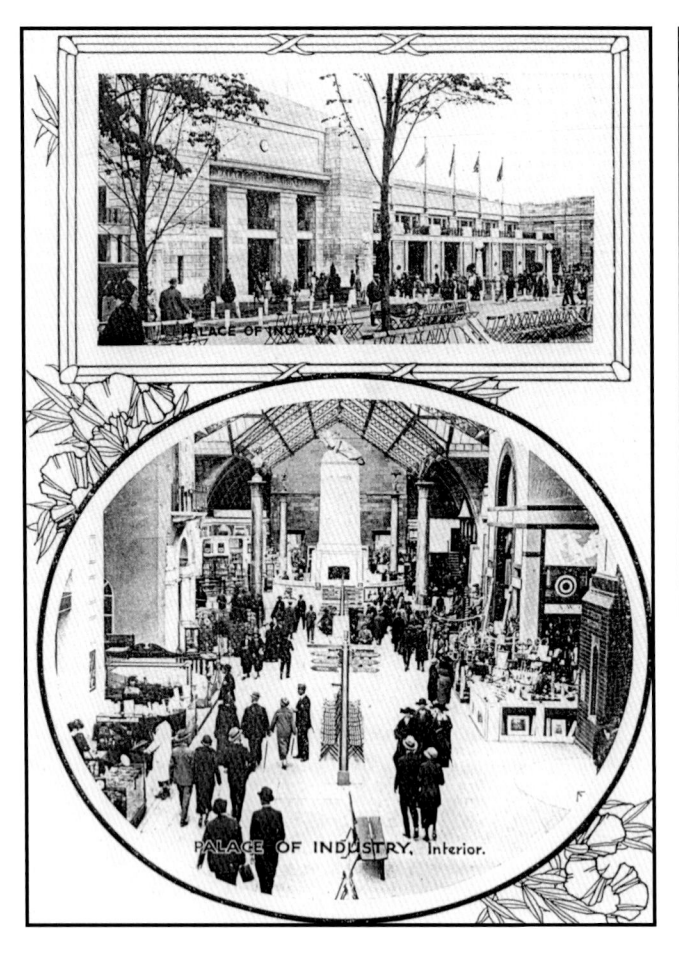

The British Empire Exhibition, Wembley, 1924-5.

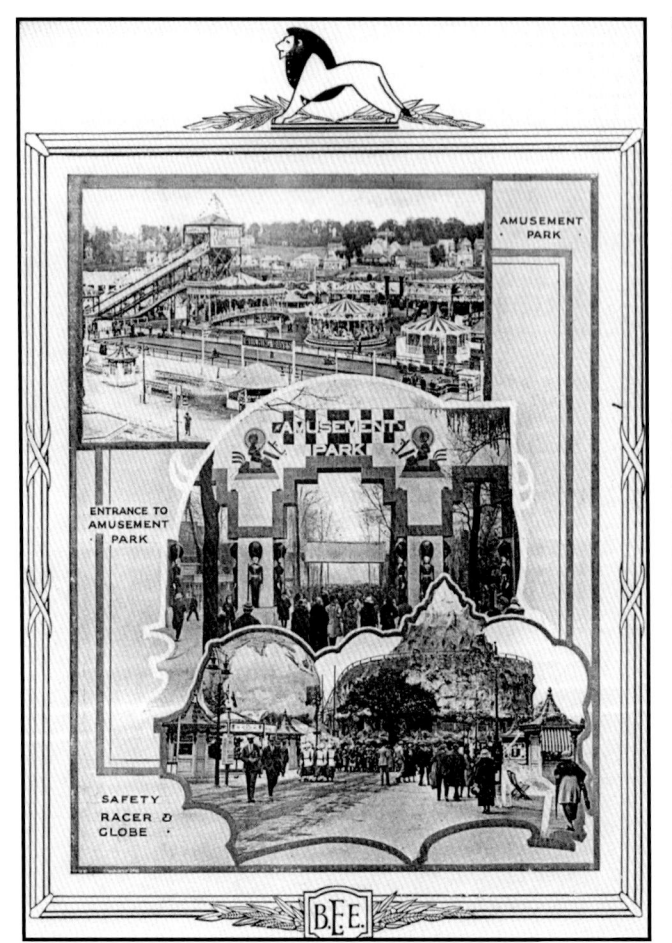

The Exhibition, though very successful during its first season, closed after the second season in 1925, as it was by then running at a loss. The site was then sold for £300,000 to Jimmy White, and most of the buildings were dismantled or moved. The only feature that remained and continued to give Wembley its international reputation was the Stadium, which Arthur Elvin (who started up in business as an assistant in one of the Exhibition cafes in 1924, and who then raised enough money to run eight cafes in 1925) bought from Jimmy White for a quarter of the value it cost to build and equip. At the time it was in a poor financial state, and no profits had been made for the previous few years, but Elvin introduced greyhound racing and speedway racing, thus gradually bringing back the crowds to Wembley Stadium.

Although 'Fairyland' with its exotic attractions had disappeared forever, Metro-land with its rustic charms was still there, and the people who came and enjoyed the pleasures of 'Fairyland' could not help but be seduced by the delights of Metro-land, and many were those who decided to make that rural arcadia their home, as the table below shows.

It can be seen how the population and the number of houses grew steadily throughout the 1920s and 1930s. The small increase in the number of houses in 1930 was a direct consequence of the crisis that struck in 1929. The tremendous increase in 1934 was not only due to the fact that Kingsbury was once more united with Wembley, but it also corresponded to the time when building costs reached their lowest level, and when cheap money became available. It is also interesting to note from the Medical Officer of Health's reports that most of the houses were built by private enterprise and were sold rather than let. In his 1923 report he states: 'Building has taken place in all parts of the district by private builders… The houses recently built in the district, especially at Wembley Park, are as important as they are imposing, and, as a good residential estate, give a style and character to the whole of that part of the district.' And in the 1925 report he added, 'Practically the whole of the houses in Wembley are modern in character and of high standard, and are kept in good condition. Since the war few houses have been erected by private enterprise which can in any way be regarded as suitable or intended for the housing of what are known as the working class. The only real attempt

Expansion of Wembley between 1921 and 1940 [61]

Year	Population	Increase of population	Acreage	Density	No of inhabited houses	Increase in inhabited houses	No of persons per house
1921	16,191	584	4,564	3.52	3.797		4.26
1922	16,450	259	4,564	3.60	4,052	255	4.06
1923	16,910	460	4,564	3.70	4,341	289	3.90
1924	18,420	1,510	4,564	4.03	5,063	722	3.63
1925	21,318	2,958	4,564	4.68	5,977	914	3.57
1926	25,320	3,942	4,564	5.54	6,882	905	3.68
1927	28,300	2,980	4,564	6.20	7,933	1,051	3.56
1928	32,710	4,410	4,564	7.16	8,741	808	3.74
1929	35,530	2,820	4,565	7.78	9,944	1,203	3.57
1930	40,094	4,564	4,564	8.78	11,231	287	3.57
1931	48,546	8.452	4,564	10.63	13,000	1,769	3.73
1932	53,420	4,874	4,564	11.70	14,000	1,000	3.81
1933	58,850	5,430	4,564	12.89	16,000	2,000	3.68
1934	92,160	33,310	6,299	14.83	26,000	10,000	3.54
1935	105,000	12,840	6,300	16.66	28,503	2,503	3.68
1936	107,550	12,840	6,300	17.07	29,307	804	3.67
1937	114,700	7,150	6,300	18.20	29,480	173	3.89
1938	118,800	4,100	6,300	18.85	29,900	420	3.97
1939	121,600	2,800	6,300	19.30	33,857	3,957	3.59
1940	117,380	9,200	6,300	18.63	33,607	-350	3.49

to meet the great demand which exists for houses of this character has been made by the Council.' This statement is then followed by these figures:

number of dwelling houses of all classes   5,977
number of new working class houses erected   27
number of working class houses   857

And if we refer back to the table, we can see that the increase in the number of houses for that year was 914.

In his 1930 report the Medical Officer of Health wrote:

'From a special count made during mid-summer 1930, it was ascertained that there were 11,231 occupied dwelling houses in the district, of these approximately 3,627 are terrace house type and there are some 1182 houses of the working class type … of these approximately 989 have been built since 1905. Of the remainder, some are dwelling accommodation over business premises, but the majority are of the detached and semi-detached villa type, having three to five bedrooms.'

Thus, as he foresaw in 1912, Wembley did gradually develop into 'a large residential suburb for the middle class'. And the following passage from the Wembley Official Guide of 1928 gives us a brief account of this change:

'Until 1924 when the British Empire Exhibition first opened, Wembley, although it had commenced some years previously to grow and become one of the most important suburbs of London, was not very well known, but the coming of the exhibition brought Wembley into prominence and people from all over the world came to know what was once a little insignificant village as a most progressive suburb. It forms part of what is known as "The Beautiful North West". It still retains many of its rural characteristics, but it is gradually changing its aspect as the estate developers cover fields with roads, houses and shops, and the ever increasing volume of motor traffic causes roads to be widened, and trees to be cut down, beautiful winding country lanes giving place to wide straight arterial roads, and rows of houses and shops shutting out from view the beautiful country beyond. Only a few years ago, many thousands of people during the spring and summer months alighted from the trains at Wembley Hill and Sudbury, and rambled along the lanes and fieldpaths, and enjoyed their picnics in the woods and fields, but now thousands of people come to Wembley because they have heard that many charmingly built houses and bungalows are been built on beautifully laid out estates, and that they can buy these houses and live in pleasant and quiet surroundings, and yet within easy reach of London. Anyone desiring to find a place in which to settle down, whether old or young, could not choose a better spot than Wembley. It is being developed on

Park Lane in 1910. *Grange Museum/Brent Archives*

Park Lane in 1926. *Grange Museum/Brent Archives*

good town planning lines, the houses are up-to-date in every respect, and are surrounded with ample air space. Estates are being laid out in a picturesque fashion; provision is made for those possessing their own cars and there is every facility for shopping and all kind of recreation. The Wembley Council are fully alive to their responsibilities, and an active interest in local affairs is taken by many residents who wish to see Wembley develop into a residential town where peace and quietness and good health may always be enjoyed.'[62]

The Medical Officer of Health was also proud to point out in his report of 1930 'that the development of the district has not been on 'ribbon lines' but that compact estates have developed.' And many estates did indeed develop. Among the numerous estate developers of the time one can mention: Callow & Wright, involved in the developing of the Wembley Hill Garden Estate; Haymills Ltd, which built in Wembley Park and Preston Road; Comben & Wakeling, which built houses on the St John Estate, in Clayton Avenue, Waverley Avenue, on the Manor Estate, on the Park Lane Estate, on the St. Augustine Estate, on the Lindsay Park Estate, in Kenton and also in Sudbury; and there were also J. Laing & Son Ltd and Richard Costain & Sons Ltd in Sudbury, and

Wembley Hill Garden Suburb in 1935. *Grange Museum/Brent Archives*

Above: Wembley Park Drive before suburban development. *Grange Museum/Brent Archives*

Opposite top: High Road Wembley in 1910. *Grange Museum/Brent Archives*

Opposite bottom: High Road Wembley in 1937. *Grange Museum/Brent Archives*

Below: The building of North Wembley Estate (Queenscourt) 1920-30. *Grange Museum/Brent Archives*

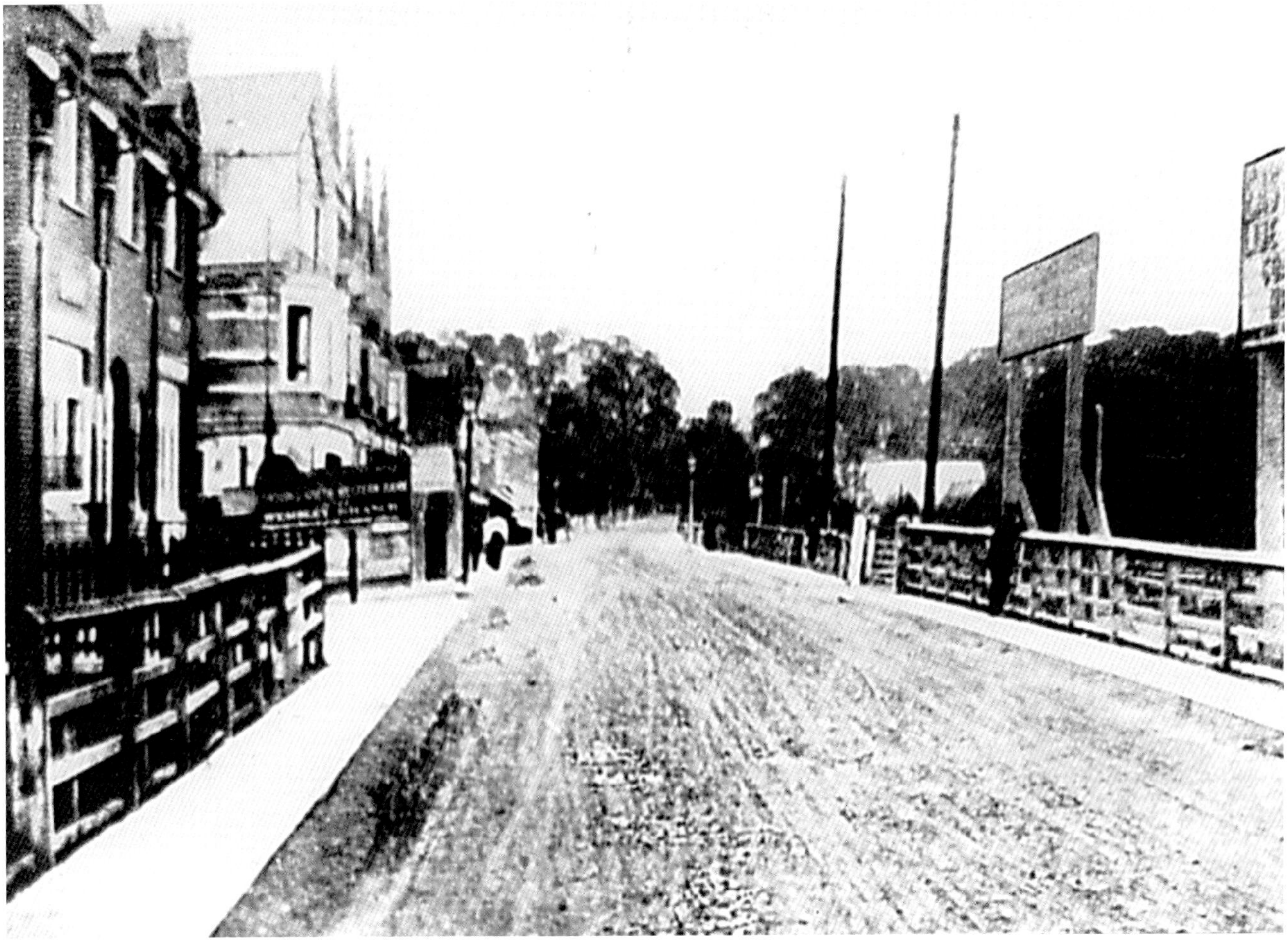

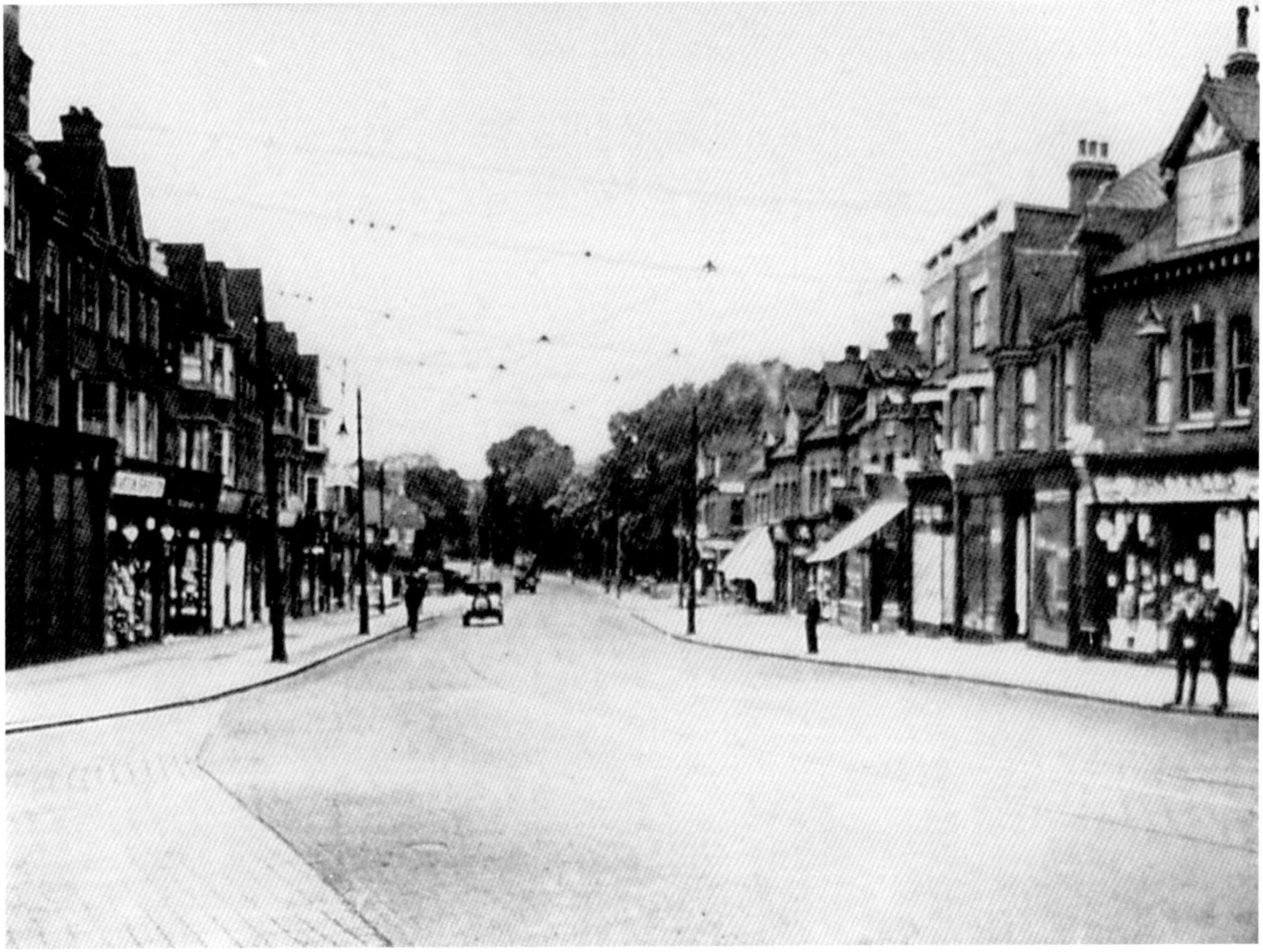

Wimpey in the Preston Road area and south-east of Wembley Hill station.

As Wembley started to grow, industries other than building industries started to develop. The first development was during the First World War when factories in connection with the manufacture of war materials began to open, but the transport facilities were not good enough then for them to expand. The second stage of Wembley's industrial development came after the British Empire Exhibition. It seemed then only fitting that a site chosen to house an exhibition to promote trade should become afterwards a centre of trade. The conditions became then more favourable, not only because a large area became available for development but also because of the great improvement in transport facilities. Since one could not expect to find all the labour force in Wembley itself, good transport services were essential, so that workers could come from the neighbouring towns such as Harrow, Kilburn, Neasden and Willesden. Some of the buildings used for the exhibition were kept and used for industrial purposes, as for instance the huge Palace of Engineering. The latter was in fact one of the few exhibition buildings built to be permanent, and one of its advantages was the system of railway lines which ran through it. Other industrial estates developed in Kingsbury, North Wembley and Alperton, but they were all under the control of the town planning schemes, so as not to spoil the residential character of the town.

In 1925 the Medical Officer of Health quotes as 'the largest employers of labour within the district Fiat Motors Ltd, Aster Engineering Co, General Electric Co, Unic Motorworks and Glacier Metal Co.' In his 1938 report he writes:

'The industries in Wembley may be grouped as follows: – engineering processes, machinery making and repairing – electrical and radio machinery – motor car engineering – foundries, metal works, construction and building materials – food manufacturers, milk treatment – ice factories – clothing factories – furniture, upholstery, glass, cork making, printing – photography and such – laundry and such – paper goods – amusements and sports equipment – rubber works – chemical gas processes.'

The difference between the two reports shows us the extent of the industrial development that took place in Wembley after the British Empire Exhibition. To all these industries one must also add the increasing number of shops and offices, which also provided work to quite a number of local people.

Amusements and entertainments offering the possibility of enjoying a pleasant social life were also provided. There were four cinemas in Wembley itself: the Wembley Hall Cinema in the Harrow Road, which opened in 1915 as the Wembley Hall Cinematograph Theatre and which became the Wembley Odeon after the Second World War;

Aerial view of Wembley showing the General Electric Company, 1930.

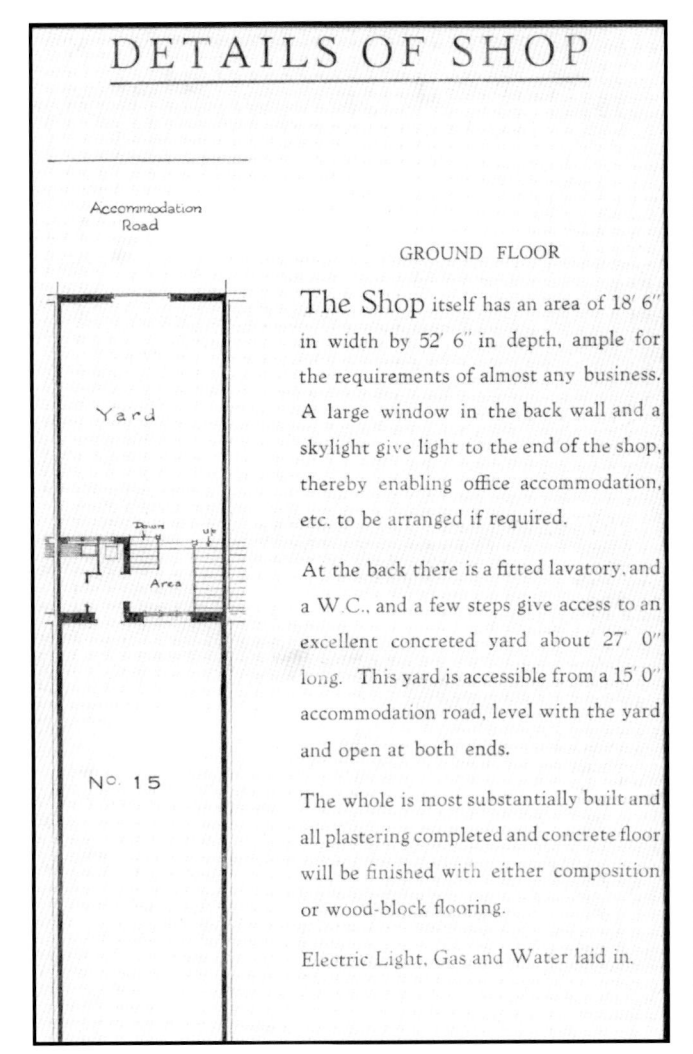

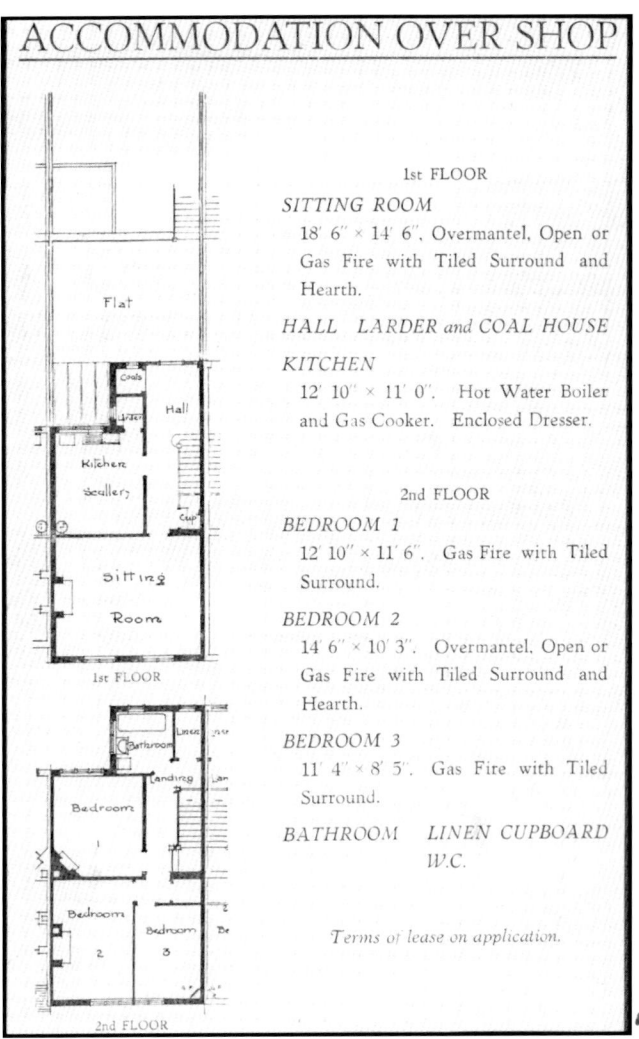

Particulars of shops and their accommodation to be let on lease at Grand Parade, Forty Avenue, Wembley.

the Elite Cinema in Empire Way, which opened in 1928 and was renamed the Capitol in 1933; the Majestic Odeon in the High Street, which opened in 1929; and the ABC Regal Cinema, which opened in Ealing Road in 1937. One could also go dancing either at the Elite Palais de Dance situated next to the Elite cinema or to one of the ballrooms next to the Majestic Odeon cinema, or take part in one of the many dancing evenings organised by various social clubs. Among the many clubs available were, for those who liked drama and music, the Choral Society (founded in 1892), the Wembley Dramatic Society (1923), and the Operatic Society (1937). for the children there were Scout and Guide organisations; for the gentlemen there was the Fairview Club (founded in 1919); and for those who enjoyed sports or games there were the Wembley Cricket Club (founded in 1900), the Wembley Rugby Football Club (1925), and the Wembley Rotary Club (1930).

As far as sport was concerned, Wembley was well provided. There were many tennis courts, golf courses and athletics grounds available in Wembley itself or in its immediate area. A municipal open-air swimming pool was opened in 1935 on the Vale Farm Estate at Sudbury. Moreover, many events were staged at the Stadium and at the Empire Pool. The Stadium had mainly become a national centre for football, but one could also watch there speedway racing and greyhound racing. The Empire Pool was opened in 1934, designed as a swimming pool that could be converted, at any time, into an ice rink or could be floored over so as to stage other events such as boxing, tennis, athletics, basketball and table tennis.

One could also attend the frequent concerts, dances and whist drives given at the St John's Hall, the Legion Hall or the Express Dairy Company Hall.

Attractive open spaces were also preserved by the Council. After the loss of Wembley Park, the Council acquired in 1914 the King Edward VII Park, a 26-acre site situated in Park Lane that was laid out as an open space and amusement centre; it was provided with a bandstand, two pavilions, a playground for children, nine tennis courts (six more were added in 1925), large bowling and putting greens, and several acres of ground especially laid out for cricket, football and hockey. Then under the town planning scheme, Wembley Council bought in 1921 and 1926 One Tree Hill, an open space of 15 acres in Alperton; in 1927 a further 23½ acres of farmland

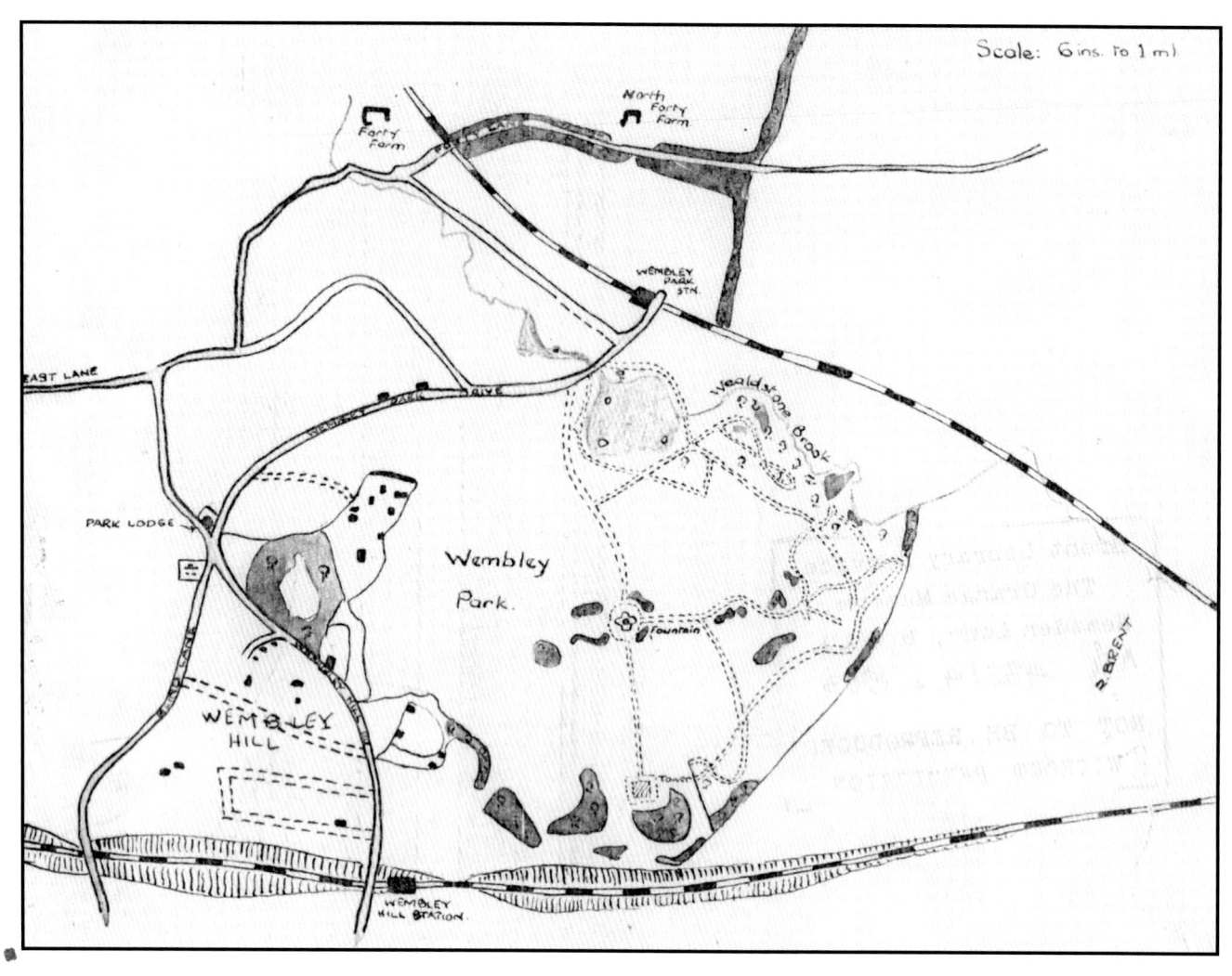

Wembley Park 1903. *Grange Museum/Brent Archives*

was acquired in Alperton Lane and became Alperton Sports Ground.

There was also a small recreational open space at Sudbury, a park at the top of Barn Hill, and finally the 200 acres of Fryent Way Regional Space, which was acquired in 1937. Educational facilities were not forgotten since a fair number of schools (state and private) gradually started to appear as the years went by and the population increased. Quite a few churches were also built. Thus Wembley provided the suburban dweller with everything he needed, and the Medical Officer of Health was right when he wrote in his report of 1927: '…the majority of inhabitants live in Wembley because of its well-known salubrity as a district – especially healthy for children with its open country, its parks and recreation grounds; for the extraordinary railway, tramway, omnibus and other facilities for approaching the great City; and for the friendly social amenities permeating the whole district…'

So Wembley, a little hamlet lost in the greenery of the Parish of Harrow until the end of the 19th century, had been turned into a big suburban town during the first half of the 20th. The process started in 1894 when it was separated from Harrow in order to form, with the hamlets of Sudbury, Alperton, South Kenton and the parish of Kingsbury, the Wembley Urban District. Unfortunately, the union with Kingsbury turned out to be unsuccessful, and in 1900 Kingsbury was excluded from the Urban District of Wembley and became a separate Urban District. In 1927 Wembley was divided into six wards: Alperton, Sudbury, Kenton, Wembley Central, Wembley Hill and Wembley Park. In 1934 Wembley and Kingsbury were once more reunited to create one of the largest Urban Districts in the country. And finally, a few years before the Second World War, to crown Wembley's astonishing record of urban development, Wembley Urban District was incorporated as Wembley Municipal Borough by virtue of a Royal Charter presented on 8 July 1937 by the Lord Mayor of London. This was a great honour for Wembley, and the event was celebrated with great pageantry. The new Municipal Borough was then divided into 12 wards: Wembley Central, Wembley Park, Tokyngton, Kenton, Preston, Alperton, Sudbury and Sudbury Court, together with another four formed from the Urban District of Kingsbury – Roe Green, Fryent, Chalkhill and the Hyde. Having grown so big, Wembley now needed a new town hall. The foundation stone of the building, to be situated in Forty Lane, was laid in 1937, and the new town hall, which contained offices, a public hall and a library, was opened in 1939.

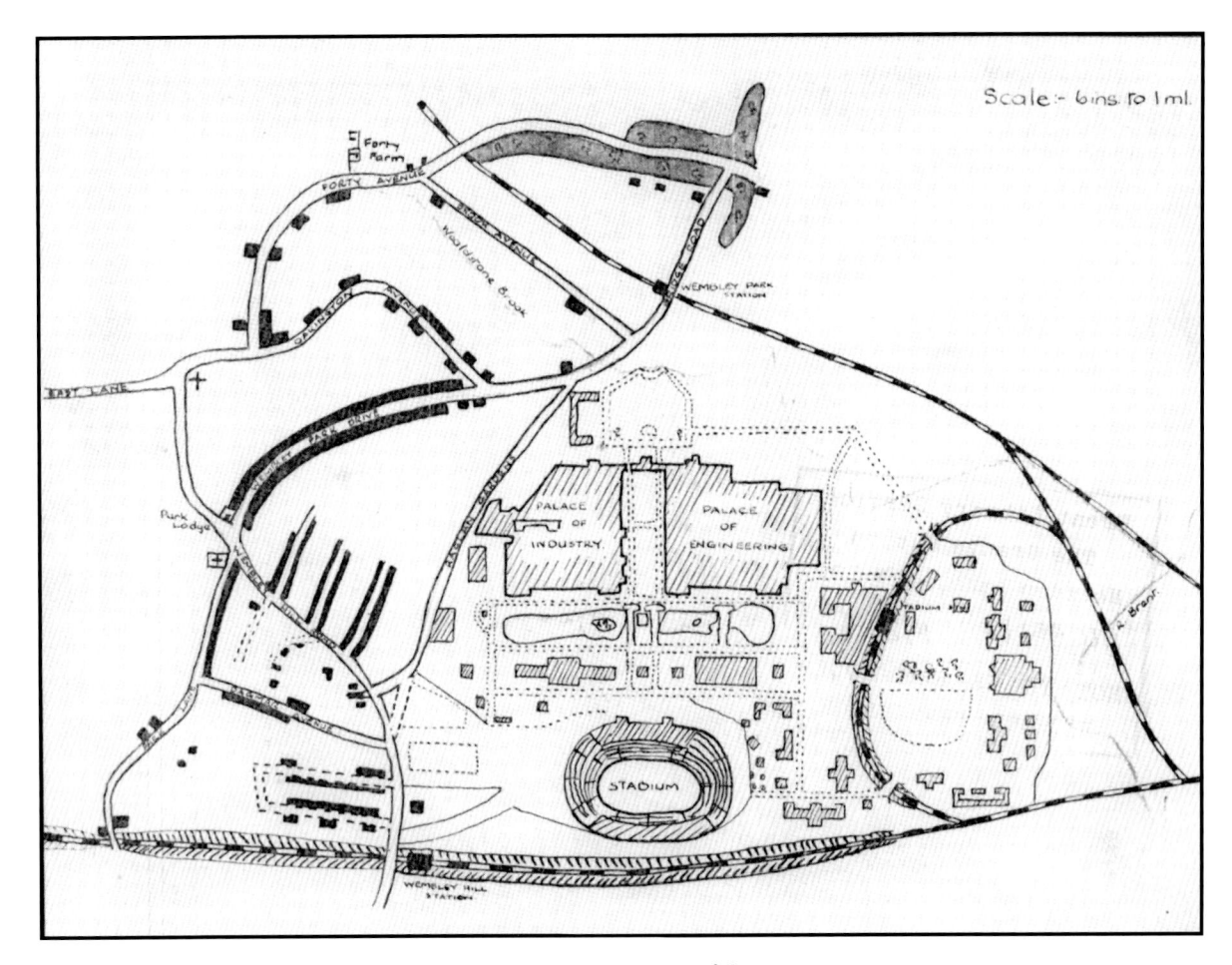

Wembley Park 1924-25. *Grange Museum/Brent Archives*

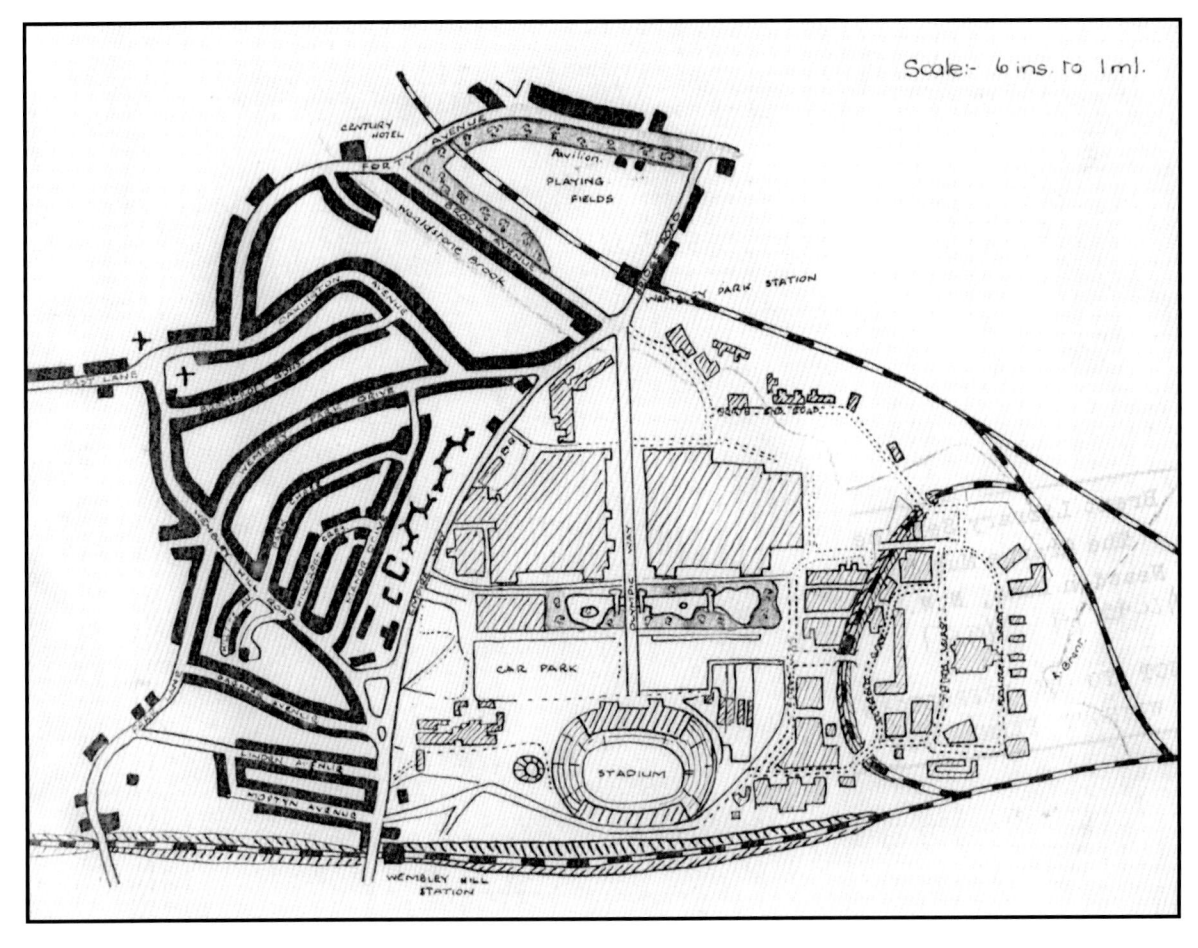

Wembley Park 1951. *Grange Museum/Brent Archives*

Wembley 1880 – photo of a 25-inch Ordnance Survey Map

Wembley 1912 – photo of a 25-inch Ordnance Survey Map

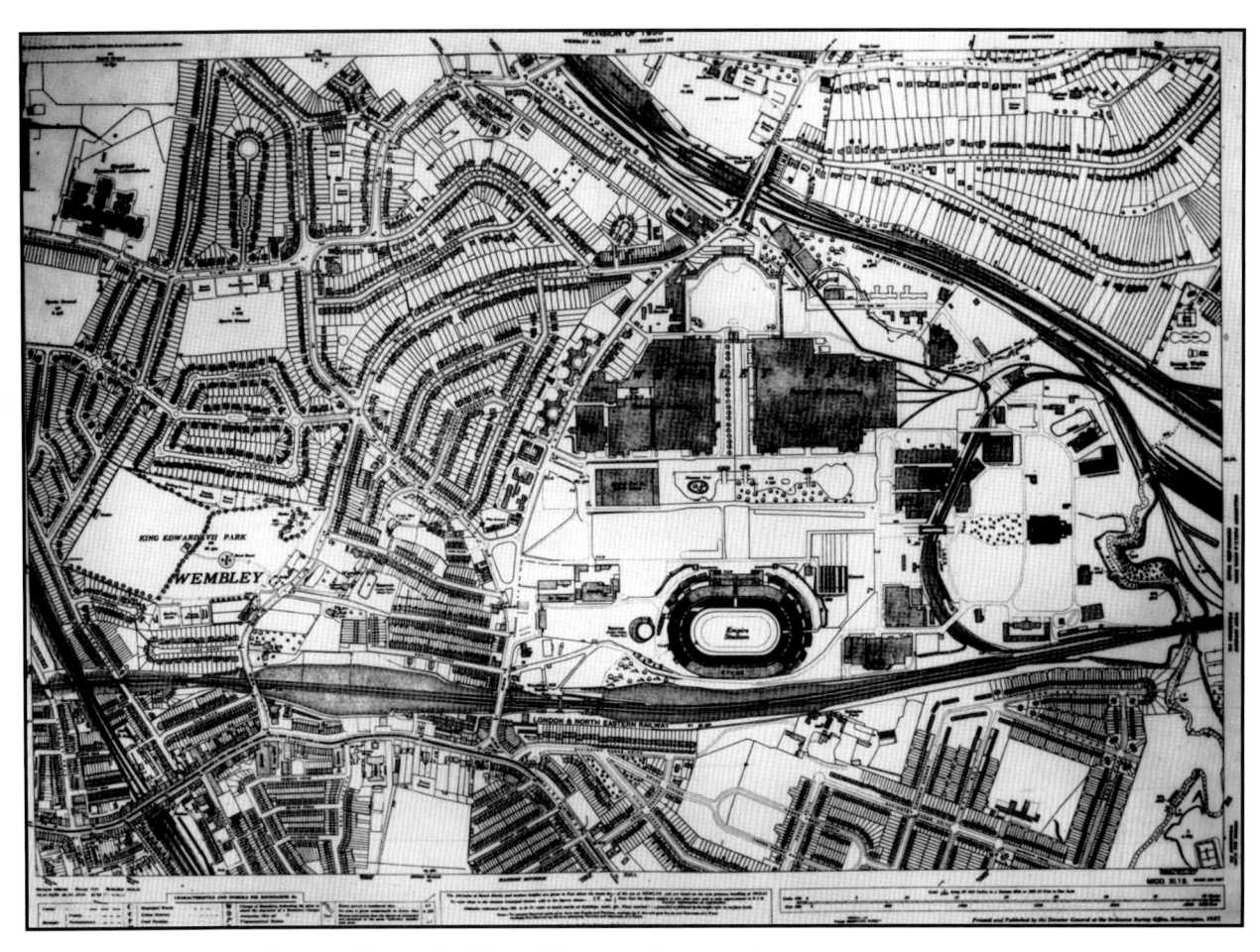

Wembley 1935 – photo of a 25-inch Ordnance Survey Map

Aerial view of Wembley Park in 1947. *Grange Museum/Brent Archives*

Conclusion

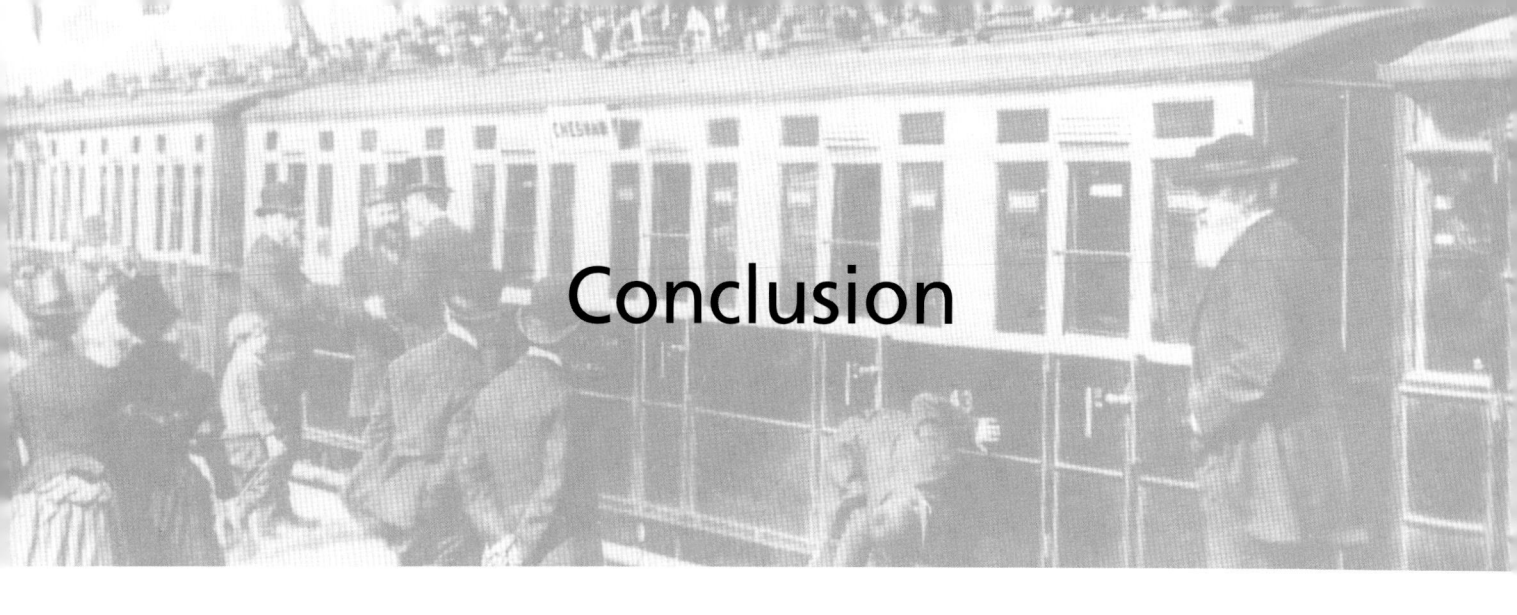

All the other towns along the Metropolitan Railway line followed the same sort of pattern of development as Wembley. The small hamlets or country villages were transformed within less than half a century into big suburban towns. This development was of course beneficial to the railway companies, which were able to increase their revenues, and to the people looking for a cosy home at the time, but to the natural environment it was unfortunately harmful. The following observation made by the Medical Officer of Health on the development of Wembley in his report of 1933 is quite relevant:

'In the course of the last two or three years important extensions of the Underground Railways have taken place, linking some of the previously less accessible parts of the country with central London. The builder has followed hard upon this improvement in transport facilities and is rapidly transforming the few remaining rural parts of Middlesex into urban communities. Whether the process of urbanisation will continue until the whole of Middlesex is converted into one huge town, it is impossible to say. The present tendency certainly is in that direction and so long as the demand for houses in semi-rural surroundings in proximity to London continues, so long will the builder endeavour to meet that demand.'

Unfortunately, what was in 1933 still an uncertainty for the Medical Officer of Health is now reality; 'the process of urbanisation' did continue and what had once been beautiful countryside where nightingales sang, and what was still the City man's Arcadia known as Metro-land, has been swamped by housing estates, factories, shops and office blocks. 'The whole of Middlesex' has been converted into one huge town. Nowadays, not many people remember the rustic charms of Wembley or of Metro-land, and soon even fewer will, since the builders are still busy pulling down or destroying what is left of the past to make room for the future – but what future?

Let us again take Wembley as an example. In the 1960s no more virgin countryside was left in Wembley that could be built upon, but a lot of people living in the area still needed to be housed, such as those living in the slums of Kilburn or Stonebridge, so the Council decided to buy by compulsory purchase order part of what had been a high-class residential area developed by the Metropolitan Railway Country Estates Company, thus threatening large properties standing in large gardens. And that was how 182 beautiful houses accommodating 550 people on the Chalk Hill Estate were pulled down between 1966 and 1970 to make room for a new estate made of concrete that was to provide 1,658 dwellings for more than 5,000 people. Planners were hoping to make of it a modern paradise where the spirit of community life would thrive, and they designed it so that all the tenants could mingle with one another and equipped it with all sorts of modern amenities such as central heating, double glazing, a Garchey refuse disposal system, one main television aerial, two multi-storey car parks, playgrounds and a paddling pool for the children, a medical centre, schools and shops. Unfortunately, this planner's paradise very soon after its completion became the tenants' nightmare and a paradise for criminals and muggers. The walls were defaced with graffiti, the walkways named by the planners 'the streets in the sky' where neighbours were meant to socialise became unsafe and littered with rubbish, and the children's paddling pool became dangerous because of the glass and rubbish that was thrown into it. People were even being murdered, and as soon as it was dark tenants barricaded themselves in and dared not go out. A national newspaper report in December 1983 dubbed the estate the 'Devil's Estate'. So, instead of creating a spirit of community and friendship, anonymity, anger and hooliganism set in. Was it then worth sacrificing 182 beautiful houses, and will all of Metro-land's houses go the same way?

The demolition of the first house in Chalk Hill Road. *Grange Museum/Brent Archives*

Not much of the atmosphere that once made Metro-land such a nice place to live remains (especially in Wembley, which has now become over-built) except perhaps north of the Metropolitan Railway line, from Rickmansworth onwards, where one can still find large open spaces of woods and meadows, and where one can still imagine for a moment what Metro-land must have been like – but for how long? Despite some of the measures that have already been taken, such as the creation of the Green Belt, more still need to be taken to avoid overcrowding and overdevelopment if what had once been a beautiful arcadia is to avoid becoming in years to come a huge mass of slums; this would then force people to move out again and invade what is at the moment preserved countryside. Metro-land is now a thing of the past, and it is up to us to prevent our environment from being spoiled by preserving the little greenery and beauty that is still left in and around London.

Farewell Metro-land

Metro-land!
Dream-land of city dwellers!
Happy-land of country lovers!
Metro-land!
The pride of a railway line,
The attraction of a time,
Once you were.
Yes, Metro-land,
People cherished thee,
People admired thee.
To Metro-land,
They all came:
At first, on a trip for the day,
And then, to decide they would stay
But soon, Metro-land,
With busy shops and cosy houses,
They covered all your open spaces.
And now, Metro-land,
You are no more but, a sweet memory,
In the hearts of all those, who once loved thee.

Appendix
The locomotives of the Metropolitan Railway

Steam locomotives

In 1861, Robert Stephenson & Company built a 2-4-0 tender steam locomotive that was designed by John Fowler. He was trying to solve the problem of the emission of steam and smoke in tunnels by designing a fireless steam locomotive that used exhaust re-condensing techniques to feed back the steam to the boiler instead of letting it escape, while a great quantity of fire bricks acted as a heat reservoir. Unfortunately, it failed its trial run and was never used for passenger service; it was subsequently nicknamed 'Fowler's Ghost', sold in 1865 to Isaac Watt Boulton, and later resold to Beyer Peacock for scrap.

Between January and August 1863 the Metropolitan Railway was operated by 22 Great Western Railway broad gauge engines of the 2-4-0T type. Six had been built by Vulcan, six by Kitson and ten by Swindon.

Between August 1863 and January 1864 the Metropolitan Railway used 12 Great Northern Railway narrow gauge engines of the 4-0-2T and 0-6-0T type, which had been built by Tayleur, Wilson and Hawthorn.

The first Metropolitan Railway locomotives were known as the 'A' class, and between 1864 and 1870 44 were built, followed by 22 of an improved type between 1870 and 1885, known as the 'B' class. They were all 4-4-0 tank engines, and the 'As' weighed 42½ tons in working order with 1,000 gallons of water in their side tanks. The coupled wheels had a diameter of 5ft 9in and the bogie wheels were 3 feet in diameter. The two inclined cylinders were 17 by 24 inches, and the stroke was 24 inches. The boiler pressure, originally 120lb per square inch, was raised to 160lb per square inch with the later engines. Their original colour was green, with copper tops and brass figures on the

'A' class locomotive No 41 at Brill on 15 March 1930. The cab was a later addition to the class. *Stephenson Locomotive Society*

Class A No 41 at Quainton Road on 25 November 1935, two years after the takeover by the London Passenger Transport board and shortly before the Brill branch closed. The locomotive still carries the Metropolitan Railway's name although the coach shows London Transport. *A. W. Camwell/Stephenson Locomotive Society Collection*

chimneys. In 1885 the colour was changed to maroon. The first 18, put into service in 1864, were each given a name, but later, when they were repainted, the names disappeared and were replaced by numbers. They were:

Number	Name	Notes
1	Jupiter	Scrapped in 1897 following accident damage; number reallocated to an 'E' class engine
2	Mars	
3	Juno	
4	Mercury	
5	Apollo	
6	Medusa	
7	Orion	Sold to the Mersey Railway in 1925 as No 2
8	Pluto	
9	Minerva	
10	Cerberus	Later sold to the Cambrian Railways as No 2
11	Latona	Later sold to the Cambrian Railways as No 12
12	Cyclops	Later sold to the Cambrian Railways as No 33
13	Daphne	Later sold to the Cambrian Railways as No 34
14	Dido	Later sold to the South Hetton Coal Company as No 6
15	Aurora	Later sold to the Cambrian Railways as No 36
16	Achilles	
17	Ixion	
18	Hercules	
19-23		Built in 1866. No 20 was later sold to the Nidd Valley Light Railway. No 23 was renumbered L45 by the London Passenger Transport Board, was withdrawn in 1949, and is now preserved in its 1903 condition
24-28		Built in 1867
29-33		Built in 1868
34-38		Built in 1868
39-44		Built in 1869

Nos 34 to 38 were built by the Worcester Engine Company. They were designed by R. H. Burnett and intended for the St John's Wood Extension Line passenger traffic. They had no class letter and were of the 0-6-0T type. Eventually, four were sold to the Taff Vale Railway between 1873 and 1875 and one to the Sirhowy Railway in 1873. Their numbers were then allocated to the first five 'B' class locomotives.

Then came the 22 'B' class 4-4-0Ts, Nos 45-66, which were in fact a modified version of the 'A' class locomotives. They were all built by Beyer, Peacock between 1879 and 1885. Nos 34 to 38 were built in

'F' class locomotive No 92. *Crecy Heritage Library*

1879. No 34 was later sold to the Nidd Valley Light Railway, and in 1907 No 36 was sold to the West Somerset Mineral Railway. Nos 50 to 59 were built in 1880, followed by Nos 60 to 64 in 1884; No 61 was later sold to the Mersey Railway as No 2. Nos 65 and 66 were built in 1885 (No 66 was subsequently sold to the Cambrian Railways as No 37). By 1919 all the 'B' class locomotives were withdrawn.

In 1891 came four 'C' class 0-4-4T steam engines numbered 67-70. They were built by Neilson & Company and designed by J. Stirling and J. J. Hanbury. Like the 'A' and 'B' classes they were used for all-purpose work. They were of the same design as some built in the same batch for the South Eastern Railway, whose Chairman at the time was also Edward Watkin. This time the cylinders were inside. Each engine weighed about 50 tons 8cwt. Unfortunately, their introduction was marred by an accident that occurred in the tunnels near Marlborough Road; a train was allowed by mistake into the section where No 67, which was hauling its first passenger train, had just stopped, smashing into the back of it and injuring 17 people. In 1901-03 all four locomotives were rebuilt with new boilers, and by 1919 had all been withdrawn.

In 1894-95 six 2-4-0T 'D' class locomotives appeared. Nos 71 and 72 were built in 1894, and Nos 73-76 the following year. They were built by Sharp, Stewart & Co and similar in design to some engines used by the Barry Railway; the first two were used on the Aylesbury-Verney Junction section and the other four, fitted with condensing gear, on the Baker Street-Aylesbury section. Unfortunately, they turned out to be insufficiently powerful for passenger traffic and ended up being used for freight duties, except for Nos 71 and 72, which were used on the Brill Branch. Between 1916 and 1922 all these engines were gradually withdrawn.

In 1896 T. F. Clark, who had been foreman of the locomotive shop, was appointed Locomotive Superintendent, and he designed the next seven locomotives, 0-4-4Ts Nos 77, 78, 1 and 79-82, known as the 'E' class. Nos 77 and 78 were built by the company at Neasden Works in 1896, Hawthorn Leslie built Nos 79 and 80 in 1900, and Nos 81 and 82 in 1901. No 1 was built in 1898 at Neasden to replace the original No 1, a 4-4-0T that had been damaged in an accident at Baker Street in September 1897 and subsequently withdrawn from service; however, it was to become famous on 30 July 1904, when it was used to haul the inaugural train on the Uxbridge branch. When the London Passenger Transport Board took over, Nos 77, 1, 80 and 81 became L46, L44, L47 and L48 respectively. No L47 was withdrawn in 1941, L46 in 1962, and L44 and L48 in 1963.

The 'E' class engines were successful and the company intended to have seven more built, but with the advance of electrification this did not happen, which explains why there is a gap in the numbering of the engines between the 'E' and 'F' classes, as Nos 83-89 were not allocated.

In 1901 came four 0-6-2 tank engines known as the 'F' class and built by the Yorkshire Engine Co. Apart from the wheel arrangement they were similar to the 'E' class, but since they were not fitted with condensing apparatus they were used mainly for freight. Numbered 90-93, when the LPTB took over they became Nos L49-L52. Nos L49 and L51 were withdrawn in 1951, L50 in 1958 and L52 in 1962.

In 1915 the Yorkshire Engine Company built four 'G' class 0-6-4T locomotives, designed by C. Jones and intended for express passenger work. No 94 was named *Lord Aberconway*, No 95 *Robert*

Metropolitan 'C' class locomotive No 68 heads towards Verney Junction in 1923. *Crecy Heritage Library*

H. Selbie, No 96 *Charles Jones* and No 97 *Brill*. In 1927 they were all sold to the London & North Eastern Railway.

The numbers 98 and 99 were never allocated.

The number 100 was allocated to an 0-4-0ST shunter built in 1884 by Hudswell Clarke & Company. It was withdrawn in 1907.

No 101 was built in 1897 and No 102 in 1899. These two 'S' class 0-6-0ST engines were designed and built by Peckett & Sons and purchased for yard work at Finchley Road and Harrow. The LPTB renumbered them L53 and L54. The former was withdrawn in 1960 and the latter in 1961.

Between 1920 and 1921 eight 'H' class 4-4-4T locomotives were designed by C. Jones and built by Kerr, Stuart & Company. They were numbered 102 and 104-110, and were intended for express passenger work. In 1937 they were transferred to the LNER.

Nos 111-116 were 'K' class 2-6-4T engines designed by G. Hally and built in 1925 by Armstrong Whitworth & Company using parts from Woolwich Arsenal. They were intended for goods traffic, and in 1937 the six locomotives were transferred to the LNER.

Nellie was an 0-6-0ST shunter built in 1869 by Manning Wardle & Company. It was purchased by the Metropolitan Railway Company in 1905 and withdrawn in 1915.

Electric locomotives

In 1905-06 the first ten electric locomotives, known as 'camel-backs', were built by the Amalgamated Railway Carriage Company and fitted with British Westinghouse electrical control equipment.

In 1907-08 another batch of ten emerged, more box-like in appearance with their flat-fronted driving cab; these were also built by the Amalgamated Railway Carriage Company, but fitted with British Thomson-Houston electrical control equipment.

In 1922-23 new electric locomotives, built by Vickers Ltd, replaced the originals. They were first given a number, but in 1926 they were given the

No 100, 0-4-0ST shunter. *Crecy Heritage Library*

0-4-4T No 77. *Crecy Heritage Library*

names of famous people real or fictitious associated with Metro-land:

No	Name	Year of disposal
1	*John Lyon*	1962
2	*Oliver Cromwell**	1962
3	*Sir Ralph Verney*	1962
4	*Lord Byron*	1962
5	*John Hampden*	1962**
6	*William Penn*	1962
7	*Edmund Burke*	1962
8	*Sherlock Holmes*	1962
9	*John Milton*	1962
10	*William Ewart Gladstone*	1962
11	*George Romney*	1962
12	*Sarah Siddons*	1962***
13	*Dick Whittington*	1962
14	*Benjamin Disraeli*	1962
15	*Wembley 1924*	1951
16	*Oliver Goldsmith*	1962
17	*Florence Nightingale*	1943
18	*Michael Faraday*	1962
19	*John Wycliffe*	1948
20	*Sir Christopher Wren*	1954

* Renamed *Thomas Lord* in 1953
** No 5 has been preserved and is in the London Transport Museum
*** No 12 has been preserved and is still in working order.

Principal dimensions of steam locomotive classes

Class	Wheel arrangment	No in class	Cylinder dimsions (in)	Boiler pressure (lb per sq ft)	Total evaporated heating surface (sq ft)(i)	Weight in working order (tons)	Weight of coupled wheels (tons)	Driving wheel diameter (ft in)	Coupled wheel-base (ft in)	Grate area (sq ft)	Water capacity (gal)	Coal capacity (tons)	Super-heating surface (sq ft)	Tractive effort (85% pressure)
A	4-4-0T	39	17x24	120	943	42.2	31	5 9	8 10	19	1,000	1	-	10,250
-	4-6-0T	5	20x24	130	1,132	45	45	4 0	14 0	22¼			-	22,100
B	4-4-0T	27	17x24	130	977	36.8	36.8	5 9	8 1	17¼	1,140	1.5	-	11,110
C	0-4-4T	4	17x26	140	922	32	32	5 6	7 5	15	1,050	1.5	-	13,550
D (ii)	2-4-0T	2	17x24	150	1,091	31.2	31.2	5 3	7 9	14½	800	1.8	-	13,950
D (iii)	2-4-0T	4	17x24	150	1,093	33.3	33.3	5 3	8 0	16¾	800	1.8	-	13,950
E (iv)	0-4-4T	3	17x26	150	1,146	33	33	5 6	7 5	16¾	1,250	2.2	-	14,990
E (v)	0-4-4-T	4	17½x26	150	1,146	33	33	5 6	7 5	16¾	1,250	2.2	-	15,320
F	0-6-2T	4	17½x26	150	1,150	47.5	47.5	5 2	16 0	18	1,430	2.5	-	16,350
G	0-6-4T	4	20x26	160	1,178			5 9	28 9	21¼	2,000	4.5	268	20,500
S	0-6-0ST	2	16x22	140	712	39	39	3 10	11 0	13¼	1,160	1.2	-	14,570
H	4-4-4T	8	19x26	160	1,178	39	39	5 9	7 9	21¼	2,000	4.5	268	18,500
K	2-6-4T	6	19x28	200	1,526			5 6	15 6	25	2,000	4	285	
No 100	0-4-0ST	1	13x20			22	22	3 3			600	.75	-	
Nellie	0-6-0ST	1	12x17		370	16.75	16.75	3 0	10 9	7	450		-	

(i) Excluding super-heating surface
(ii) Nos71 and 72
(ii) nos 73-76
(iv) NOs1, 77, 78
(v) Nos 79 - 82

Figures are generally of original production, e.g. boiler pressure of the earlier classes were gradually increased to 160lb./sq. inch.

Bibliography

Written sources

Aldcroft, Derek H.: *Building in the British Economy Between the Wars* (Allen & Unwin, 1968, London)
The Interwar Economy Britain 1919-39 (Batsford, 1970, London)

Baker, C.: *The Metropolitan Railway* (The Oakwood Press, 1951, London), pp76

Barker, T. C. and Robbins, Michael: *A History of London Transport*, Volume 1 (1975), pp414, and Volume 2 (1976), pp550 (George Allen & Unwin, London, paperback edition)

Barman, Christian: *The Man Who Built London Transport* (a biography of Frank Pick) (David & Charles, 1979, London)

Bayley, Stephen: *The Garden City* (Open University Press, 1975, London)

Benest, K. R.: *Metropolitan Electric Locomotives* (Lens of Sutton, 1963, Surrey), pp44

Betjeman, John: *Collected Poems* (John Murray, 1980 paperback edition [first published 1958], London), pp427
Metro-land, television film first shown on BBC in 1973

Bowley, Marian: *Housing and the State 1919-1944* (George Allen & Unwin, 1945, London), pp283

Briggs, Milton and Jordan, Percy: *Economic History of England* (Universal Tutorial Press, 1967, London)

Bruce, Graeme J.: *The Big Tube, a short illustrated history of London's Great Northern and City Railway* (London Transport, 1970), pp169
Steam to Silver (London Transport, 1970), pp56

Brunel's Tunnel and Where it Led, booklet produced by the Brunel Exhibition Project, 1980, London

Bundock, J. D.: 'Speculative Housebuilding and Some Aspects of the Activities of the Speculative Housebuilders within the Greater London Outer Suburban Area, 1919-1939', Volumes 1 and 2 (unpublished thesis, University of Kent at Canterbury, December 1974), pp808

Burnett, John: *A History of the Cost of Living* (Pelican Books, 1969, London)

Casserley, H. C.: *The Later Years of Metropolitan Steam* (D. Bradford Barton Ltd, 1978, London), pp96

Clarke, L.: various unpublished articles on the Brill Branch, the Wotton Tramway and the Aylesbury & Buckingham Railway

Clayton, R.: *The Geography of Greater London* (Cambridge University Press, 1964, Cambridge)

Cleary, E. J.: *The Building Society Movement* (Elek, 1965, London)

Cockman, F. J.: *The Railways of Hertfordshire* (Hertfordshire Library Service in association with the Hertfordshire Local History Council, 1978), pp80

Coles, C. R. L. *Railways Through the Chilterns* (Ian Allan Ltd, 1980, London), pp128

Concise Dictionary of National Biography 1901-1950 (Oxford University Press, 194?, Oxford)

Coppock, J. T. and Prince, H. C., editors: *Greater London* (Faber & Faber, 1964, London), pp405

Course, Edwin: *London Railways* (B. T. Batsford Ltd, 1962, London)

Country Homes in Metro-land, Volume No 9, July-September 1917

Creese, Walter L.: *The Search for Environment: The Garden City before and after* (Yale University Press, 1966), pp360

The Daily Telegraph, 10 January 1863

Dark, Arthur: *From Rural Middlesex to London Borough. The Growth and Development of Harrow illustrated with maps* (London Borough of Harrow, 1981, Harrow), pp41

Davies, R. and Grant, M. D.: *Forgotten Railways: Chilterns and Cotswolds* (David & Charles, 1975, London), pp256

Day, John R.: *The Story of London's Underground* (London Transport, 1979 edition, [first published in 1963], London), pp168

Densham, P.: *The Locomotives of the Metropolitan Railway 1863-1923* (Denton Equipment, for the Metropolitan Model Railway, January 1944)

Diamond Jubilee of the Metropolitan Railway, 1863-1923, brochure published by the Metropolitan Railway Company

Dickens, Charles: *Great Expectations* (Penguin Books, 1973 edition, [first published in 1860-61], London), pp168

Douglas, Hugh: *The Underground Story* (Robert Hale Ltd, 1963, London), pp208

Dow, George: *Great Central*, Volume 2: *Dominion of Watkin 1864-1899* (Ian Allan, 1962, London), pp422, and Volume 3: *Fay sets the Pace 1900-1922* (1965), pp439
Railway Heraldry (David & Charles, 1973, London), pp269

Druett, W. W.: *Harrow Through the Ages* (Kings & Hutchings Ltd, Hillingdon Press, 1956 edition, [first published in 1935], Hillingdon)

Pinner Through the Ages (Kings & Hutchings Ltd, 1937, Hillingdon), pp175

Dyos, H. J.: 'Workmen's Fares in South London' in *The Journal of Transport History*, Volume 1 (1953)
  'Railways and Housing in Victorian London' in *The Journal of Transport History*, Volume 2 (1955)
  'Some Social Costs of Railway Building in London' in *The Journal of Transport History*, Volume 3 (1957)
  Victorian Suburb – A Study of the Growth of Camberwell (Leicester University Press, 1977 edition, [first published in 1961], Leicester), pp240

Dyos, H. J. (editor): *The Study of Urban History* (Arnold, 1968, London)

Dyos, H. J. and Wolff, Michael (editors) *Victorian City, Images and Realities* (Routledge & Kegan Paul, 1973, London and Boston), Volume 1 pp1-428, Volume 2 pp431-956

The Economist, 25 July 1885, p912

Edmonds, Alexander: *History of the Metropolitan District Railway Company to June 1908* (London Transport, 1973, London)

Edwards, Dennis: 'How the "Met" came to Watford' in *The Hertfordshire Countryside*, Volume 25, No 145, May 1971, pp20 and 21
  'Walter Atkinson: Builder of the Harrow and Uxbridge Railway' in *Underground* No 12 (Underground Society, 1983, London), pp30
  Yesterday in Ickenham (Ickenham Residents Association, 1982), pp15

Edwards, Dennis and Pigram, Ron *Metro-Memories* (Midas Books, 1977, Tunbridge Wells), pp128
  The Romance of Metro-land (Midas Books, 1979, Tunbridge Wells), pp128
  The Final Link (Midas Books, 1982, Tunbridge Wells), pp144
  The Golden Years of the Metropolitan Railway (Midas Books, 1983, Tunbridge Wells), pp128

Elsas, M. J.: *Housing Before and After the War* (P. S. King & Staples Ltd, 1942, London), pp69

The Estates Gazette supplement, 20 March 1909, London

The Evening News, 30 September 1933

The Evening Standard, 13 November 1973: 'The Great Suburban Superboom'

Ferneyhough, Frank: *The History of Railways in Britain* (Alban Book Services Ltd, 1975, London)

Follenfant, H. G.: *Reconstructing of London's Underground* (London Transport, 1974, London), pp184

Gadsden, E. J. S.: *Metropolitan Steam* (Roundhouse Books, 1963, Northwood, Middlesex), pp43

Girling, Brian, edited by Clive Smith: *Harrow as it was* (C. R. Smith (Publications), 1975, Hendon), pp31

Gloag, John: *The Englishman's Castle* (Eyre & Spottiswoode, 1945, London)

Graves, Charles: *London Transport Carried On: an Account of London at War, 1939-1945* (London Passenger Transport Board, 1947, London), pp77

Graves, Robert and Hodge, Alan: *The Long Week-end: A Social History of Great Britain, 1918-1939*, (Faber & Faber, 1950, London), page 472

Grossmith, G. and W.: *The Diary of a Nobody* (Penguin Books, 1965, London)

Hall, Peter: *London 2000* (Faber & Faber Ltd, 1963, London)

Halsey A. H., editor: *Trends in British Society since 1900, a Guide to the Changing Social Structure of Britain* (Macmillan, St Martin Press, 1977, London)

Hardy, Brian: *London Underground Rolling Stock* (Capital Transport Publishing, 1981 edition, [first published in 1976], Harrow Weald, Middlesex), pp113

Harrow Before Your Time (Pinner and Hatch End WEA Local History Group, 1972, Harrow), pp80

Hastie, Tom: *Home Life* (Batsford, 1967, London)

Havers H. C. P.: *Underground Railways of the World – Their History and Development* (Temple Press Books, 1966, London), pp197

Hewlett, Geoffrey, editor: *A History of Wembley* (Brent Library Service, 1979, Wembley), pp259

Hodges, Sir William: *A Treatise on the Law of Railways, Railway Companies and Railway Investments*, seventh edition by John M. Lely, Esq., H. Sweet and Sons, Volume 1 (1888) and Volume 2 (1889), London

House of Commons, 1884-85, XXX, Q. 10479

Howard, Ebenezer: *Garden Cities of Tomorrow* (Faber a& Faber, 1974 edition, [first published in 1892], London), pp168,

Hawkins, F.: *An Introduction to the Development of Private Building Estates and Town Planning* (Estates Gazette Ltd, 192?, London, pp368

Howson, H. F. *London's Underground* (Ian Allan Ltd, 1962 edition, [first published in 1951], London), pp125

Hughes, M. V.: *A London Family Between the Wars* (Oxford University Press, 1979 edition, [first published in 1940], Oxford), pp180

Jackson, A. A.: *Inside Underground Railways* (Ian Allan Ltd, 1964, Shepperton-on-Thames, Middlesex), pp64
  Semi-Detached London (George Allen & Unwin Ltd, 1973, London), pp381
  London's Local Railways (David & Charles, 1978, London), pp384

Jackson, A. A. and Croome, D. F.: *Rails Through the Clay* (George Allen & Unwin, 1962, London)

Jenkins, Alan: *On Site 1921-1971* (Heinemann, 1971, London), pp226

Jones, Ken: *The Wotton Tramway (Brill Branch)* (The Oakwood Press, Locomotion Papers No 75, 1974, London), pp60

Julian, Julian: *An Introduction to Town Planning* (Charles Griffin & Company, 1914, London), pp149

Kellett, J. R.: *The Impact of Railways on Victorian Cities* (Routledge & Kegan Paul, 1969, London), pp467

Lee, Charles E. *Sixty years of the Northern* (London Transport, 1967, London), pp28
  100 years of the District (London Transport, 1968, London), pp32
  The Bakerloo Line (London Transport, 1973, London), pp23
  The Piccadilly Line (London Transport, 1973, London), pp26
  The Metropolitan Line, A Brief History (London Transport, 1975 edition, [first published in 1972], London), pp32
  The East London Line and the Thames Tunnel – A Brief History (London Transport, 1976, London), pp24

Levey, Michael: *London Transport Posters* (Phaidon Press Ltd, 1976, London) pp80

Lewis, Roy and Maude, Angus: *The English Middle Classes* (Phoenix

House, 1949, London), pp320
The Listener, 26 August 1976, p240 and p241: 'All Stations to Amersham – Sir John Betjeman in Metro-land'
London Passenger Transport Act 1933, 23 Geo, 5, Ch. 14
London Transport: *The Last Drop – London Transport Steam 1863-1971*, 1973 edition, [first published in 1971], London), pp24
March, D. C.: *The Changing Social Structure of England and Wales, 1871-1961* (Routledge & Kegan Paul, 1965, London)
McAllister, Gilbert and Elizabeth: *Town and Country Planning* (Faber, 1941, London)
McGrandle, Leith: *The Cost of Living in Britain* (Wayland Publishers, 1973, London), pp128
The Metropolitan & Great Central Joint Railway Illustrated Guide of 1910
The Metropolitan Inner Circle Completion Act 1874, 37 & 38 Vic., CH. cxcix
The Metropolitan & London & North Eastern Railways: *Country Walks in Middlesex, Hertfordshire and Buckinghamshire with sketch maps of routes*, Nos 3 and 4
The Metropolitan Railway Act 1887, 50 & 51 Vic., Ch. cxxxvi
The Metropolitan Railway Company: *Metro-land* (1916, 1917, 1923, 1925, 1928, 1930, 1931 and 1932)
The Metropolitan Railway Company: *Near and Far* (May 1912)
Montgomery, John: *The Twenties* (Allen & Unwin, 1970, London)
Mowat, Charles Loch: *Britain Between the Wars 1918-1940* (Methuen & Co Ltd, 1955, London), pp698
Nock, O. S.: *Underground Railways of the World* (Adam & Charles Black, 1973, London), pp288
Oliver, Paul, Davis, Ian and Bentley, Ian: *Dunroamin* (Barrie & Jenkins, 1981, London), pp224
Passingham, W. J.: *Romance of London's Underground* (Sampson Low, Marston & Co Ltd, 1936, London), pp243
Pawley, M.: *Home Ownership* (Architectural Press, 1978, London)
Peacock, T. B.: *Great Western Suburban Services* (Oakwood Press, 1978, London), pp107
Pevsner, Nikolaus: *Middlesex* (Buildings of England, Penguin Books, 1951, London), pp204

Priestley, J. B.: 'Houses' in *The Saturday Review*, 11 June 1927, p897, 898 and 899
Quennell, Marjorie and C. H. B.: *A History of Everyday Things in England 1851-1948*, five volumes (B. T. Batsford, 1961 edition, [first published in 1948], London)
The Railway Magazine, 1915, Volume 36, p499, advert about Metro-land
Rasmussen, Steen Eiler: *London the Unique City* (Pelican Books, 1960, London)
Reissman, Leonard: *The Urban Press – Cities in Industrial Societies* (The Free Press, 1970, New York), pp255 (also published in London by Macmillan)
Richards, J. M.: *The Castles on the Ground* (John Murray, 1973 edition, [first published in 1946], London), pp96
Memoirs of an Unjust Fella (Weidenfield & Nicolson, 1980, London), pp279
Robbins, Michael: *A New Survey of England: Middlesex* (Collins, 1953, London), pp456
'Baker Street for the Midlands?', unpublished lecture, 10 March 1961
'Railways and Willesden', reprinted from *Transactions of the London & Middlesex Archaeological Society*, Volume 26, 1975, pp309-18
'Transport and Suburban: Development in Middlesex down to 1914', extract from *Transactions of the London & Middlesex Archaeological Society*, Volume 29, 1976, pp129-136
Roebuck, J.: *The Making of Modern English Society from 1850* (Routledge & Kegan Paul, 1973, London)
Rose, Douglas: *The London Underground – A Diagrammatic History* (Author, 1980, North Finchley)
Sharp, Dennis: *The Picture Palace* (Hugh Evelyn, 1969, London)
Sharp, Thomas: *Town Planning* (Penguin Books, 1940, London)
Sinclair, Robert: *Metropolitan Man: The Future of the English* (George Allen & Unwin, 1937, London)
St George, H.: 'Neath the Shade of Ruislip Poplars', music by Fred Parnum (Handel & Co, 1909, London)
Sully, H. B.: *A Short History of the Cinema in Middlesex 1910-1965* (Middlesex Local History Council Bulletin No 18, 1965)

Taylor, A. J. P.: *English History, 1914-45* (Oxford University Press, 1965, Oxford)
Taylor, Nicholas: *The Village in the City* (Temple Smith, 1973, London), pp239
Thorns, C. David *Suburbia* (Paladin, 1973, St Albans), pp175
The Times, 23 April 1934
The Times Supplement on the Centenary of the London Underground, 24 May 1963
Trevelyan, G. M.: *Illustrated English Social History*, four volumes (Longmans, 1942, London)
The Uxbridge Gazette, special edition, 30 June 1904
The Victoria History of Counties of England: History of Middlesex, Volumes 4 and 5, edited by R. B. Pugh (Oxford University Press, 1971, 1976, Oxford)
Ward, Mary and Neville: *Home in the Twenties and the Thirties* (Ian Allan Ltd, 1978, London), pp128
Ward, Zena: 'Let's Go To Wembley', music by N. M. Blair (Lareine Company, 1924, London)
Waugh, Evelyn: *Vile Bodies* (Penguin Books, 1980 edition, [first published in 1930], London); one of the characters is named Lady Metroland
White, H. P.: *A Regional History of the Railways of Great Britain*, Volume 3 *Greater London* (Phoenix House, 1963, London), pp227
Wilkins, Harry: *Greenhill from Village to Harrow Town Centre* (London Borough of Harrow, 1981, Harrow), pp88
Williams, Guy R.: *London in the Country – The Growth of the Suburbia* (Hamish Hamilton, 1975, London), pp191
Wilsher, Peter: *The Pound in your Pocket* (Constable, 1970, London)

Study of Haymills Houses Ltd's records (especially those concerning the Barn Hill Estate) – thanks to Mr G. A. Cox
Study of large scrapbook belonging to the Metropolitan Railway Country Estates Company and containing various brochures, adverts, newspaper cuttings, photos, etc – thanks to Sterling Homes Ltd (Gerrards Cross)

Study of the Minute Books of the Metropolitan Railway Country Estates Company – thanks to Mr Penlington, Secretary of Guardian Royal Exchange Assurance Ltd

**Written sources available only at the Greater London Record Office, Clerkenwell Road, London EC1
The Metropolitan Railway Company Records: Accession 1297**

Met1/1 to Met1/64: Minute Books of the Company from 1853 to 1933

Met1/70 to Met1/75: Law and Lands Committee from 1870 to 1911

Met1/97 to Met1/106 and Met1/119 to Met1/123: Minutes of Meeting of Officers between 1908 and 1933

Met1/107 to Met1/119: Board Reports (1903-1933)

Met1/124: Reports and Correspondence about the London & Aylesbury Railway, the Metropolitan & St John's Wood Railway, etc (1873-1877)

Met1/125: The Metropolitan & St John's Wood Railway (1877-1879)

Met1/126: Elevation of Finchley Road station (1879-1880)

Met1/127 to Met1/130: The Aylesbury & Buckingham Railway Reports from 1866 to 1879

Met3/1: Agreement with the Great Central Railway as to conveyance and leases of land (11 June 1913)

Met3/2: Agreement with the London & North Western Railway concerning the alteration and improvements at Verney Junction (29 November 1895)

Met3/3: Agreement with the Aylesbury & Buckingham Company for the acquisition of the railway by the Metropolitan Railway Company (13 November 1889)

Met3/6: Wembley Park station, plan of signalling and track layout (1932)

Met4/8: Copy of the correspondence with the Manchester, Sheffield & Lincolnshire Railway concerning the negotiations for use of the Metropolitan line for the London end of its railway (1894-1898)

Met4/9 to Met4/13: Guard Books with collections of things

Met4/16: Collection of reports and pamphlets from 1928 to 1933

Met4/21: Diaries

Met7/1: Memorial from the people of Rickmansworth wanting a more central station (October 1885)

Met7/2: Petition from the people of Eastcote (March 1905)

Met7/3: Petition from the people of Northwood (January 1931)

Met7/4: Memorial from the people of St John's Wood and Marlborough Road regarding the closing of their stations (1929)

Met7/5: Memorial from the people of Northwood (May 1927)

Met7/7: Memorial of the people of Hillingdon (1932)

Met7/8: Memorial from the people of Watford (1926)

Met7/11: Memorial from the people of Wembley Park (1930)

Met10/89: Development of Northwick Park Estate and the construction of the Northwick Park and Kenton station

Met10/93: Proposed intermediate station between Willesden Green and Neasden and the Dollis Hill Estate (1899-1908)

Met10/123: Preston Road Halt

Met10/125: Construction of Sandy Lodge station

Met10/131: Harrow Bessborough and Belmont Estates request a station at West Harrow (1907-1912)

Met10/132: North Harrow station (1913-1917)

Met10/133: West Harrow station (1913-1917)

Met10/134: North Harrow and West Harrow stations (1910-1914)

Met10/148: Development of land at Sandy Lodge (1911-1914)

Met10/149: Development of land at Moor Park and Sandy Lodge (1920-1924)

Met10/150: Agreement for a siding road at Moor Park (1924-1928)

Met10/151: Alteration of the name of Sandy Lodge station (1924-1930)

Met10/152: Lord Leverhulme's Moor Park Estate and the Metropolitan Railway Country Estates Company

Met10/153: Moor Park and Sandy Lodge Estates plans (1910-1925)

Met10/154: Land for slip at Moor Park (1928-1929)

Met10/196: British Empire Exhibition at Wembley (1924-1925) and the construction of Wembley Park station (1921-1929)

Met10/197: Article from the *Telegraph* of 10 December 1926 about the aftermath of the British Empire Exhibition

Met10/198: Wembley Park 1924

Met10/199: The Never Stop Railway at the British Empire Exhibition (1924-1925)

Met10/317: Lengthening of platforms at Rayners Lane and Ickenham (1918-1922)

Met 10/322: Metropolitan Railway Country Estates Company

Met 10/323: Metropolitan Railway Country Estates Company at Neasden and Wembley (1919-1921)

Met10/327: Metropolitan Railway Country Estates Company's land and property at Kingsbury Garden Village, Neasden, Chalk Hill Estate and Hillingdon (1921-1928)

Met10/328: Proposed relief line from Willesden Green to Edgware Road (1925-1926)

Met10/329: Relief line from Willesden to Edgware Road (1925-1930)

Met10/330: Relief line from Willesden to Edgware Road and the Metropolitan Railway Act of 1926; alternative scheme for a proposed relief line (West Hampstead to Great Portland Street)

Met10/551: Proposal for a 'Metro-Magazine' for the staff (1926-1932)

Met10/652: Richmond line, agreement with the London & South Western Railway on though bookings from Richmond (1931-1932)

Met10/665: Correspondence with the Metropolitan District Railway relating to alterations and improvements at Rayners Lane Junction (1930-1932)

Met10/685: Application for a subsidy by the Metropolitan Railway Country Estates Company for the development of the Weller Estate at Amersham (1930)

Met10/699: Housing Development Summary of the District of Kilburn-Brondesbury to Uxbridge, Amersham and Watford (1930-1933)

Met 10/696: Correspondence with the Metropolitan District Railway Company about the reconstruction of Rayners Lane station (1929-1931)

Met10/702: Agreement on the exchange of land between the Metropolitan Railway Company and the Metropolitan Railway Country Estates Company, on the Weller Estate at Amersham (1930-1931)

Met 10/712: Growth of population in Metro-land and a Housing Development Summary of the District of Kilburn-Brondesbury to Uxbridge, Amersham and Watford (1928)

Met10/730: Ruislip Manor (1910-1917)

Met10/756: Metropolitan Railway Surplus Lands Committee (1929-1930)

Met10/758: Watford line and the London Passenger Transport Board Bill

Met19/1: Illustrated Guide to the Metropolitan Railway Extensions (1905)

Met10/2: Illustrated Guide to the Metropolitan Railway Extensions (1903)

MTCC1/1: Metropolitan Tower Construction Company Limited (7 October 1891 to 11 December 1899)

MTCC1/2: Metropolitan Tower Construction Company Limited (from 3 August 1933 to 19 July 1899)

WPE 1/1 to WPE 1/5: Wembley Park Estate Company Limited Minutes Books of General Meetings from 9 January 1890 to 24 September 1930

Written sources available at Harrow Library of Local History, Civic Centre, Harrow

Bate, J. R.: 'Metro-land', article in the *Abbey National Review*, Volume 4, No, June 1961

Bennett, A. E. and Barley, H. V.: *London Transport Railways* (a list of opening, closing and renaming of lines and stations) (David & Charles, London, 1963)

Charles Booth's London, selected and edited by Alfred Fried and Richard Elman (Hutchison, 1969, London), pp342

Census of England and Wales for the years 1901, 1921, 1931, 1951

Collins, M. F. and Pharoah, T. M.: *Transport Organisation in a Great City* (the case of London) (George Allen & Unwin, 1974, London) pp660

Cooper, E. and Bednall, D.: *Pinner Streets, Yesterday and Today* (P.H.E.L.H.A.J., 197?, Pinner, Middlesex), pp48

Cutler, A.: *Guide to Ideal Homes in North Harrow*, 1926

Dark, A.: 'Metro-land' (historical notes on Metro-land)

Gadsden, E. J. S.: *The Duke of Buckingham's Railways* (Bledlow Press, 1962, London)

Green, Frank and Wolff, Sidney: *London and Suburbs Old and New* (Souvenir Magazine Limited, 1933, London), pp300

Harris, Mary: 'The Disappearance of Greenhill, Middlesex, 1837-1967', unpublished special essay written for Sidney Webb College, W1

'Harrow Miscellany', written by members of Harrow WEA Local History Class, 1972-1975

The Harrow Observer and Gazette:
15 April 1932, p7, an estate with an appeal, features of the Harrow Garden Village
29 August 1930, London's latest garden suburb
4 July 1930, p5, pioneer builder's anniversary

Kitchen, Frank: 'The Rise of Harrow in the Plain, 1880-1914', unpublished special essay for teachers' certificate examination for Brighton Polytechnic

London Aspects of Change, edited by the Centre for Urban Studies (Macgibbon & Kee, 1961, London), pp344

May, Trevor: 'Road Passenger Transport in Harrow in the Nineteenth and Early Twentieth Centuries' in *Journal of Transport History*, February 1971, p18 to p38

Nash, T. F.: a brochure on Nash Houses (1933)
New Ideal Homesteads: a brochure on the houses they built on the Belmont Park Estate in 1934

Pugh, Hilary: 'The Origins of a London Suburb – the Economic Social and Administrative Development of Harrow (1841-1861)', special essay written in 1968

Radio Times, 22 February 1973, p6, 'The Arcadia beyond Neasden'
15 March 1973, p4, 'Out and about with Sir John in Metro-land'

Sekon, G. A.: *Locomotion in Victorian London* (Oxford University Press, 1976, London), pp384

Shelley, Kay: 'Nostalgic Trip to Metro-land', *Middlesex Advertiser*, 14 June 1979, p8

Sheppard, Francis: London *1808-1870, The Infernal Wen* (Secker & Warburg, 1971)

'The Early History of the Metropolitan District and Metropolitan Railways in Wembley', Wembley Transport Society Publication No 3, July 1963, pp46

Trent, Christopher: *Greater London* (Phoenix House, 1965, London), pp282

Written sources available at the Grange Museum of Local History at Neasden

Bass, Koward: *Glorious Wembley (The Official History of Britain's Foremost Entertainment Centre)* (Guinness Superlatives Ltd, 1982, Enfield, Middlesex), pp175

A brochure on Costin Houses dated 1939; reference Ace. 1036

Hegan, H.: 'The development of public transport in Wembley', article written on 20 June 1977; reference Acc. 1614/7

Elsley, Rev H. W. R.: *Wembley Through the Ages* (*Wembley News*, 1953, pp250)

The Engineer, 8 September 1893, p239 and p240 (article on the Tower of Wembley)

Goddard, Dr C. E. A.: 'Wembley', article published in the *Middlesex Quarterly*, 1951, No 1 (Autumn)

Golland, Richard: *Watkin's Folly*

The Harrow Observer and Gazette, 14 September 1906, p3, article on the demolition of Watkin's Tower

Miss Jones: 'Thesis on the British Empire Exhibition at Wembley 1924-25', written in 1976

The Railway Gazette, 19 September 1924, p374, article on the railway and other exhibits at the British Empire Exhibition

Sale, T. W.: 'The Never Stop Railway', *The Railway Magazine*, November 1933, Volume LXXIII, No 437

Thorogood, J. E.: 'Memories of Wembley of seventy years ago' (*Wembley News*, 30 April 1948)

The Times, 24 September 1965, p12, article on 'From a painter's paradise to an architect's domain'

The Wembley History Society Journal: all issues published between 1952 and 1983

The Wembley Medical Officer of Health's Reports: all reports between 1895 and 1940

The Wembley News: all publications for the years 1923, 1924, 1925
15 November 1935, article on the origins of Wembley
26 February 1937, supplement on local industries
28 August 1970, article on the history of Wembley
The Wembley Official Guide for the years 1928, 1931, 1939
Wembley Charter Day, a brochure published for the occasion on 8 July 1937; reference M.P. 352

Written sources available at the Guildhall Library, London

Baker, Benjamin: 'The Metropolitan and Metropolitan District Railways', reference Pam 15241
The Economist: Volume 44, 1886, p920, 'The proposed division of the Metropolitan Railway'
Volume 30, 1872, p1017 and p1018, 'The decline of the Metropolitan Railway'
Ellis, Luke: 'Guide to the Metropolitan Railway extension to Harrow and Chesham', London, 1891, *The Railway*; reference SL 48 52
Galloway, Richard Hodgson: 'The London Corporation and Metropolitan Railway, 1865'; reference A.2.5. No.4 in 1
Keen, P. A.: 'Metropolitan Railway Road Services' in *The Journal of Transport History*, Volume 1, 1953-54, p216 top, 237; reference St. 159
Lee, C. E.: 'Mixed gauge to Hammersmith', *The Railway Magazine*, Volume 110, 1964, p472 top, 479; reference Pam 11127
'The East London Line and the Thames Tunnel', 1976; reference Pam 13553
'The Metropolitan Railway in its prime', *The Railway Magazine*, Volume 109, 1963, p93 to p102; reference Pam 15381
Metropolitan & Great Central Joint Committee, 1 January 1931; reference SL 48/52
The Metropolitan Railway: Reports of the Directors to the half yearly general meeting of proprietors (1854-1881); reference SL 48/52
The Metropolitan Railway: The London Metropolitan Railway from Paddington to Finsbury Circus, July 1862; reference Gr. 6.1.4
The Metropolitan Railway: a 15% paying line, 1868; reference Pam 2119
The Metropolitan Railway: arbitration between the Metropolitan Railway Company and the Metropolitan District Railway Company, 1878; reference SL 48/52
The Metropolitan Railway: an illustrated guide, 1880; reference Pam 2562
The Metropolitan Railway Rules and Regulations, June 1904; reference SL 48/52
Parliament, House of Commons: a Bill for the making of railways, for completing the Metropolitan Outer Circle, 1879; reference Fo. Pam 4122
The Railway Magazine: 'Railway connections at King's Cross by "Fowler's Ghost"', Volume 108, 1962, p297 top, 304; reference Pam 11122
Robbins, Michael: 'Fowler's Ghosts', *The Railway Magazine*, Volume 109, 1963, p390 to p394; reference Pam 11125
Statutes of Great Britain: Chap. cxvii, Vic. 1865, an Act to confer further power upon the Metropolitan Railway Company
Westinghouse Brake and Saxby Signal Company: the re-signalling of Edgware Road station, Metropolitan station, 1927; reference Fo. Pam 4643
Willox, William: 'Signalling on the Metropolitan Railway', photocopy from the Institution of Civil Engineers Minutes Proceeding, Volume 214, 1922; reference Pam 15239

Oral sources

Interview and correspondence with Mr Charles Beety, former Solicitor of the Metropolitan Surplus Lands Company and the Metropolitan Railway Country Estates Company
Interview with Sir John Betjeman on 5 March 1982
Interviews and correspondence with Mr G. A. Cox, Chairman of Haymills (Contractors) Ltd
Interview with Sir Horace Cutler, Leader of the GLC at the time, on 4 May 1982
Interviews with Mr Dennis Edwards and attendance at his lectures on Metro-land
Interview with Mr Geal, former employee of the Metropolitan Railway Company
Correspondence with Mr Edward Mirzoeff, Senior Producer, Documentary Features, at BBC Television
Interview with Mr Penlington, Secretary of the Guardian Royal Exchange Assurance, concerning the Metropolitan Railway Country Estates Company
Interview and correspondence with Mr Michael Robbins
Interview with Mary Ward (architect) about the life during the interwar period
Attendance at meetings of the London Underground Railway Society

Further reading

Benest, Kenneth R.: *Metropolitan Electric Locomotives* (London Underground Railway Society, 1984)
Boynes, David: *The Metropolitan Railway* (NPI Media Group, 2003)
Durnin, Stephen: *London Underground Stations* (Capital Transport Publishing, 2010)
Emmerson, Andrew: *The London Underground* (Shire Publications, 2010)
Foxell, Clive: *The Metropolitan Line: London's First Underground Railway* (The History Press Ltd)
Images of 150 Years of the Metropolitan Railway (The History Press Ltd)
Echoes of the Met Line (The History Press Ltd)
Shadows of the Metropolitan Railway (The History Press Ltd)
Rails to Metro-land (2005)
Glover, John *Metropolitan Railway* (Glory Days) (Ian Allan Ltd, 1998)
London's Underground (Ian Allan Ltd, 2003)
Goudie, Frank: *Metropolitan Steam Locomotives* (Capital Transport, 1990)
Green, Oliver: *Metro-land: British Empire Exhibition 1924 Edition* (Southbank Publishing, 2004)
McCormack, Kevin: *London Underground Steam* (Ian Allan Ltd, 2011)
Simpson, Bill: *A History of the*

Metropolitan Railway, Volume 1: *The Circle and the Extended Lines to Rickmansworth* (Lamplight Publications, 2003)
A History of the Metropolitan Railway, Volume 2: *The Railway from Rickmansworth to Aylesbury including Halton Camp Railway* (Lamplight Publications, 2004)
A History of the Metropolitan Railway: Aylesbury to Verney Junction and the Brill Branch (Lamplight Publications, 2005)
Snowdon, James R. *The Metropolitan Railway Rolling Stock* (Wild Swan, (2002)

Notes

[1] H. P. White: *A Regional History of the Railways of Great Britain*, Volume 3: *Greater London* (Phoenix House, London, 1963), page 1
[2] W. J. Passingham: *Romance of London's Underground* (Sampson Low, Marston & Co Ltd, London, 1936), page 4
[3] W. J. Passingham, op cit, page 7
[4] Frederick S. Williams, *Our Iron Roads*, 5th edition, 1884
[5] *The Daily Telegraph*, Monday 12 January 1863
[6] T. C. Barker and M. Robbins: *A History of London Transport, Volume 1* (George Allen & Unwin Ltd, London, 1975), page 117
[7] T. C. Barker and M. Robbins, op cit, page 25
[8] Hugh Douglas, The Underground Story, Robert Hale Ltd, London 1963, page 4
[9] *The English Illustrated Magazine*, article called 'The Romance of Modern London' (August 1893).
[10] C. Baker: *The Metropolitan Railway* (The Oakwood Press, London, 1951) page 18
[11] Ibid, page 20
[12] Michael Robbins: Baker Street for the Midlands?, unpublished lecture, 10 March 1961
[13] Ibid
[14] T. B. Peacock: *Great Western London Suburban Services* (Oakwood Press, London, 1978) page 18
[15] *The Uxbridge Gazette*, Special edition, 30 June 1904, page 3
[16] C. Baker, op cit, page 36
[17] T. C. Barker and M. Robbins, op cit, page 256.
[18] A. Jackson and D. F. Groome: *Rails Through The Clay* (George Allen & Unwin, London, 1962), page 239
[19] A. Jackson: *London's Local Railways* (David & Charles, London, 1978), page 306
[20] Ibid
[21] Ibid, page 307
[22] *The Economist*, 25 July 1885, page 912
[23] Report of the Board Meeting of 24 March 1886 (British Transport Historical Records, Acc. 1297 Met. 1/14)
[24] Ibid
[25] Ibid
[26] *Illustrated Guide to the Metropolitan Railway Extensions*, 1905 (British Transport Historical Records, Acc. 1297 Met. 19/1)
[27] From *Near and Far*, a brochure about pleasant home districts on the north side of London served by the Metropolitan Railway, published by the Metropolitan Railway Company in May 1912
[28] House of Commons, 1884-5, XXX, Q, 10479
[29] Prospectus of Ruislip Manor Ltd, page 2 (British Transport Historical Records, Acc. 1297 Met. 10/730)
[30] Information compiled from *Town Planning in Practice*, a brochure published in 1911 (British Transport Historical Records, Acc. 1297 Met. 10/730)
[31] British Transport Historical Records, Acc. 1297 Met. 1/26
[32] Ibid
[33] Speech delivered at Wolverhampton by Lloyd George in November 1918
[34] British Transport Historical Records, Acc. 1297 Met. 10/322
[35] Information compiled from the Minutes of the Board Meeting, 14 January 1919 (British Transport Historical Records, Acc. 1297 Met. 1/28)
[36] British Transport Historical Records, Acc. 1297 Met. 10/321
[37] Information compiled from the British Transport Historical Records, Acc. 1297 Met. 10/322
[38] Memorandum by Mr Pritchard, Solicitor, 22 May 1919 (BritishTransport Historica1Records, Acc. 1297 Met. 10/322)
[39] Board Meeting, 29 May 1919 (British Transport Historical Records, Acc. Met. 10/322)
[40] British Transport Historical Records, Acc. 1297 Met. 10/152
[41] *The Railway Magazine*, Volume 36, 1915, page 499
[42] *Near and Far* (Metropolitan Railway Company, 1912), page 11
[43] G. R. Sims: 'My Metro-land' (*Metro-land*, Metropolitan Railway Company, 1923)
[44] Leaflet published by the Metropolitan Railway Company in the early 1920s
[45] *The Harrow Observer and Gazette*, 29 August 1930
[46] Ibid, 4 July 1930
[47] Ibid
[48] 'Speculative Housebuilding and Some Aspects of the Activities of the Speculative Housebuilder with the Greater London Outer Suburban Area 1919-39', J. D. Bundock, Volume 2, unpublished thesis, University of Kent at Canterbury, page 699
[49] 'Country Homes in Metro-land', leaflet published in the early 1920s by the Metropolitan Railway Country Estates Company
[50] *Evening News*, 30 September 1933
[51] Charles Dickens: *Great Expectations*
[52] Ibid
[53] Ibid
[54] British Transport Historical Records, Acc. 1297 Met. 10/125
[55] 'Neath the Shade of the Ruislip "Poplars"', song composed by H. St George (words) and Fred Farnum (music) and published in London in 1909 by Handel & Co
[56] The Estates Gazette's supplement of 20 March 1909, London
[57] British Transport Historical Records, Acc. 1297 Met. 33 App.2, page 137, 11 February 1915
[58] Ibid
[59] Figures based on the Wembley Medical Officer of Health's reports for the years quoted
[60] 'Let's Go To Wembley!', words by Zena Ward, music by N. M. Blair (London, Lareine & Co)
[61] Figures based on the Wembley Medical Officer of Health's reports for the years quoted
[62] Wembley Official Guide of 1928, page 11

Index

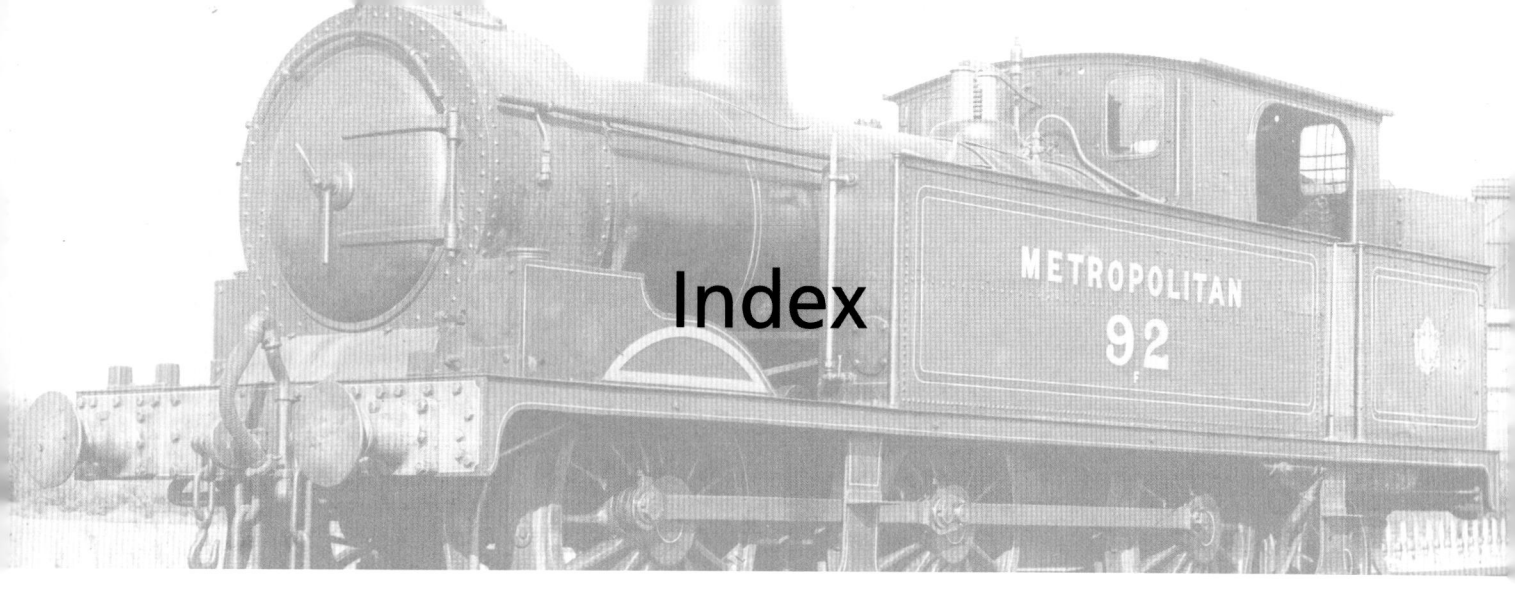

Aberconway, Lord 60, 68, 148
Addison Acts 108
Addison, Dr Christopher 108
Addison Road, Kensington 28, 30, 34.38. 62, 66
Aldersgate 30, 92, 95
Aldgate 30, 36, 37, 40, 61, 66, 95
Aldgate East 40, 77
Alperton 128, 129, 130, 131, 138, 140
Amalgamation 75,76, 83
Amersham 45, 47, 77, 90, 92, 93, 95, 97, 104
Armstrong Whitworth & Co 68, 149
Ashbury Railway Carriage & Iron Co 25, 47
Ashbury stock 56
Aveling & Porter geared steamed locomotives 47, 52
Aylesbury 45, 47, 49, 50,52, 53, 55, 56, 61, 62, 66, 77, 85, 91, 92, 93, 95, 97, 148
Aylesbury & Buckinghamshire Railway 42, 47, 50, 52, 53, 54
Aylesbury line 49, 55, 56
Aylesbury Railway Co 47, 53, 56

Baker Street 18, 22, 31, 42, 43, 45, 46, 52, 53, 56, 60, 61, 62, 63, 64, 66, 75, 77, 83, 87, 88, 90, 91, 91, 92, 95, 97, 98, 102, 104, 105, 129, 131, 148
Bakerloo Line 64, 73, 77
Banbury 49,50
Barn Hill, Wembley 116, 140
Bayswater, Paddington & Holborn Bridge Railway 14
Bayswater station 35, 92
Bell, John 54, 55
Betjeman, John 79
Beyer, Peacock & Co 25, 26, 27, 146
Bishop's Road station 28
Bishopsgate 30, 36, 39,
Bogie stock 56
Bouverie Street power station 66
Brake 18. 27, 56, 71, 72, 73
Brent, River 55, 66, 98, 123
Brill, Bucks 52, 53, 76
Brill branch 48, 54, 55, 77, 95, 148
Brill locomotive 68, 148
British Empire Exhibition, Wembley 128, 130, 131, 132, 133, 134, 138
British Railways 61, 77
British Thomson-Houston Ltd 71, 72
British Transport Commission 77
British Westinghouse Co 64, 65, 66, 71, 72, 73
Broad Street 38
Brompton 33, 34
Brunel, Sir Marc Isambard 13, 14, 15, 23
Buckingham, Duke of 49, 50, 52
Buckingham & Brackley Railway 50
Buckinghamshire 47, 59, 77, 87, 89, 90, 91, 118
Buckinghamshire Railway Co 50, 53
Building society 109, 110, 114
Bushey 59, 63

Canfield Place 55
Canons Park 63, 64
Car (also carriage, coach and compartment) 24, 25, 26, 27, 54, 56, 68, 70, 71, 72, 73, 88, 92, 96, 97
Carriage, see Car
Cassiobury Park, Watford 60
Cattle Market, Copenhagen Fields .15
Cecil Park Estate 81, 82
Cedars Estate, Rickmansworth 90, 98, 99
Central London Railway 65, 92
Chalfont and Latimer 83, 93, 95, 97. 120
Chalfont Road 46, 56, 92, 95, 116, 120
Chalk Hill, Wembley 98, 129, 144
Chamberlain Act 108
Channel Tunnel 42, 43
Chenies Estate 104, 106
Chesham 44, 45, 46, 47, 55, 56, 77, 92, 93, 95, 97, 118, 120
Chorleywood 45, 75, 92, 93, 95, 97, 98, 100, 105, 111, 116, 120
Church Siding 52
Circle Line, see Inner Circle
City & South London Railway 65
Clark, Charles W. 64
Clark, T. F. 68, 148
Claydon 50. 91
Clerkenwell 18
Clerkenwell Tunnel 18, 30
Coach, see Car
Colne Valley 57, 93
Compartment, see Car
Congestion 7, 8, 13, 14, 29, 55, 62, 64, 75
Country Homes in Metro-land, publication 89, 95, 97
Country Walks, publication 89, 90, 118
Craven Brothers of Sheffield 56
Croxley Green 59, 60, 95, 120
Crystal Way 7, 9

Deptford Road 39
Detached house 81, 82, 83, 90, 98, 99, 100, 101, 102, 105, 106, 115, 120, 130
Drayton Park 61, 66
Dreadnought 68, 73

Ealing 58, 102, 131
Ealing & South Harrow Railway 58, 59
Earl's Court 34, 38, 65, 102
East & West Junction Railway 53
East London Railway 13, 30, 36, 37, 39, 40, 41
Eastcote 59, 63, 77, 92, 93, 95, 100, 101, ,102, 103, 117, 118
Eastcote Hill Estate, Eastcote 101 102
Edgware, Middlesex 59, 63
Edgware Road 14, 16, 22, 24, 26, 30, 38, 62, 66, 92
Eiffel Tower 123, 126
Electric Traction Joint Committee 65
Electrification 56, 61, 64, 65, 66, 71, 77, 84, 107, 127, 148
Electrify 29, 30, 41, 50,61, 65, 71, 129
Elm Grove Estate, Ruislip 101
Essex Road 61
Euston Road 18, 66
Euston Square 16, 18, 62, 92
Euston station 30
Euston Tunnel 30

Fares 22, 30, 36, 60, 64, 65, 75, 90, 92, 95
Farringdon, Lord 60
Farringdon Road 30, 31, 66
Farringdon Street 13, 18, 20, 22, 23, 28, 30, 31, 37, 93
Finchley Road 30, 31, 43, 55, 61, 62, 63, 64, 68, 77, 92, 95, 149

Finsbury Park 61
Fleet (river – sewer – valley) 12, 14, 18
Fleet Valley Improvement Committee 14
Forbes, James Staats 36, 37, 42, 58
Fowler, Sir John 22, 23, 24, 28, 30, 33, 146
Fowler's Ghost 23, 24, 146
Fumes 13, 25, 32, 66

Ganz & Co 65
Garden Estates Ltd 84, 85
Garden suburb, garden city, garden village 84, 98,102, 104,121,128, 129, 135
Gauge, broad 18, 23, 24, 25, 26, 28, 43, 57
Mixed 18, 23, 28
Narrow 28
Standard 18, 25, 26, 28, 52, 57
General Post Office 15, 30
Gibson, Henry 86, 87, 98, 102
Gloucester Road 34, 38, 66
Golf 83, 85, 89, 116, 117, 118, 120, 128
Gower Street 12, 18, 22, 38
Grand Junction Canal 57
Grand Union Canal 60, 130
Grange Estate, Pinner 82
Great Central Railway (also see Manchester, Lincolnshire & Sheffield Railway) 55, 59, 68, 84, 97, 129, 131
Great Eastern Railway 36, 37, 40
Great Missenden, see Missenden
Great Northern Railway 15, 18, 19, 24, 25, 28, 30, 39, 42, 54, 55, 61, 62, 146
Great Western Railway 15, 23, 24, 25, 26, 28, 29, 30, 50, 52, 53, 55, 57, 58, 97, 146
Greenwich 8, 66
Gridiron Bridge, Farringdon 30

Hammersmith 28, 40, 41,66, 131
Hammersmith & City Railway (or line) 28, 29, 38, 40, 41, 62, 95
Hampstead Junction Railway 30, 31
Harrow 43, 53, 55, 58, 59, 60, 61, 66, 67, 68, 72, 77, 82, 91, 93, 94, 95, 97, 104, 111, 112, 113, 114, 116, 119, 120, 122, 123, 138, 140, 149
Harrow & Rickmansworth Railway 45
Harrow & Uxbridge Railway 58, 59
Harrow Garden Village 90. 95, 102, 103, 104, 105, 111, 112, 113, 114, 116
Harrow South Junction 55
Hawthorn, Leslie 148
Haymills Ltd 109, 110, 111
Hendon 85
Hertfordshire 79, 87, 89, 90, 91, 93, 118
Hillingdon 59, 93, 95, 101, 102, 120
Hillingdon Mount Estate, Hillingdon 101, 102
Homes in Metro-land, house seeker's guide, publication 91, 101

Ickenham 58, 59, 85, 92, 93, 95
Illustrated guide to the Metropolitan Railway Extensions, publication 82, 88
Inner Circle 33,37, 38, 40, 41, 62,66, 77
Inner Circle Completion Co 36

Jones, Charles 68, 148
Jones, R. A. 52
Jubilee Line 64
Jubilee stock 56

Kensington 28, 33, 34, 37, 65, 77
Kenton 43, 83, 128, 140
Kerr, Stuart & Co 68, 148, 149
Kingsbury 42, 43,63, 64, 91, 94, 95, 98, 128, 133, 138, 140
Kingsbury and Harrow Joint Committee 43
Kingsbury Garden Village, Neasden 98
King's Cross 12,13, 14, 15, 17, 18, 19, 20, 22, 23, 26. 30, 37, 38, 55, 62, 77, 95, 97

Latimer Road 28, 38, 66
Leinster Gardens, dummy houses 33, 34
Lewis Omnibus Co Ltd 60
Lighting in railway carriages 26, 37, 56, 71
Lillie Bridge 36
Liverpool Street 30, 36, 39, 40, 61,92, 93, 95, 97
Lloyd George, David 86, 107
Locomotives 20, 23,24, 25, 26, 27, 31, 37, 43, 45, 46, 50, 52, 53, 56, 59, 62, 66, 67, 68, 69, 70, 71, 72, 73, 76, 77, 146, 147, 148, 149, 150
London & Aylesbury Railway 47
London & North Eastern Railway 60, 62, 68, 77, 129, 148, 149
London & North Western Railway 30, 38, 43, 47, 49, 50, 54, 59, 131
London & South Western Railway 29
London, Brighton & South Coast Railway 39, 40, 41
London, Chatham & Dover Railway 30, 36, 40
London, Midland & Scottish Railway 61, 63
London Passenger Transport Board 60,64, 66, 68, 73, 75, 77, 83, 104, 147, 148
London Transport 41, 68, 77
London Transport Board 77
London Transport Executive 77
Lots Road power station, Chelsea 65

Manchester 26, 42, 53, 54, 55, 79
Manchester, Sheffield & Lincolnshire Railway 42, 54, 55, 56
Manning Wardle locomotive 52, 149
Manor Farm Estate, Ruislip 90, 100, 101
Marlborough Road station 62
Marylebone 55, 60, 87, 123, 131
Metro-land 62, 73, 79, 84, 87, 88, 89, 90, 91, 93, 95, 96, 111, 113, 115, 116, 117, 119, 120, 121, 133, 144, 145
Metro-land, publication 82, 83, 87, 89, 90, 91, 93, 94, 95, 97 98, 102, 105, 111, 112, 117, 118, 120
Metropolitan Amalgamated Railway Carriage & Wagon Co 71, 72, 73
Metropolitan and District Joint Committee 40
Metropolitan and Great Central Joint Committee 55, 87
Metropolitan and St John's Wood Railway 30, 43, 47, 146, 147
Metropolitan Board of Works 8, 36
Metropolitan Cattle Market, Smithfield 15
Metropolitan District Railway 33, 34, 36, 37, 38, 40, 41, 58, 65, 81, 84, 129, 131
Metropolitan Railway Country Estates Ltd 84, 86, 88, 89, 90, 98, 99, 100, 102, 104, 105, 106, 111, 113, 121, 128, 129, 144
Metropolitan Railway Surplus Lands Committee (and Company) 79, 80, 81, 82, 83, 84, 87, 97
Metropolitan Vickers Electrical Co Ltd 71, 72, 73
Middle Circle 38
Middle classes 86, 88, 104, 114, 116
Middlesex 79, 81, 82, 87, 89, 91, 93, 117, 118, 144
Midland Railway 30, 31, 43, 97
Missenden 53, 92, 93, 94, 97, 118, 120,
Moor Park 60, 94, 95, 97, 118, 120, 120
Moorgate 28, 30, 33, 61, 62, 66
Moorgate Street 28, 30, 31, 36, 61, 95, 97

Nationalisation 41, 75, 77, 105
Near and Far, publication 81, 82, 83, 89, 92, 93, 95, 97, 116
Neasden 43, 55, 59, 61, 63, 64, 68, 77, 85, 91, 95, 98, 111, 116, 138, 148
Neilson & Co 148
New Cross 30, 39, 40, 41
New Cross Gate 39
North London Railway 38, 61
North Metropolitan Co 15
North Western Estates Syndicate Ltd 86, 87
Northern Line 61
Northolt Junction 84
Northwick Park 61, 83, 94, 95, 116, 120
Northwood 45, 84, 85, 93, 95, 97, 120
Notting Hill Gate 33, 35, 92
Notting Hill station 28

Old Kent Road 39
Old Street 61
Oldbury Carriage Co 27
Olympia 28, 30, 38
Outer Circle 38
Oxford & Aylesbury Tramroad 52, 53

159

Oxford, Aylesbury & Metropolitan Junction Railway Co 52

Paddington 14, 15, 16, 20, 23, 28, 30, 33, 34, 38, 55, 57, 131
Parson, John 16, 24, 42
Pearson, Charles 9, 13, 14, 15, 22, 30, 84
Peckett & Sons 149
Pick, Frank 76, 77
Pinner 45, 81, 82, 83, 92, 93, 95, 98, 102, 11, 118, 119, 120
Pochin, H. D. 42, 80
Pollitt, William 55
Poole Street power station 61
Portland Road 18, 22, 92
Power station 59, 61, 64, 65, 66, 68
Power supply 64, 65
Praed Street 16
Preston Road 61, 64, 83, 93, 95, 128
Princes Risborough 49, 50, 52, 53, 55
Pullman cars 96, 97
Pybus, P. J. 63, 77

Quainton Road 46, 48, 49, 50, 52, 54, 55, 91, 95
Queensbury 64
Quex Road 62

Rayners Lane 58, 59, 77, 85, 87, 90, 102, 104, 105, 106, 111, 112, 113, 120
Rayners Lane Junction 59
Regent's Canal 9, 31, 62
Reid, E. S. 104, 112
Relief line 62
Rickmansworth 45, 46, 47, 55, 60, 66, 68, 72, 73, 77, 90, 91, 93, 95, 96, 97, 98, 99, 100, 106
Rolling stock 20, 25, 36, 39, 50, 56, 61, 62, 68 to 73, 146 to 150
Rotherhithe 13, 37
Rotherhithe Tunnel 39
Rothschild, Baron Ferdinand 53
Ruislip 55, 59, 66, 77, 84, 85, 88, 90, 93, 95, 100, 101, 118, 119, 120
Ruislip Building Co Ltd 84
Ruislip Garden City 84, 85
Ruislip Manor 59, 77, 84, 85, 100, 101, 114, 118
Ruislip Manor Ltd 85, 95
Rummens, Francis 49
Russell, Hon Frank K. C. 86

St Mary's station 40, 41
St Pancras 30, 62
Sandy Lodge see Moor park
Saunders, Charles 24, 36
Selbie, Robert Hope 68, 85, 86, 90, 91
Semi-detached house 81, 82, 83, 90, 98, 100, 101, 102, 105, 112, 113, 115, 120, 127, 130, 134
Shadwell 39
Sharp, Stewart & Co 148
Shepherd's Bush 28
Shoreditch 39, 40

Signalling on the railway 18, 24, 64, 66
Sims, George R. 88, 91
Smithfield 15, 28, 30, 133
South Eastern & Chatham Railway 30, 68
South Eastern Railway 8, 30, 36, 39, 40, 41, 42, 55, 56
South Harrow 58, 59, 102, 117, 118, 129
South Kensington 33, 34, 38, 41, 62, 92
South London Railway 39
Southern Railway 41
Stanmore 59, 63, 64, 128
Stanmore branch (or line) 64, 73, 77
Stephenson, Robert 12, 23, 146
Stoke-Mandeville 47, 92, 95, 97
Suburb 82, 84, 85, 86, 89, 112, 114, 115, 121, 122, 130, 134
Suburban 14, 45, 55, 57, 59, 61, 64, 68, 79, 84, 85, 89, 97, 107, 114, 115, 116, 119, 120, 140, 144
Suburbia 7, 39, 102, 107, 115, 116, 120
Sudbury 122, 128, 129, 130, 131, 134, 139, 140,
Swiss Cottage 31, 43, 77

Tennis 83, 90, 101, 102, 117, 119, 120, 123, 139
Thames Tunnel 13, 14, 15, 39
Tickets 20, 21, 37, 90, 91, 92, 93, 95
Towcester & Buckingham Railway 54

Tower Hill 33, 40

Underground 9, 12, 13, 14, 27, 28, 33, 41, 75, 76, 77, 80, 106, 144
Uxbridge 58, 59, 63, 66, 77, 85, 92, 93, 95, 97, 102, 116, 120, 129
Uxbridge & Rickmansworth Railway 58
Uxbridge branch 57, 58, 61, 62, 148
Uxbridge Gazette 58, 59
Uxbridge Road Junction 28, 38

Verney, Sir Harry 50, 52
Verney Junction 50, 52, 53, 55, 62, 68, 77, 91, 95, 97, 148

Waddesdon 48, 50, 52, 53, 95
Wapping 13, 39
Watford 59, 60, 63, 95, 120
Watford branch 59, 60
Watford Corporation 59
Watford Joint Railway Committee 59
Watford Junction 47, 59
Watkin, Sir Edward 36, 37, 40, 42, 43, 45, 47, 49, 50, 54, 55, 57, 80, 81, 123, 124, 125
Watkin Tower, Wembley 55, 124, 125, 126, 127
Wealdstone Brook 63
Weller Estate, Amersham 90, 104
Wembley 63, 85, 119, 121, 122, 123, 127, 128, 129, 130, 131, 133, 134, 135, 136, 137, 138, 139, 140, 143, 144
Wembley Hill station 55, 125, 129, 130,

131, 134
Wembley Park 55, 59. 63, 64, 65, 72, 77, 85, 93, 95, 98, 111, 118, 120, 122, 123, 124, 125, 127, 128, 129, 130, 131, 135, 136, 139, 140, 141, 143
Wembley Park Estate Co 98, 127, 128, 129
Wembley Stadium 127, 130, 133, 139
Wendover 47, 92, 93, 95, 97
Wescott 50, 52, 95
West Brompton 52, 95
West Hampstead 31, 32, 43, 95
West Harrow 59, 95
West London Extension Railway 34
West London Railway 28, 34, 38
Westbourne Park 28, 38
Westminster 33, 34
Wheatley Act 109
Where to Live, publication 98, 102, 103, 113
Whitechapel 39, 40, 41, 66
Whitechapel and Bow Extension 58
Whitechapel branch 36
Whitechapel Junction Railway 40
Whitworth, Benjamin 42
Widened Lines 30, 31, 62
Willesden 128, 131, 138
Willesden Green 31, 43, 45, 62, 66, 72, 85, 91
Willesden Junction 6, 38
Wimpey 111
Winslow 50, 95
Wood Siding 52, 54, 95
Worcester & Broom Railway 54
Worcester Engine 31, 147
Wotton 48, 52, 95
Wotton Tramway 49, 52, 53
Wycombe Railway 50, 53

Yerkes, Charles Tyson 65
Yorkshire Engine Co 56, 68, 148